30p

QuarkXPress® 5 Made Simple

Tom Gorham

OXFORD AMSTERDAM LONDON NEW YORK PARIS
SAN DIEGO SAN FRANCISCO SINGAPORE SYDNEY TOKYO

Made Simple
An imprint of Elsevier Science
Linacre House, Jordan Hill, Oxford OX2 8DP
200 Wheeler Road, Burlington MA 01803

First published 2003

British Library Cataloguing in Publication Data
A catalogue record for this book is available from the British Library

ISBN 0 7506 55054

Typeset by Tom Gorham using QuarkXPress
Icons designed by Sarah Ward © 1994
Printed and bound in Great Britain by Scotprint, Haddington

Contents

Preface

Some things are obvious: if you're keen to pursue a legal career you study law. If you want to be a painter you go to Art school. And if you're going to publish magazines or work in the printing industry, or you just want to get creative with your computer, you need to know QuarkXPress.

QuarkXPress is the page layout program that has dominated desktop publishing for more than a decade. It is used in the production of almost every newspaper and magazine in Britain – as well as a number of books like this one. The application's domination looks set to continue with QuarkXPress 5, which adds support for important features such as layers and tables (see *Quark basics*, Chapter 2). The program also recognises the importance of the Internet by including the ability to generate Web pages from the same familiar interface (see *XPress on the Web*, Chapter 12)

While these new features are covered in detail in *QuarkXPress 5 Made Simple*, users new to Xpress will want to learn the basics of the program. I've concentrated on areas new users may find difficult: in particular how fonts work in Chapter 5 and how to incorporate pictures into your documents in Chapter 7.

QuarkXPress has a fearsome reputation, but it is one that is undeserved. I have aimed to make it as easy as possible to understand how to create documents for print and Web with impressive results as quickly as possible. With this knowledge, you should be mastering Xpress in no time.

Tom Gorham, 2002

Take note

Most of the screenshots in this book are taken from the Mac version, but you will see a few from Windows too. I've mixed things for two reasons: first, to show how the program works nearly identically on different platforms (where there are differences I have pointed them out); and second to ensure you are comfortable with XPress no matter what platform you are asked to use it on. Versatility should never be underrated!

1 Getting started

The QuarkXPress page

A QuarkXPress document contains a number of windows and palettes that float above the document.

The pasteboard

This is an area outside the page boundary. Items placed on the pasteboard don't print unless they overlap the page itself.

The ruler

The ruler can help you accurately place items on your page.

> **Tip**
>
> **Many of the default settings for page elements can be set via the Preferences menu.**

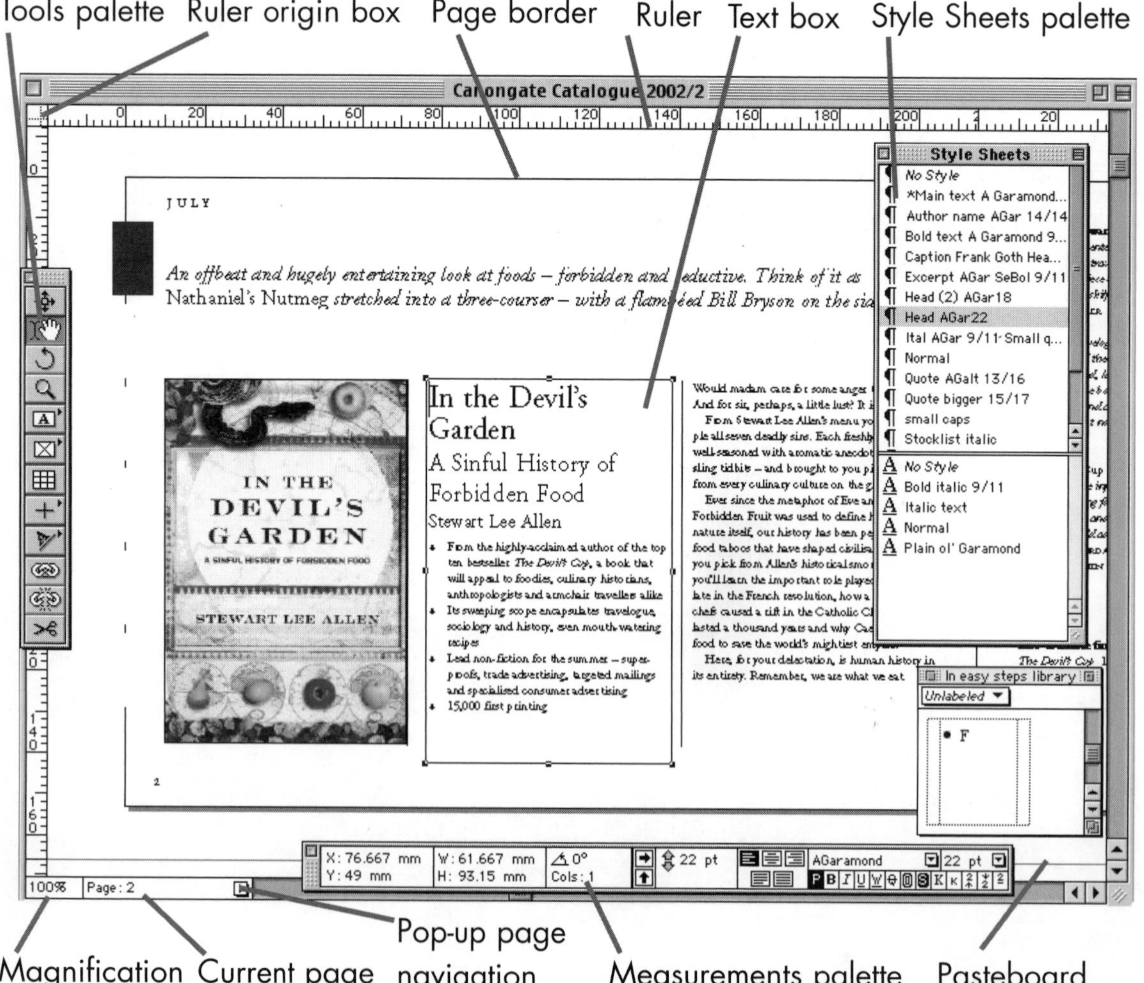

Ruler Origin

This box allows you to alter the point at which the ruler starts, and is useful if you want to measure the distance between two objects on a page. To change ruler origin, click inside this box and drag your mouse to the point where you want the ruler to start: horizontal and vertical guide lines will help you find the right spot. To revert to the original ruler settings, simply click once more in the Ruler Origin box.

Floating palettes

The Style Sheets palette shown opposite is an example of the many floating palettes that QuarkXPress uses (others include Colour and Document Layout palettes).

Boxes

There are three types of boxes that can be created in XPress: text boxes, picture boxes and contentless boxes.

Tools palette

This palette holds many of the tools XPress uses and allows you to switch between them to create a document. For more about the Tools palette, see page 6.

Pop-up navigation

Press and hold on the disclosure triangle to the left of this and you can scroll through the pages of the current document, starting at the current page. Release the mouse over the page you want to view.

Document magnification

This allows you to set the level of magnification on the page to any value between 10 and 800 per cent. To find out other ways of adjusting views in a document, see page 19.

Take note

QuarkXPress can't claim to do everything, but one of the benefits of the program is that it is extensible through XTensions. XPress ships with a number of these in its XTensions folder. There are literally hundreds of XTensions available to perform a variety of tasks, from checking documents for errors that might cause problems when you send it to press, to tools that allow you to add realistic shadows behind objects on the page. Installing XTensions is simple: just drop the XTension inside the XPress XTension folder and relaunch XPress.

Menus

Menus are vital in QuarkXPress, so it's a good idea to take a moment to examine what they do. Although each holds a plethora of options, each menu is arranged logically to hold related commands.

The **File** menu allows you to open, create and save documents and libraries. It's also the menu to use to import or export text and pictures, print a document or quit the program.

The **Edit** menu allows you to select, find or change text and pictures. You can also set document and application preferences and amend colours and other styles.

The content of the **Style** menu varies according to the currently selected object in your document. If you have selected a text box, you can modify its contents using this menu. If a picture box is active, the Style menu allows you to

Edit
Undo Deletion ⌘Z
Cut ⌘X
Copy ⌘C
Paste ⌘V
Clear
Select All ⌘A
Subscribe to...
Subscriber Options...
Show Clipboard
Find/Change ⌘F
Preferences ▸
Style Sheets... ⇧F11
Colours... ⇧F12
H&Js... ⌥⌘H
Lists...
Dashes & Stripes...
Print Styles...
Program Language ▸
Tagging Rules...
Jabberwocky sets...
Underline Styles...
Meta Tags...
Menus...

The Edit menu lets you edit text and pictures as well as many document-wide settings.

Style
Font ▸
Size ▸
Type Style ▸
Colour ▸
Shade ▸
Horizontal/Vertical Scale...
Kern...
Baseline Shift...
Character... ⇧⌘D
Character Style Sheet ▸
Text to Box
Alignment ▸
Leading... ⇧⌘E
Formats... ⇧⌘F
Tabs... ⇧⌘T
Rules... ⇧⌘N
Paragraph Style Sheet ▸
Flip Horizontal
Flip Vertical
Hyperlink ▸
Anchor ▸
Underline Styles ▸

The Style menu when text is selected.

File
New ▸
Open ▸
Close ⌘W
Save ⌘S
Save as... ⌥⌘S
Revert to Saved
Get Text... ⌘E
Save Text... ⌥⌘E
Append... ⌥⌘A
Export ▸
Save Page as EPS... ⌥⇧⌘S
Collect for Output...
Document Setup... ⌥⇧⌘P
Page Setup... ⌥⌘P
Print... ⌘P
Quit ⌘Q

The File menu includes a number of important functions.

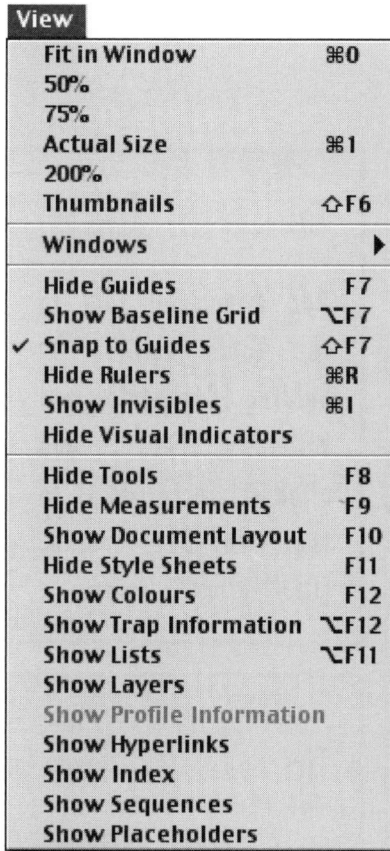

Utilities
Check Spelling
Auxiliary Dictionary...
Edit Auxiliary...
Suggested Hyphenation... ⌘H
Hyphenation Exceptions...
Usage...
XTensions Manager...
Component Status...
PPD Manager...
Use German (Reformed)
QuarkLink
Profile Manager...
Show Tagged Content
Guide Manager...
Build Index...
Jabber
Tracking Edit...
Kerning Edit...
Remove Manual Kerning
Line Check
Convert Old Underlines

make adjustments to the size, rotation and colour of the image contained within it. Click on a line and you can alter its width and colour. If creating Web documents or PDFs, you can also assign hyperlinks in this menu.

The **Item** menu, greyed out until you click on an item such as a box or line, contains functions that change the shape and content of boxes as well as altering how text runs around them. This menu also lets you group and lock boxes into position.

The **Page** menu lets you insert, delete and move pages in your document, as well as set up Master guides that establish the margins of your pages. The **Display...** submenu lets you switch between master page and standard page views. For more on master pages, see page 44.

A miscellaneous set of functions are included in the **Utilities** menu. Here you can check on the active fonts and pictures in your document (via the **Usage...** submenu), check your spelling and keep track of the XTensions in your document.

In the **View** menu, you can adjust document view sizes, view guides and baseline grids as well as toggle the visibility of the various palettes.

Item
Modify... ⌘M
Frame... ⌘B
Runaround... ⌘T
Clipping... ⌥⌘T
Duplicate ⌘D
Step and Repeat... ⌥⌘D
Delete ⌘K
Group ⌘G
Ungroup ⌘U
Constrain
Lock F6
Merge
Split
Send to Back ⇧F5
Bring to Front F5
Space/Align... ⌘,
Shape
Content
Edit
Point/Segment Type
Delete All Hot Areas
Super Step and Repeat...
Convert Text to Table...
Table
Gridlines
Rollover

Tools palette

The QuarkXPress Tools palette contains most of the basic tools you need to put together documents.

Item and Content tools

The two tools you will need to become familiar with quickly are the top two: the Item and Content tools. You must click on the Item tool before you can move items, such as boxes and lines, on a page. To enter text or images inside a box, you must select the Content tool first.

One or other of the Item and Content tools will be selected by default.

Tools are selected by clicking once on them. To select an item in a pop-out menu (indicated by small triangles), click and hold on the visible tool.

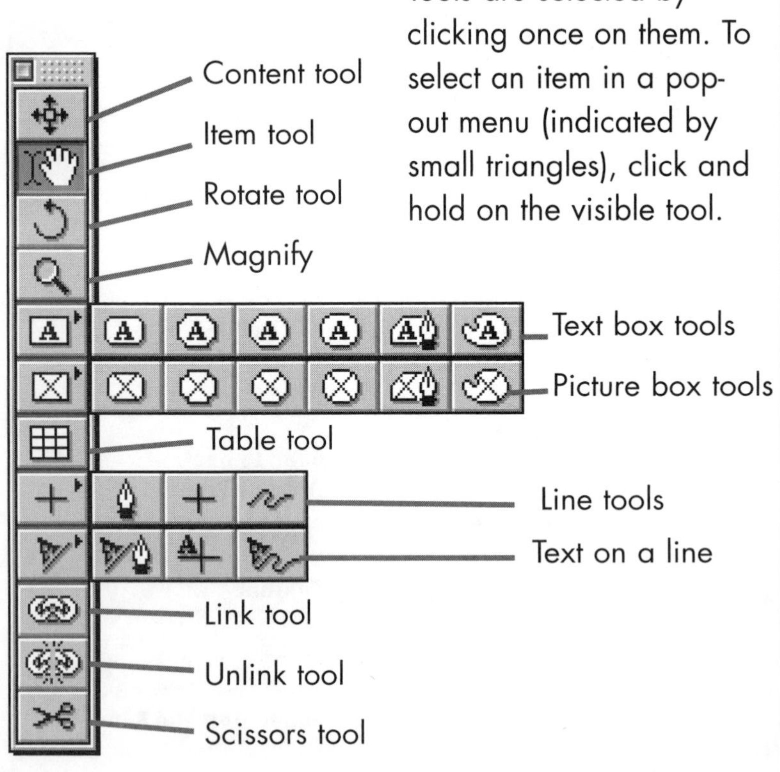

Tip

Add a pop-out tool to the Tools palette by holding [Ctrl] (Mac and Windows) while you click it. To return it to the pop-out menu, [Ctrl]-click it again.

Tip

Many Quark problems can be solved by replacing its Preferences file (held in the Preferences folder inside the XPress application folder), but deleting it loses any application preferences you have set (see page 13 for more about Preferences. Store a spare copy of your Preferences file in a safe place, so you can revert to it at any time.

Rotate

The Rotate tool rotates items manually. Select this tool, click on the box or line you want to rotate. Click on your desired axis point and then drag the image to rotate it around this point.

Tip

Double-clicking the Magnify, Text, Picture and Line tools opens the Document Preferences window, where you can adjust their default settings, such as their default colour. For more on setting preferences, see page 13.

Magnify

This tool enlarges or reduces the document window size by a set percentage. To use it, select it and click once on the document window. The window will expand. [Option]-click (Mac) or [Alt]-click (Windows) to zoom out instead.

Text box tools

These create boxes to hold typed or imported text. The default tool creates rectangular boxes, but you can also create oval, rounded corner, concave corner, freehand or Bézier boxes using the pop-up options.

Picture box tools

These create picture boxes to hold images. The default tool is rectangular, but you can also create oval, concave corner, freehand or Bézier boxes using the pop-up options.

Tip

Instead of using mouse clicks to select tools, use a keyboard shortcut. To switch to the tool below the currently selected tool, press [Command-[Option]-[Tab] (Mac) or [Ctrl]-[Alt]-[Tab] (Windows).

Table tool

This tool, new in XPress 5, creates tables to hold text, pictures or both.

Linking and Unlinking tools

These link and unlink text boxes. To see how to use these tools, see page 54.

Scissors tool

The Scissors tool is used to cut lines and text boxes.

Measurements palette

The **Measurements** palette offers a handy alternative method of accessing functions otherwise found in the **Style** menu or **Modify** dialog box (see page 10). Not only can you see the current status of objects and their contents, you can also edit them directly by clicking on their values in the palette.

The content of the palette varies according to the currently selected tool or item.When the Item tool is selected in the **Tools** palette and a text box is selected in the document window, the Measurements palette looks like this:

Take note

Horizontal and vertical box positions are measured from the ruler origin, usually the top left of the document.

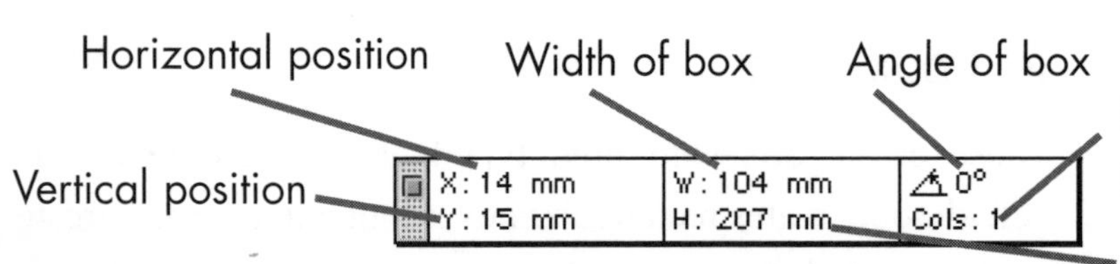

The horizontal box position: shows the horizontal position of the current text box measured from to the ruler origin. In most cases this will be the top left corner of the document.

The vertical box position: the vertical position of the box relative to the ruler origin.

Angle of box: the angle of rotation of the currently selected box from 0 to 360. (You can also manually rotate items using the **Rotate** tool in the **Tools** palette.)

Number of columns: the number of columns in the selected text box.

When the **Content** tool is selected, the palette contains the following additional fields:

Tip

Move between fields in the Measurements palette by clicking in the palette and pressing [Tab] to move forward one field and [Shift]-[Tab] to go backwards.

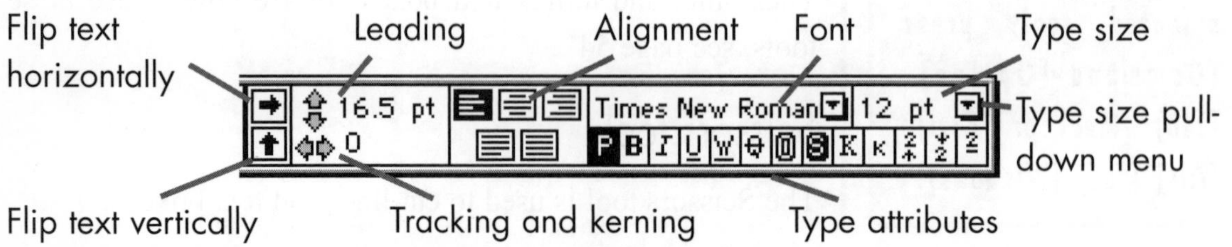

When an image is selected with the **Item** or **Content** tool, the palette looks like this:

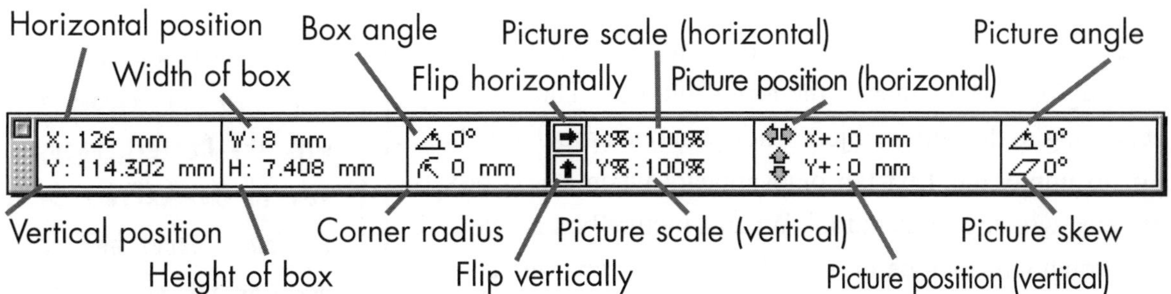

Take note

If you enter a value in a field that XPress doesn't understand an error message appears. You must return to the field and correct the error before you can continue.

The corner radius specifies the curvature of the corner of the picture box. Rectangular boxes will have a radius of zero.

The picture flip, scale, position, angle and skew all refer to the picture inside the box, rather than the box itself.

The picture scales allow you to set the scale of the picture inside its box. A value of 100 per cent displays the picture at its original size. The smallest scale available is five per cent; the maximum is 1,000 per cent – or ten times the original size of the image.

Picture position refers to the position of the picture within the box, while picture angle describes its angle within the box.

When a line is selected, the palette will look like this:

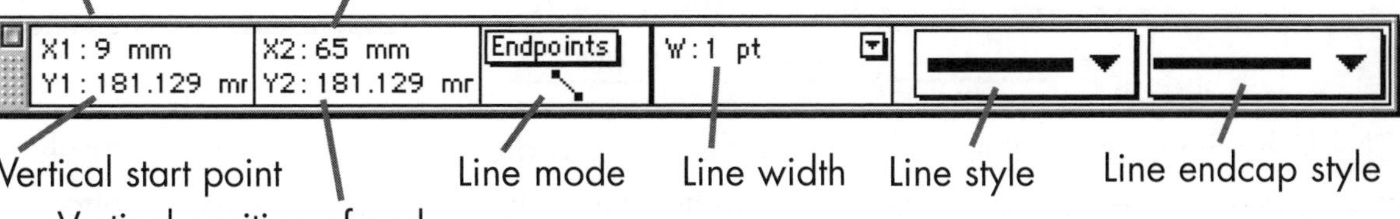

The beginning and end of a line – its start and end position – is measured from the ruler's origin. The Line mode, style, width and Endcap options are selected from a pull-down menu. We will look at these further in Chapter 2.

Modify dialog box

The **Item** menu's **Modify** dialog box is probably the most important dialog box in QuarkXPress. With it, you can adjust the properties of almost any object on the page or its contents.

You access the information in the Modify dialog box by clicking on one the tabs at the top of the box. The tabs vary according to the active object when you open the dialog box. For example, the Text tab only appears when a text box is selected with the Content tool. When a picture box is selected, additional tabs include Frame, clipping and runaround.

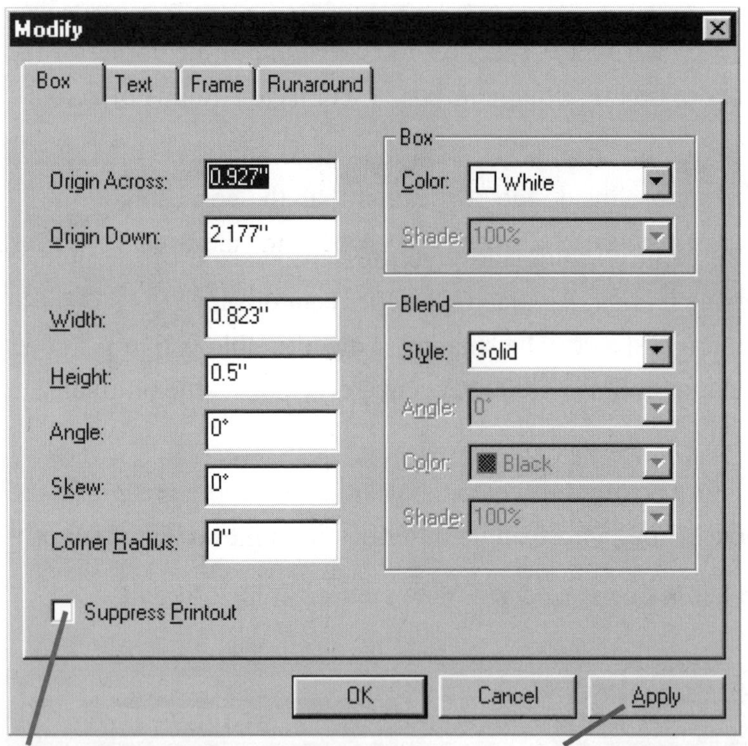

Check the Suppress Printout box to stop a box or line from printing. This option can save ink if you only want to print out part of a page, but you'll have to remember to turn it on later!

Most XPress dialog boxes include an Apply button that allows you to preview the effect of your choice. The dialog box stays active during this preview and if you choose not to proceed, just click Cancel and no changes will be made.

Tip

The Modify dialog box can also be accessed with the Context menu, new in QuarkXPress 5. For more about how to use Context menus, see page 11.

Tip

The quickest way to open the Modify dialog box, one even experienced XPress users seem to forget about, is to double-click the object you want to modify with the Item tool active.

Context menu

Tip

Click outside a box and another context menu allows you to access global preferences, print or save and export the document as a PDF or HTML file.

QuarkXPress 5 now sports another useful way to access its features: the Context menu. Click on a box or on text then right-click (Windows) or [Ctrl]-click (Mac) and a drop-down menu appears that can be used to quickly modify the selected item or its contents. Like the Measurements palette and the Dialog box, the contents of the menu vary depending on the currently selected item.

For example, if a text box is selected with the Item tool, the Context menu allows you to move boxes backwards and forwards and to copy and paste them. If a text box is selected with the Content tool, even more features are offered. You can import and save text, apply style sheets and convert any text you have selected in the box into a table. If no text has been selected, this option is greyed out.

If an image box is selected, you can additionally import pictures, adjust image box size, create hyperlinks for Web documents and PDFs from this menu. You can also change the box type from Picture to Text or None.

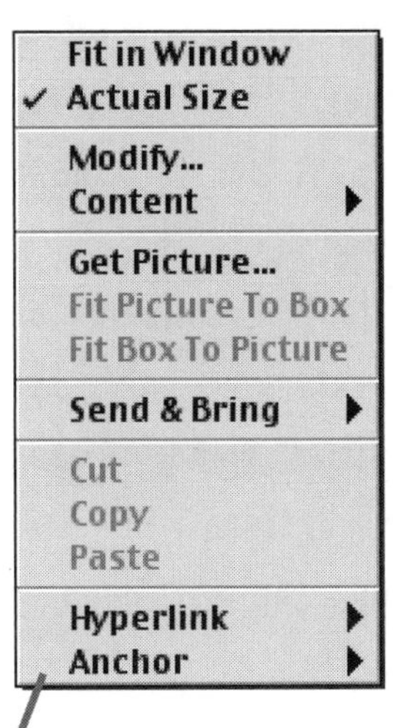

Context menu when image box is selected.

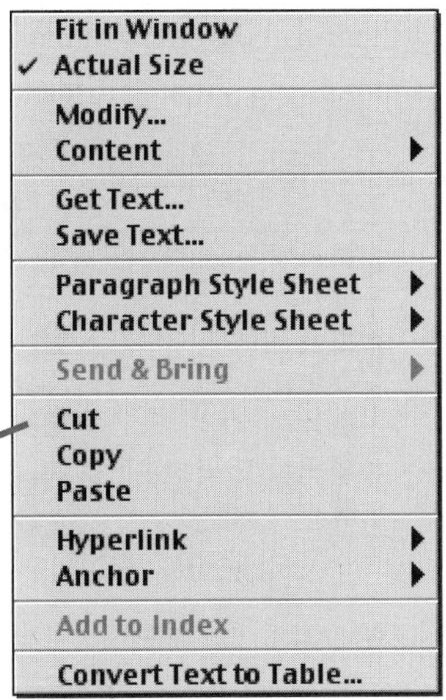

Context menu when text box is selected with the Content tool.

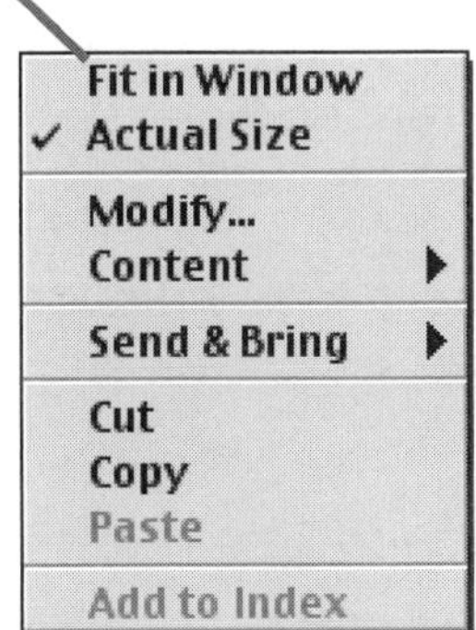

Context menu when text box is selected with the Item tool.

Other palettes

Document Layout palette

The Document Layout palette provides a visual overview of your document, by showing thumbnail representations of pages in your document. With this palette you can create and organise pages (see Chapter 3). To open the palette, point to **View** and select **Show Document Layout**.

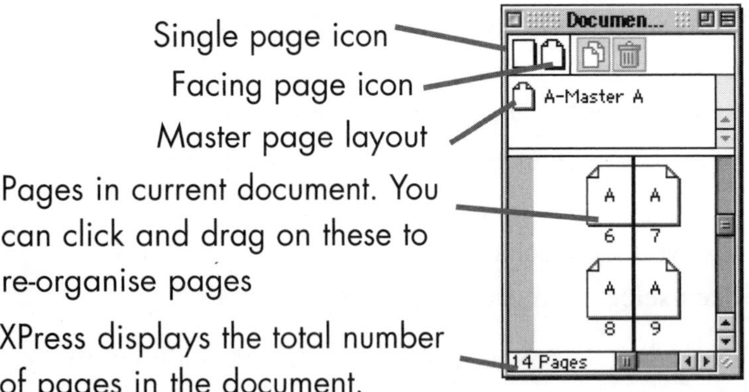

Colours palette

The Colours palette organises the colours used in the document, allowing you to apply them to box backgrounds, text and frames. To open the palette, point to **View** and select **Show Colours**.

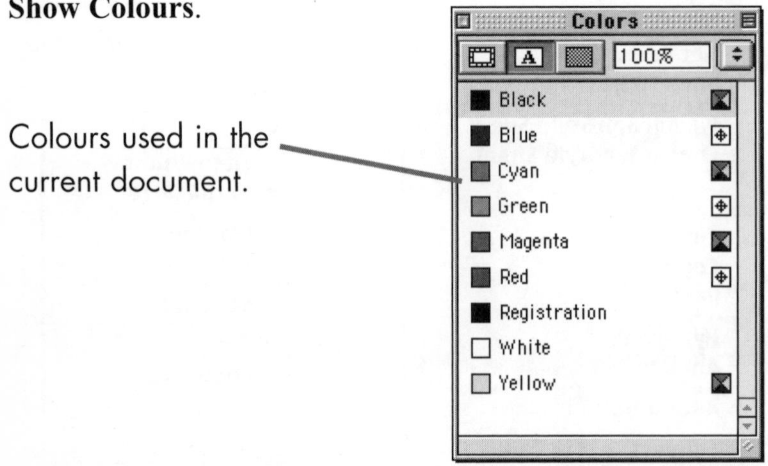

Tip

How do you find Help in QuarkXPress? XPress 5 no longer ships with printed manuals; documentation in only available in PDF format. There is limited Help available within the program: click on Help Topics in the Help menu. A less well-known source of help is available by clicking on QuarkLink in the Utilities menu. Among the options in this menu, you can connect directly to an XPress tutorial.

Tip

You can turn all palettes on and off via the View menu.

Basic steps

1 Point to Edit and click Preferences...
2 Choose Preferences from the sub-menu.
3 Select the relevant preferences option.
4 Make adjustments to the default values.
5 Click OK.

Preferences

The **Preferences** dialog box holds many of the default settings for the program – such as how fast you can scroll through your document – and your document in particular. We won't examine the dozens of options here, but it's worth examining the Preferences box to see what you can change. You'll be surprised how flexible XPress is.

Aside from the main Preferences dialog box, there are other options accessible from the Preferences menu, including those for indexes, fractions, and colour management. Third-party XTensions often add extra options to this menu too.

Not every preference setting must be set in the Preferences menu. If you create a new style sheet, colour, list or hyphenation setting while there are no open XPress documents, the new settings will appear on every subsequently opened document. Otherwise these settings will be particular to the document you are currently working in.

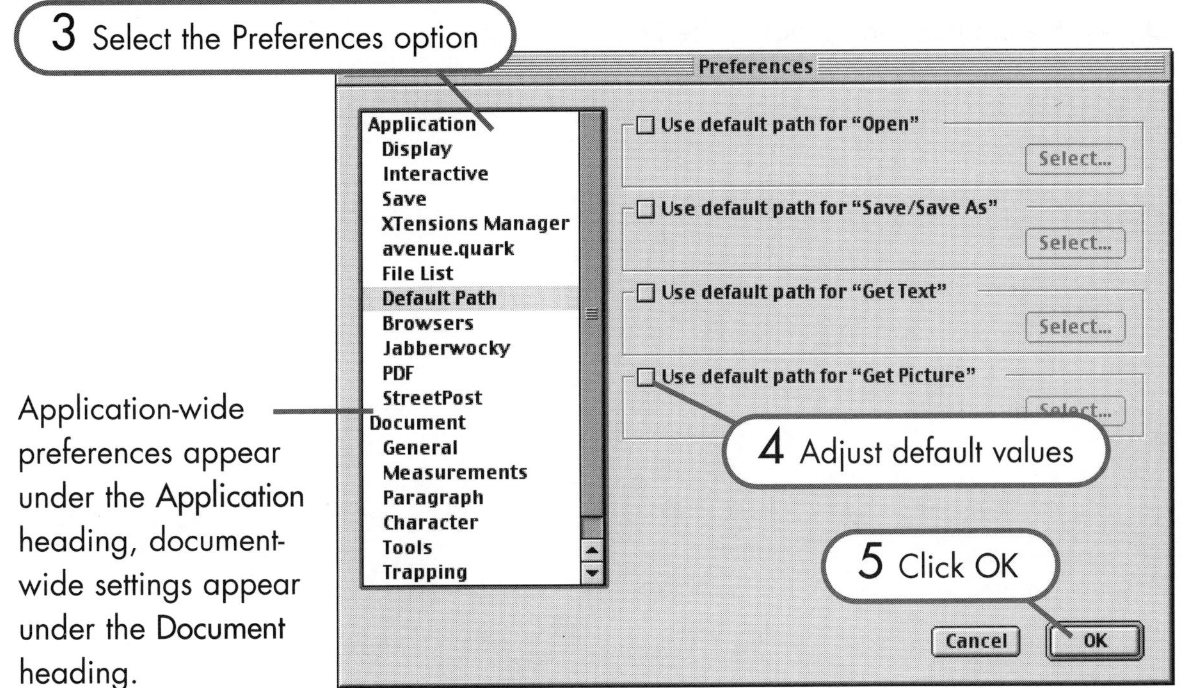

Application-wide preferences appear under the Application heading, document-wide settings appear under the Document heading.

Summary

- The QuarkXPress interface is made up of document windows, palettes and dialog boxes.
- Most of XPress's functions can be accessed from the menu bar, the Modify dialog box or one of the palettes.
- The Tools palette holds most of the tools you need to create a document. You can use keyboard shortcuts to switch tools rather than mouse-clicking on them.
- The Measurements palette is a useful method of viewing and editing objects and their contents.
- The Modify dialog box is the primary source for editing objects and their contents.
- You can use the Context menu to access commonly used functions.
- The Preferences dialog box is the home to most application and document-wide preferences.

2 Quark basics

Rulers and guides

Rulers reside on the top and left of the document window. You can toggle their visibility by pointing to the **View** menu and selecting **View Rulers** or **Hide Rulers**.

By default, rulers measure from the top left of the current page, but as we've seen, the ruler origin can be altered.

Ruler guides

Ruler guides are non-printing lines that help align boxes and other page elements. To create Ruler guides, first make sure both rulers and margin guides are visible (select **Show Guides** and **Show Rulers** from the **View** menu). If you click and hold on the horizontal or vertical ruler the cursor changes to a double-headed arrow. Drag this across the page – you will see an outline of the guide as move it. Guides can be subsequently moved – just drag them their new position – or removed by dragging them back to the ruler or off the document pasteboard.

As well as making guides invisible (select **Hide Guides** from the **View** menu) you can make them visible only above certain zoom percentages. Choose the zoom percentage you want (see page 19 on ways to do this) and hold [Shift] as you drag the guide. It will now only be visible at that percentage and above.

If you select Snap to Guides in the **View** menu, objects that you place near to the guide will automatically 'snap' to it, which makes aligning objects easier and more accurate

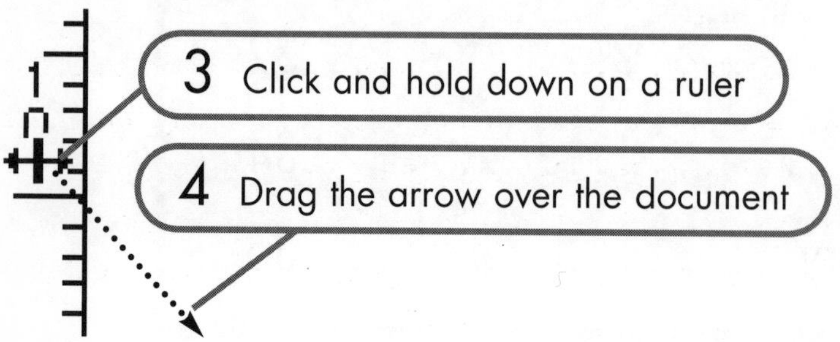

Basic steps

1 Point to View.
2 Select Show Guides.
3 Click and hold down on a ruler. The cursor changes to a double-headed arrow.
4 Drag over the page and release the mouse button.

Tip

Rulers display co-ordinates in millimetres, inches or picas according to the default set in the Measurements pane of the Preferences box. In the General pane of the same box you can choose whether guides appear in front of or behind page elements (choose in front); and set a 'snap' distance, which specifies how close an object must be to a guide before it 'snaps' to it.

Navigating

Tip

The Grabber hand is a useful scrolling tool. Hold [Option] (Mac) or [Alt] (Windows) and click and drag on the document window. It now follows you around.

Tip

You can adjust the speed of page scrolling in the Interactive pane of the Preferences dialog box. There are two other Preferences options: Speed Scroll, provides an extra speed boost for scrolling and Live Scroll updates the page automatically as you scroll. You can get the same effect (Mac only), if you hold [Option] while dragging the scroll box.

One of the most important early lessons to learn about QuarkXPress is how to navigate through documents.

Using the scroll bar

Each QuarkXPress document has vertical and horizontal scroll bars. If you click on the arrows at the bottom of the vertical scroll bar or the right of the horizontal scroll bar, you move up and down or across the page. You can also click and drag the scrolling box in the scroll bar to travel through the document. You can leap through a complete window at a time by clicking in the grey area of the scroll bar above or below the scrolling box.

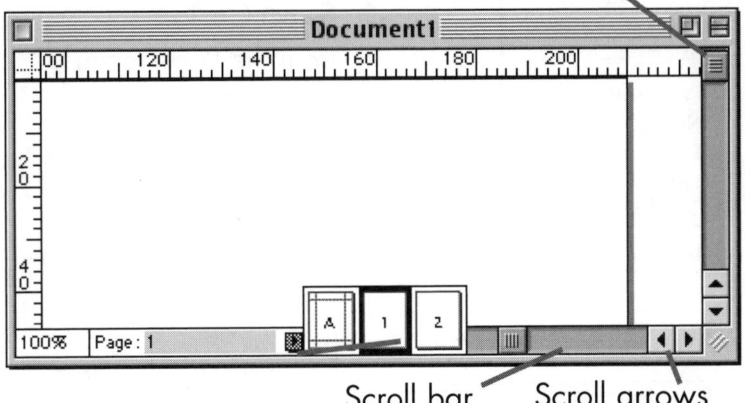

Page navigation

Scrolling isn't ideal if you want move through entire pages at a time. There are three main methods of navigating through a document: using the navigation field and pop-up window at the bottom of the document window, via the Document Layout palette, or through the **Page** menu. All three methods have their uses.

Basic steps

What about moving between documents? You can switch between document windows within XPress by pointing to **View** and selecting **Windows**. This shows a list of open XPress documents, and you can use this to switch between documents. The listed documents can also be tiled – displayed next to each other – or stacked above one another.

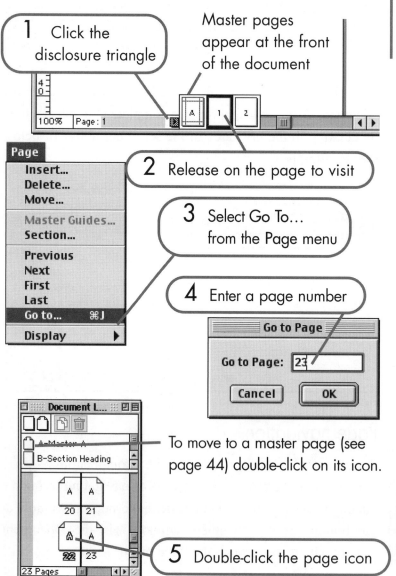

- ❑ To move pages

1 Click on the disclosure triangle.

2 Hold the mouse down and scroll through the page icons. Release when the desired page is highlighted.

Or

3 Point to Page and click Go To…

4 Enter a page number and click OK.

Or

5 Double-click on a page in the Document Layout palette. The current page is highlighted.

1 Click the disclosure triangle

Master pages appear at the front of the document

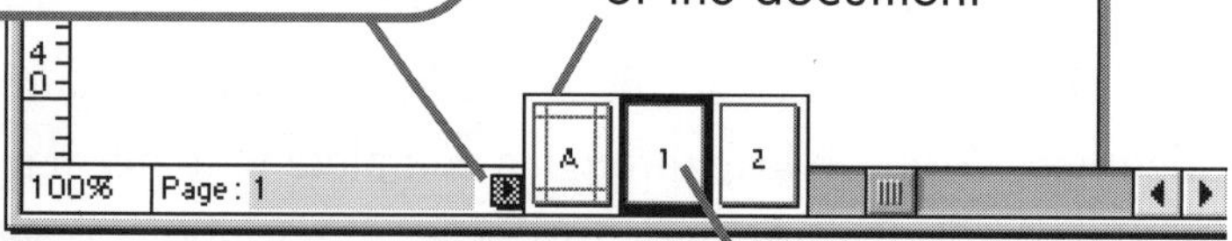

2 Release on the page to visit

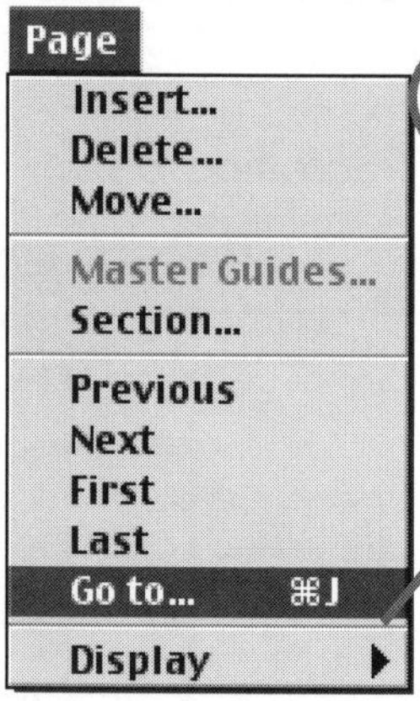

3 Select Go To… from the Page menu

4 Enter a page number

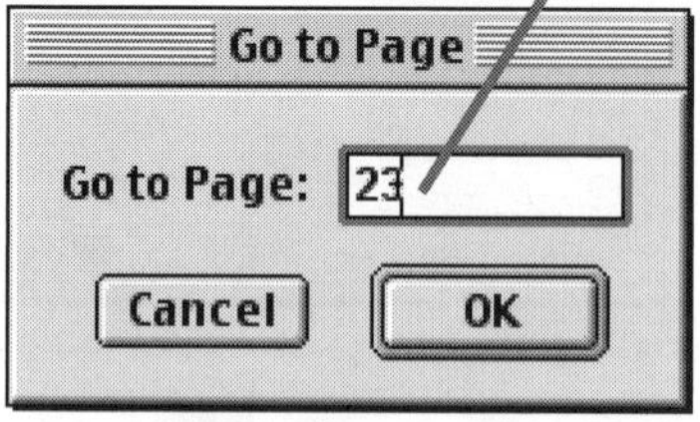

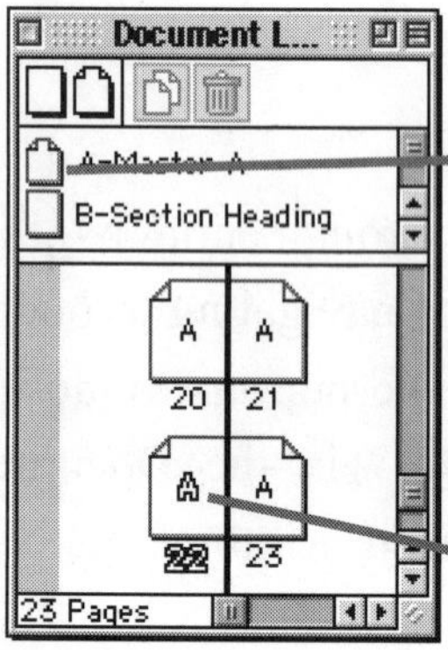

To move to a master page (see page 44) double-click on its icon.

5 Double-click the page icon

Take note

The page shown in the Page Navigation field is the one visible at the top left of the open window, even if only a corner of it can be seen.

Basic steps

1 Select View.

2 Click on a preset size.

Or

3 Click on the Zoom tool.

4 Click on the document window.

Or

5 Click and drag the mouse over the area to magnify. Then release the mouse. The selected area will fill the screen.

Or

6 Enter a value in the View Percent field at the bottom of the document window.

7 Click [Return] (Mac) or [Enter] (Windows).

Changing views

When creating XPress documents, you need to continually zoom out to check the overall layout and zoom in to view things in more detail. You can choose from several preset views in the **View** menu, but there are a number of alternative methods of zooming in and out.

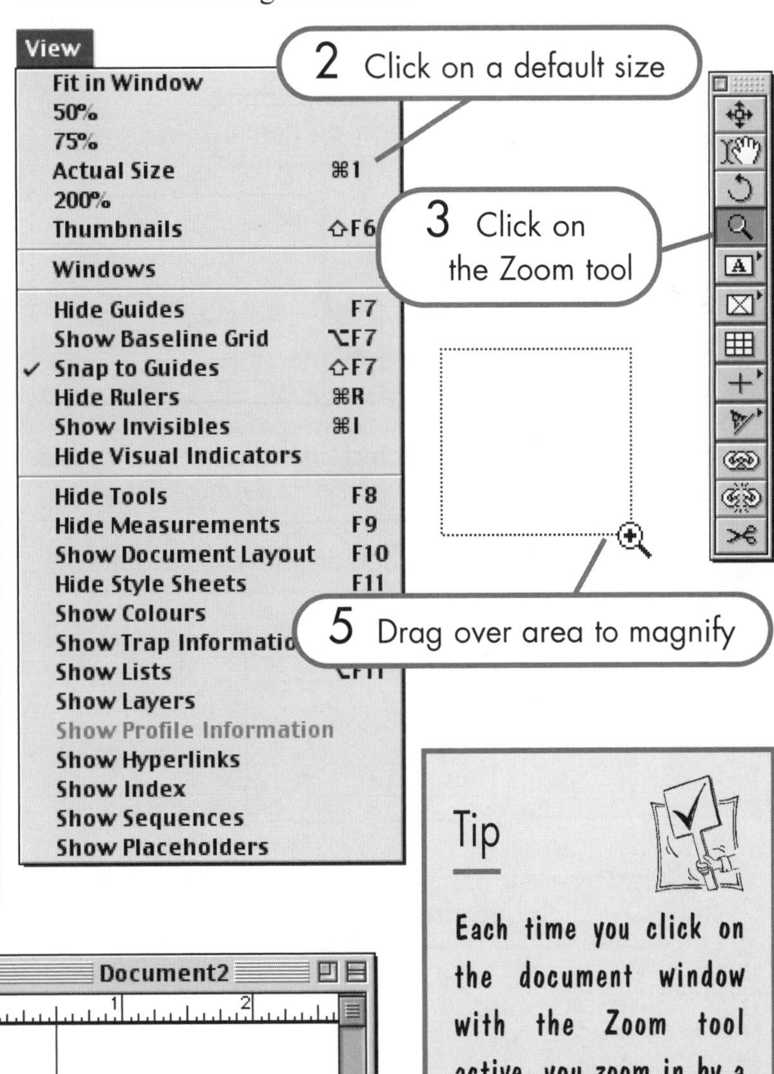

6 Enter a value

Document2

67%

Page : 1

Tip

Each time you click on the document window with the Zoom tool active, you zoom in by a preset amount set in the Preferences dialog box.

Selecting and moving

To manipulate items in the document window, you need to select them. This is done with the Item or Content tools. Generally, the Item tool is used to select items, while the Content tool is used to select the contents of those items.

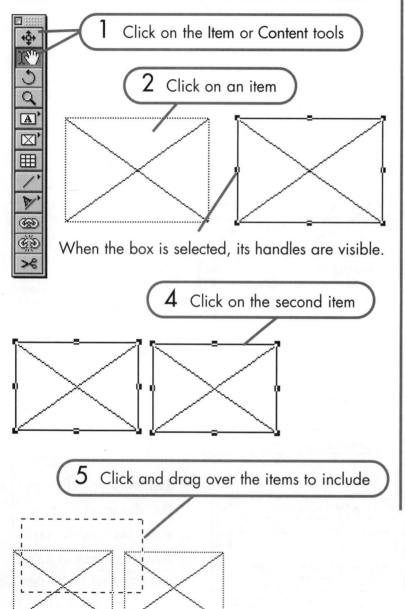

1 Click on the Item or Content tools

2 Click on an item

When the box is selected, its handles are visible.

4 Click on the second item

5 Click and drag over the items to include

Basic steps

- ❑ To select one item

1 Select the Item or Content tools.

2 Click on an item.

- ❑ To select more than one item.

3 Hold [Shift].

4 Click on the second item.

- ❑ Repeat the process to select more items.

Or

5 Drag the mouse over the items to include.

Tip

To select all items on a page, click on the Item tool and choose Select All from the Edit menu.

Basic steps

- ❑ To group items
1. Select the items to group.
2. Point to Edit.
3. Select Group.

Tip

Another way to deselect every item in a group, is press [Tab] when the Item tool is selected.

Tip

For more control over objects on a page, you can lock them in position. Select the item or group of items, point to Item and select Lock. If you try to move these items, XPress won't let you. To unlock locked items, select Unlock from the Item menu.

Deselecting items

To deselect a single item or deselect every item in a multiple selection, just click the mouse on a part of the document away from the item or items. To deselect a single item when more than one is selected, items, Hold **[Shift]** and click on the item to deselect. Every other item apart from the one you [Shift]-clicked will remain selected

Grouping items

As you've probably discovered by now, managing more than one item in this way can prove unwieldy. XPress allows you to group items, so you can treat them as a single item.

Now whenever you use the Item tool to click on an item in this group, the whole group will be selected. You can still select an individual item in the group by clicking on the Content tool first. To ungroup items, click once on the group and select **Ungroup** from the **Item** menu.

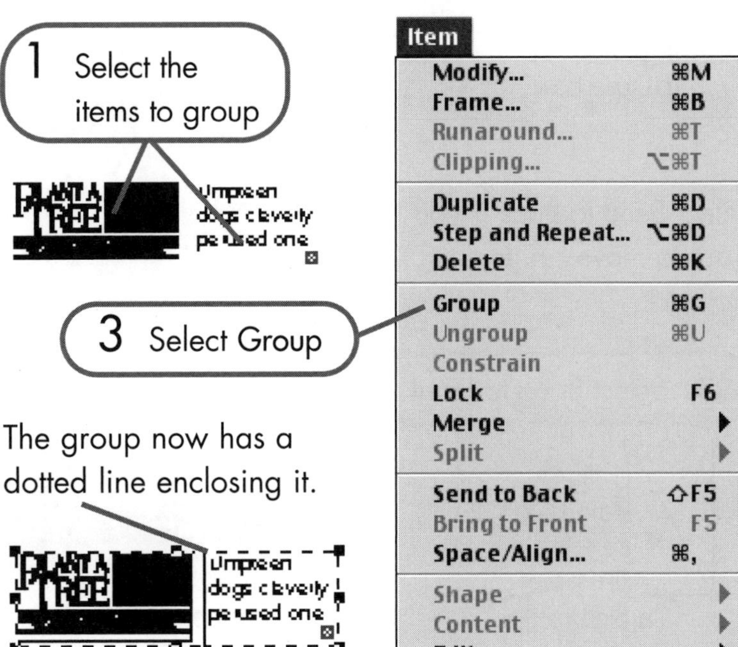

Moving items

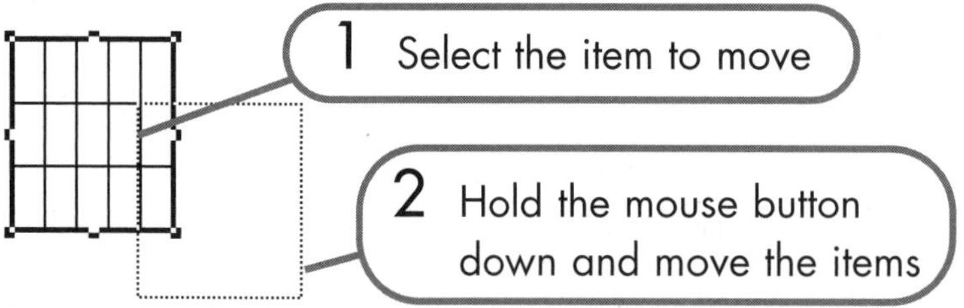

To keep an item in the same plane (vertical or horizontal) as you move it, hold [Shift] as you drag.

Layering items

If you place overlapping items on the page, they are layered on top of each other. The last-placed object on the page is always the topmost item, but you can adjust the layering to bring background items to the front and vice-versa.

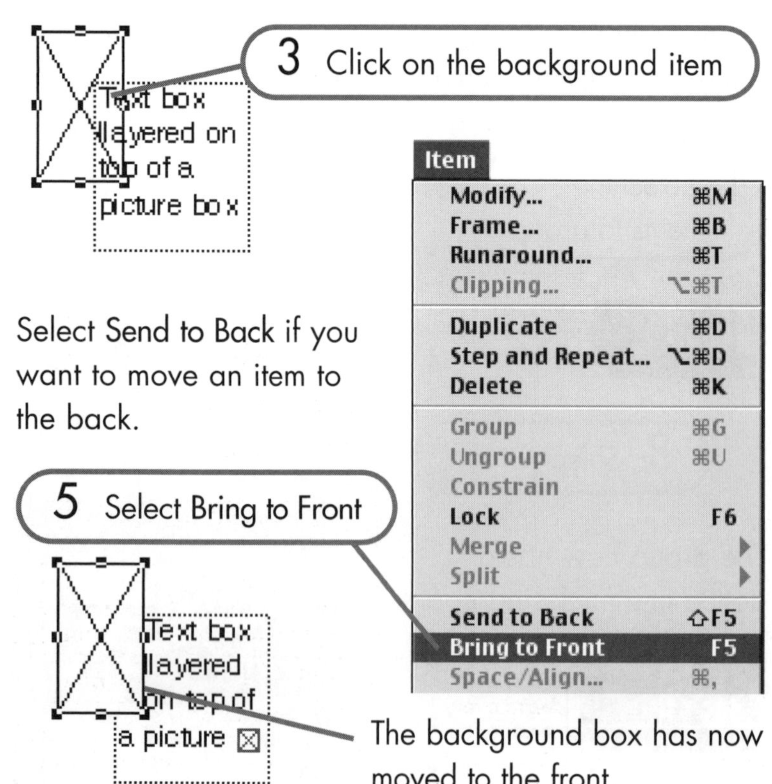

Basic steps

1. Select the Item tool.
2. Hold the mouse button down and move the item to its new position.

- ❑ To bring an item to the front

3. Click the background item.
4. Point to Item.
5. Select Bring to Front.

Tip

To select a item hidden below another, press [Command]-[Option]-[Shift] (Mac) or [Ctrl]-Alt]-[Shift] (Windows) while clicking on the item above it. Continue using this key combination to drill further down. To keep control of a hidden item once selected, keep the mouse button down after selecting it.

Copying

Basic steps

1 Select the item.

2 Point to Item and select Duplicate.

❑ Using Step and Repeat

3 Point to Item and select Step and Repeat…

4 Enter the number of times you want the item to repeat and the distance between each copy.

5 Click [OK].

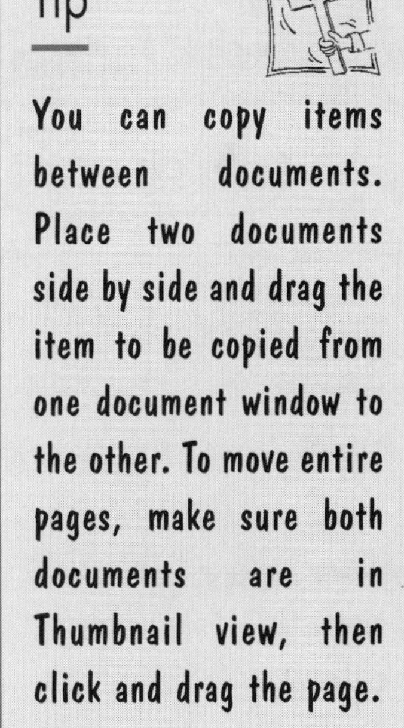

Tip

You can copy items between documents. Place two documents side by side and drag the item to be copied from one document window to the other. To move entire pages, make sure both documents are in Thumbnail view, then click and drag the page.

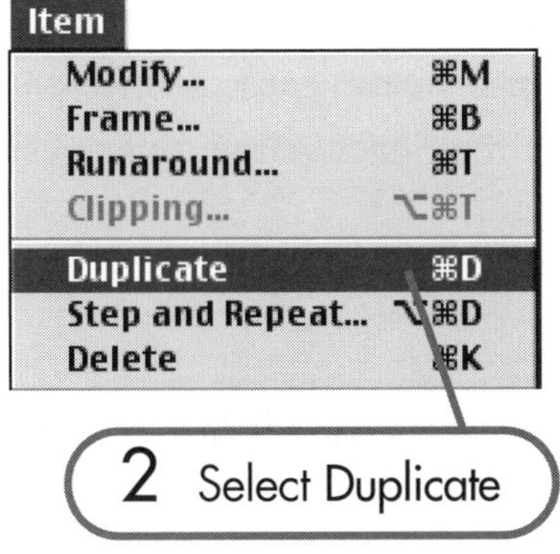

Take note

If duplicated boxes do not fit inside the pasteboard, you will get an error message.

Step and repeat

A more powerful method of duplicating items is the **Step and Repeat** command, which allows you to duplicate an item up to 99 times and specify the horizontal and vertical distance between each copy.

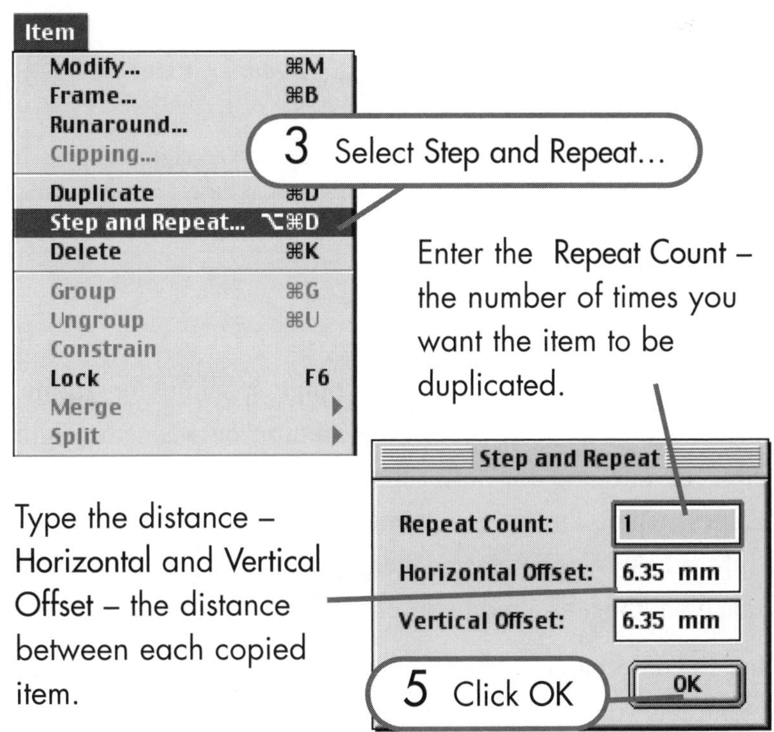

Spacing and aligning

Unless you're precise when you line page items up to page guides, it's easy to misalign them or leave gaps of different sizes. A way around this is to use the Space/Align tool.

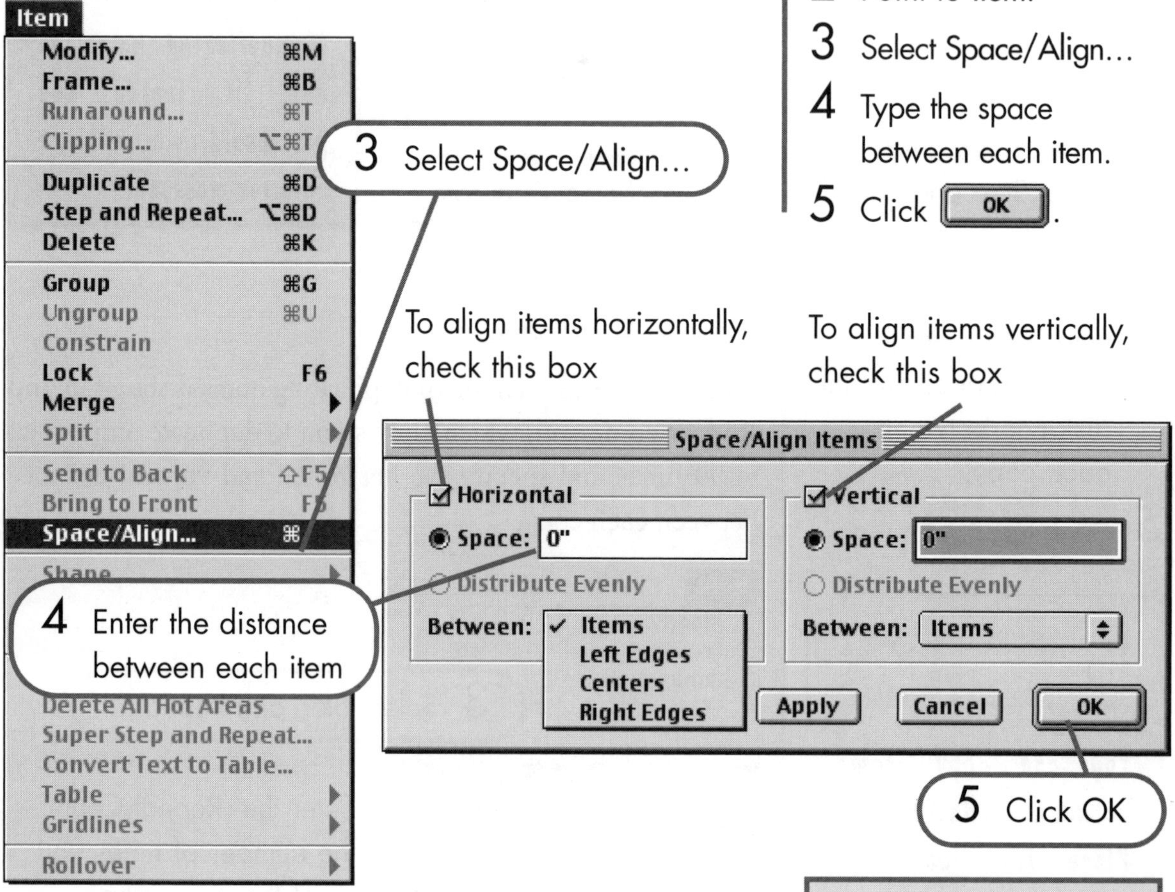

Basic steps

1. Select more than one item to align.
2. Point to Item.
3. Select Space/Align…
4. Type the space between each item.
5. Click OK.

3 Select Space/Align…

To align items horizontally, check this box

To align items vertically, check this box

4 Enter the distance between each item

5 Click OK

The options available for Horizontal spacing are **Items**, where the space will be a fixed amount between the right edge of one and the left edge of another; **Left** or **Right Edges**, where the measurement will be between the left or right edges of the selected items; and **Centres**, where the space will be measured between centres of the items.

Instead of left and right edges, the Vertical Alignment pop-up menu lets you measure from **Top** or **Bottom** edges.

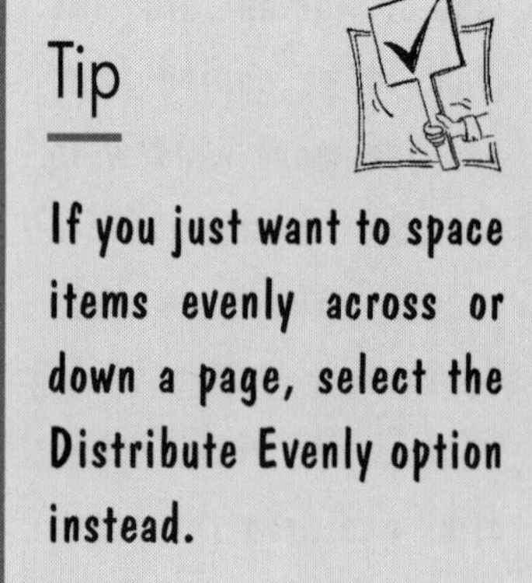

Tip

If you just want to space items evenly across or down a page, select the Distribute Evenly option instead.

Rotating items

Basic steps

1 Select an item.

❑ Using the Measurements palette

2 Click in the Measurements palette.

3 Type an angle.

❑ Using the Modify dialog box

4 Point to Item and select Modify.

5 Type an angle.

❑ Using the Rotate tool

6 Click the Rotate tool.

7 Click the mouse to create an axis point.

8 Drag to make a lever.

9 Move the mouse up and down to rotate.

6 Click on the Rotate tool

There are three ways of rotating items: via the Modify dialog box, the Measurements palette or the Rotate tool.

Using the Modify box or Measurements palette

The Modify dialog box and the Measurements palette allow you to rotate page items about their own axis – as if the centre of rotation was the centre of the item.

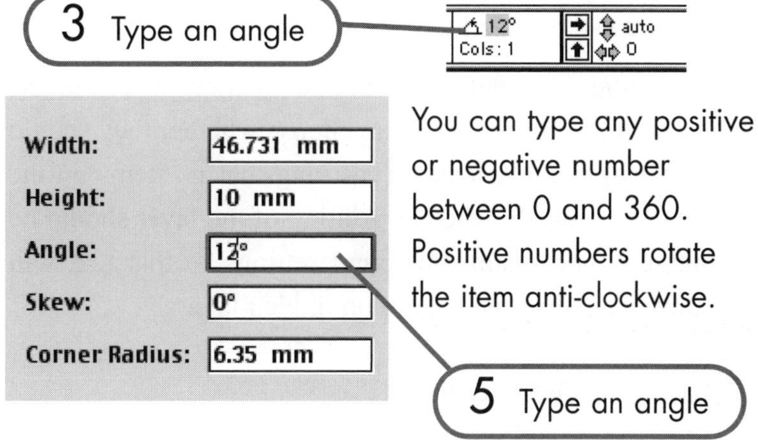

You can type any positive or negative number between 0 and 360. Positive numbers rotate the item anti-clockwise.

Using the Rotate tool

The Rotate tool is more versatile: you can set an axis for rotation, around which the item will revolve.

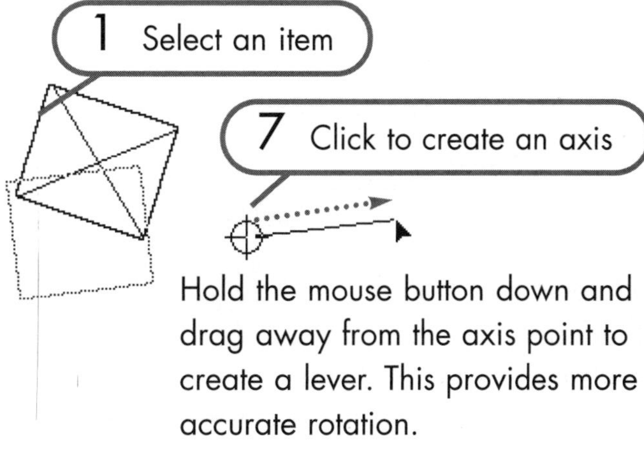

Hold the mouse button down and drag away from the axis point to create a lever. This provides more accurate rotation.

Layers

Basic steps

- ❑ To create a new layer
1. Point to View.
2. Select Show Layers.
3. Click the New Layer icon.

The new Layers feature in XPress 5 allows you to keep elements of your document on separate layers. Why might you want to do this? Simply because it makes managing objects on your document much easier. Layers can be hidden from view or set to not print, so you can keep all the elements you want to print on one layer and place instructions or notes on a separate layer.

New layers are active by default, so every item added after a layer is created is added to that layer.

You can adjust the default behaviour of new layers in the Preferences Dialog box. You can choose whether they should be visible by default, locked (ensuring that no items on the layer can be moved), whether printing of the layer should be suppressed), and retain runaround settings so that text will still flow around items that are on hidden layers.

Tip

One use for layers is in creating multi-language documents. Text in different languages can be kept in a single document, but stored on separate layers.

Creating a new layer

3 Click the New Layer icon

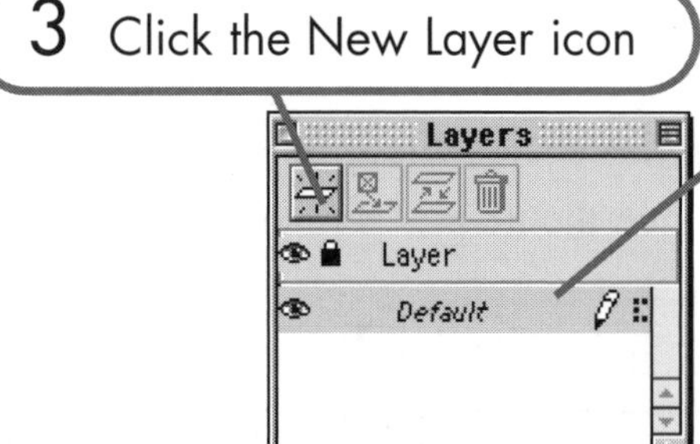

To delete a layer, highlight it in the palette and click the Delete Layer icon. Note that you can't delete the default layer.

A visual indicator appears at the top of every layered item. Its colour corresponds the the colour of the layer in the Layers palette.

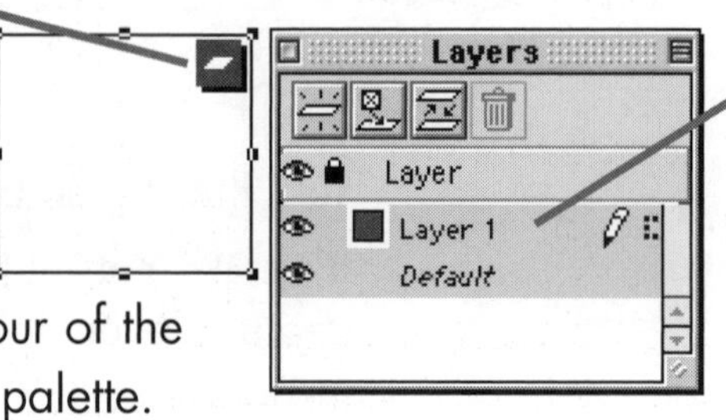

A new layer appears in the palette

Basic steps

❑ To copy a layer

1 [Ctrl]-click the layer's name in the Layers palette.

2 Select Duplicate layer from the menu.

❑ To hide a layer

3 Click on the layer's Visible icon in the Layers palette.

❑ To move an item to another layer

4 Select the document item to move.

5 Click the Move Item to Layer button in the Layers palette.

6 Choose a layer to move it to.

Tip

You can merge separate layers together. [Shift] click two or more layers in the Layers palette and click the Merge Layers button

Duplicating layers

When you duplicate a layer, you also copy the items and contents contained in that layer.

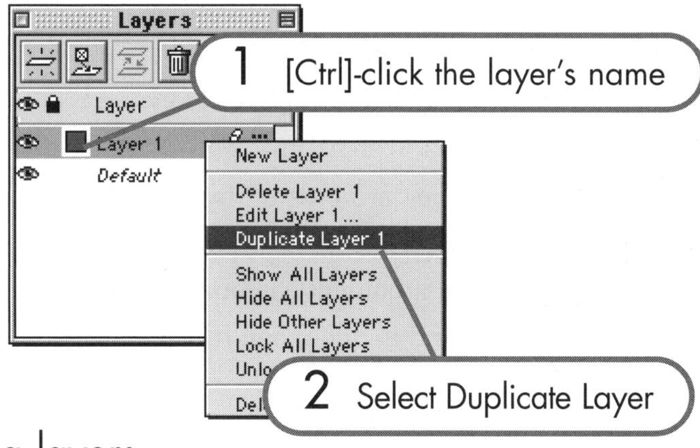

Hiding layers

Layered documents are ideal for creating multi-purpose publications, with different text on each layer. You can toggle the visibility of each layer – items on hidden layers do not print.

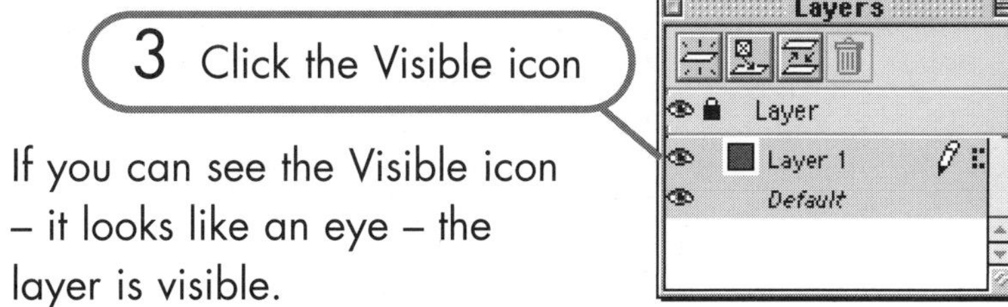

If you can see the Visible icon – it looks like an eye – the layer is visible.

Moving items between layers

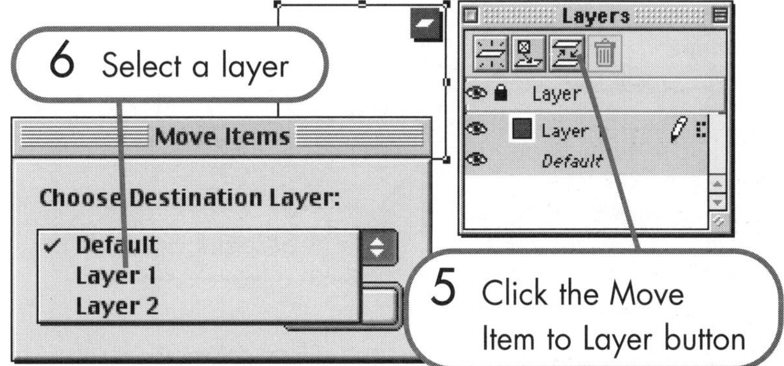

Boxes

Boxes are the cornerstones of an XPress document, containing the text, images and colours. There are two main types of box: text or picture. A third type, contentless, is designed simply to hold colours or shades.

Creating boxes

Text and picture boxes are created by clicking their respective icons on the Tools palette and dragging over the document area. To create a contentless box, you need to create a text or picture box and then change its content to 'None'.

Basic steps

1 Select the picture or text box tool.
2 Click once to start drawing the box.
3 Drag the crosshair over the document window to complete the box.
4 Release the button.

❑ To change the box type.

5 Select the box you want to convert.
6 Point to Item.
7 Select Content.
8 Choose the type of box to convert to.

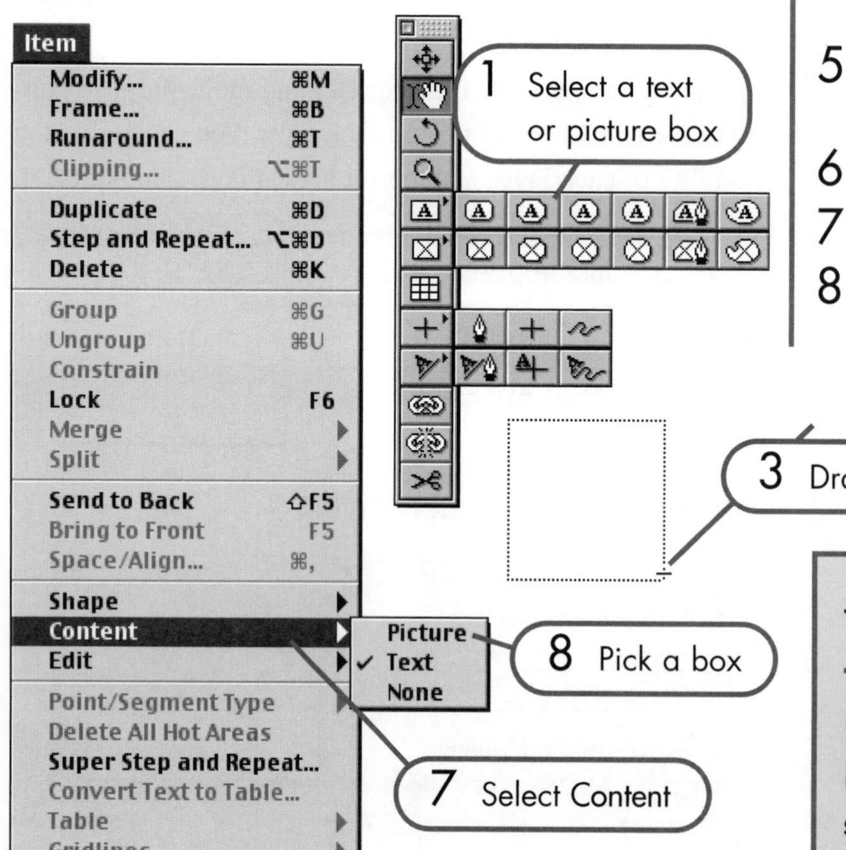

Take note

Box contents may be lost during the conversion, so save before changing box shapes.

Resizing and reshaping

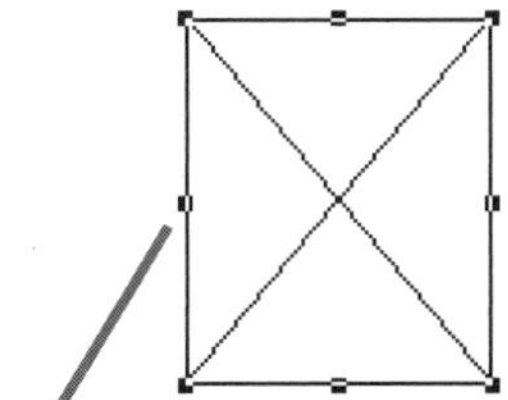

Click on one of the eight handles of the bounding box and drag in the desired direction.

You can resize a box by clicking and dragging one of its bounding handles – these are the small squares that become visible when you click on a box – or by entering new values in either the Measurements palette or the Modify dialog box.

To scale the contents of a box proportionally as you increase its size, hold down **[Ctrl]** and **[Shift]** (Windows) or **[Shift]**, **[Option]** and **[Command]** (Mac) as you drag the handles of the box in the desired direction.

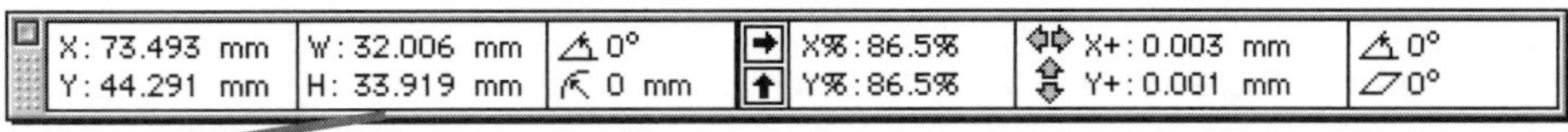

Enter new values in the Width and Height fields in the Measurements palette.

Basic steps

1 Select the box.
2 Point to Item.
3 Select Shape.
4 Click on a Shape.

Take note

You can change boxes into lines. If you convert text boxes containing text they automatically change to text paths.

Reshaping boxes

The shape of a box is chosen when you create it by selecting one of the text or picture boxes icons from the Tools palette. But you're not stuck with this choice: you can change it easily later via the **Shape** option in the **Item** menu.

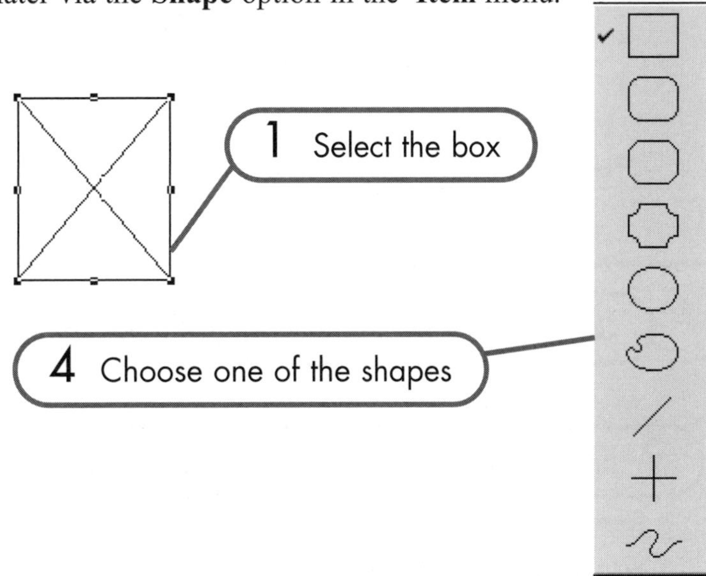

Changing corner radius

Although you can select rounded corner boxes as text or picture box shape in the Tools palette, you can also manually alter the roundness of the box corners.

Picture box with a corner radius of 0.

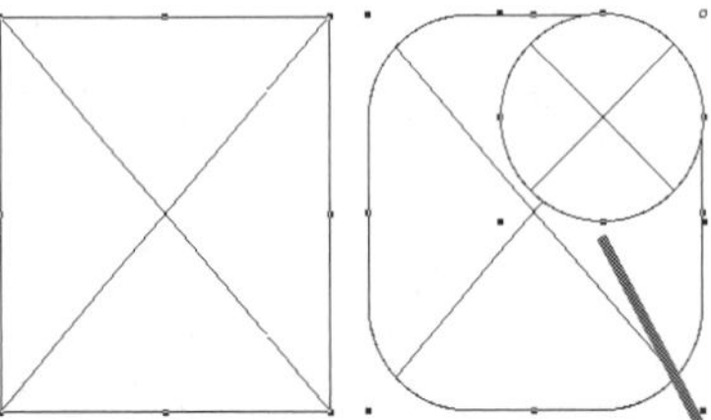

Picture box with a corner radius of 8mm. It has the same curve as a circle with an 8mm radius.

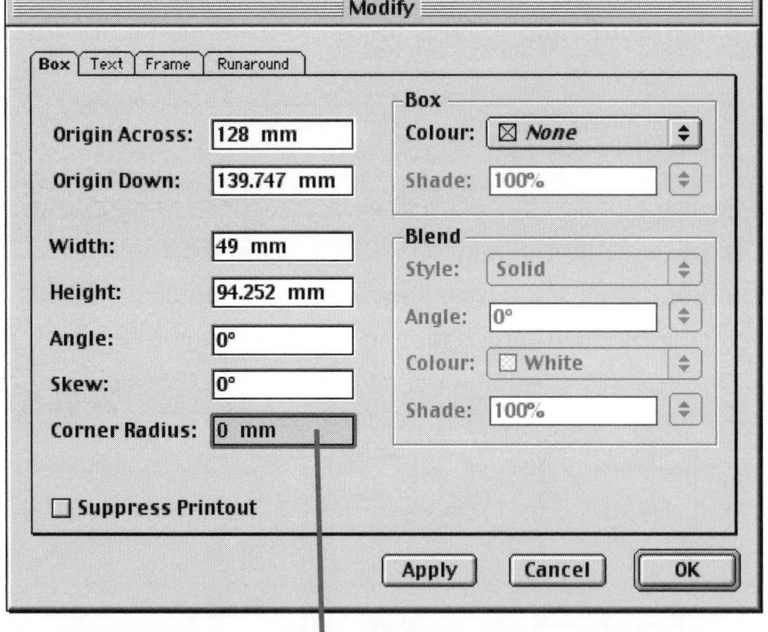

5 Enter a value in the Corner Radius field

9 Enter a value in the Corner Radius field

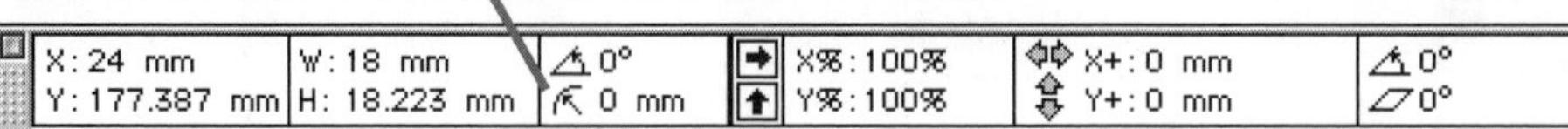

Basic steps

1 Click on a box.
2 Point to Item.
3 Select Modify.
4 Click the Box tab.
5 Enter the corner radius.
6 Click OK.

Or

7 Click on a picture box.
8 Open the Measurements palette.
9 Type the corner radius.

Take note

The corner radius of Bezier, oval or freehand boxes can't be adjusted; nor can you use the Measurements palette to adjust the radius of text box corners.

Frames

Basic steps

1 Select a box.
2 Point to Item.
3 Select Frame.
4 Click the Frame tab.
5 Choose the width and colour of the frame.
6 Choose a style from the drop-down menu.
7 Click OK.

The style is previewed in this window.

In print documents, frames are the borders that surround text and picture boxes for artistic effect. They can be created in a range of styles and you can even edit your own frame for that personalised effect.

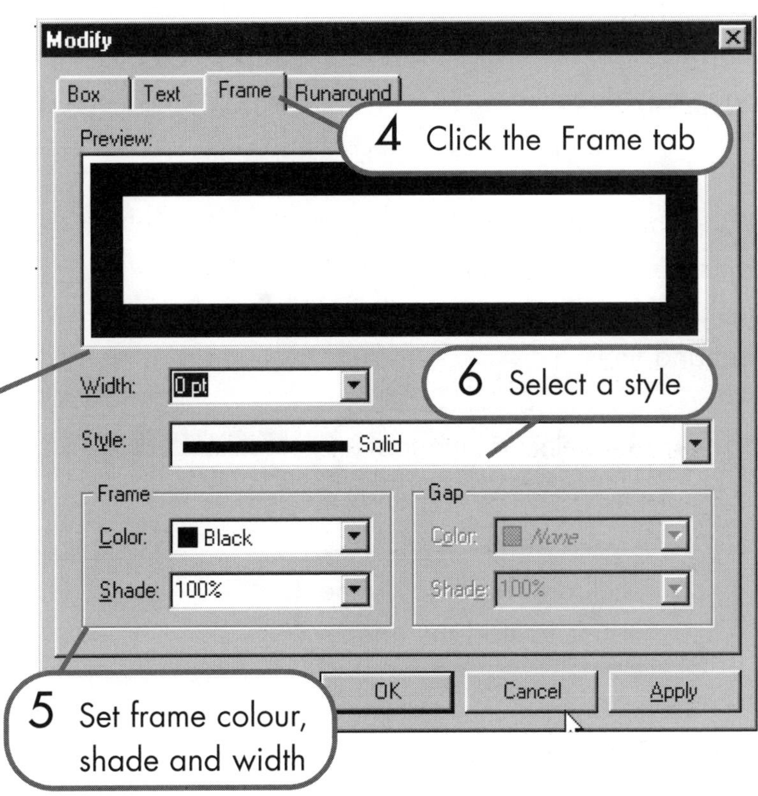

The style of a frame is selected from a drop-down menu:

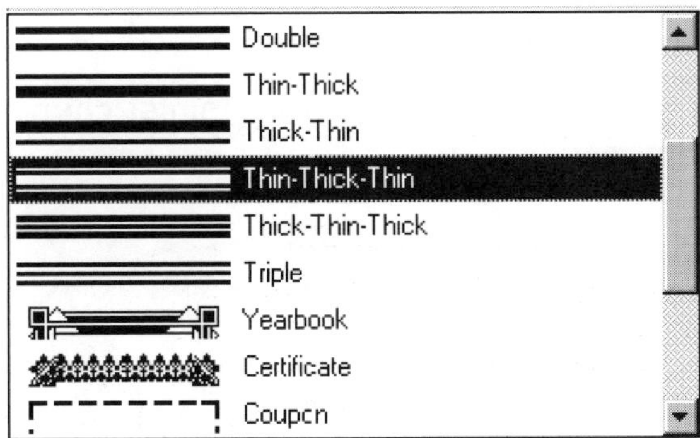

Tip

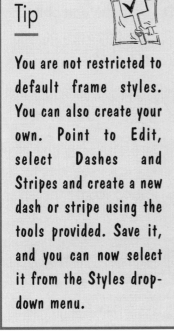

You are not restricted to default frame styles. You can also create your own. Point to Edit, select Dashes and Stripes and create a new dash or stripe using the tools provided. Save it, and you can now select it from the Styles drop-down menu.

Lines

Basic steps

QuarkXPress 5 supports four different types of line; including straight line tools and Bézier and freehand tools for creating curves and complex lines. For more about Bézier and freehand lines, see Chapter 9.

Line This draws a straight line in any direction

Bézier Line This creates lines mixing straight and curved segments

Orthogonal Line This draws horizontal or vertical straight lines

Freehand Line This creates freehand lines

1 Select a Line tool

2 Click and hold down the mouse to start the line

Resizing and rotating lines

5 Click one end of the line

The pointer changes to a hand icon.

6 Drag

Drag sideways to lengthen or shorten the line. Drag up or down to rotate it.

7 Enter measurements

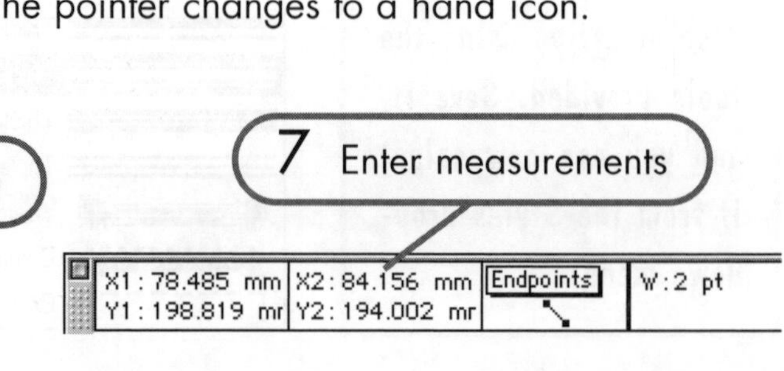

- ❑ To create a line

1 Select a Line tool.

2 Click and hold down the mouse in the document window to start the line.

3 Drag the crosshair and release at the end of the line.

- ❑ To move or rotate a line

4 Select the Item or Content tools.

5 Click on one end of the line.

6 Drag the end of the line sideways or up and down.

Or

7 Type a value in the Measurements palette.

Basic steps

1. Click on a line.
2. Click and hold down on the Line Style or Endcap boxes in the Measurements palette.
3. Choose a line style or Endcap from the drop down list.

Or

4. Click on a line.
5. Point to Item.
6. Select Modify.
7. Enter line style and arrowhead.
8. Click OK.

Tip

You can't change a line's thickness by clicking and dragging. Enter a value in the Width field of the Measurements palette or use the Modify dialog box instead.

Line styles and arrows

Who said lines should be simple? You can turn plain lines into arrows by adjusting their endcaps; or create dotted lines by adjusting their styles. What's better, you can even create your own style for that personal touch.

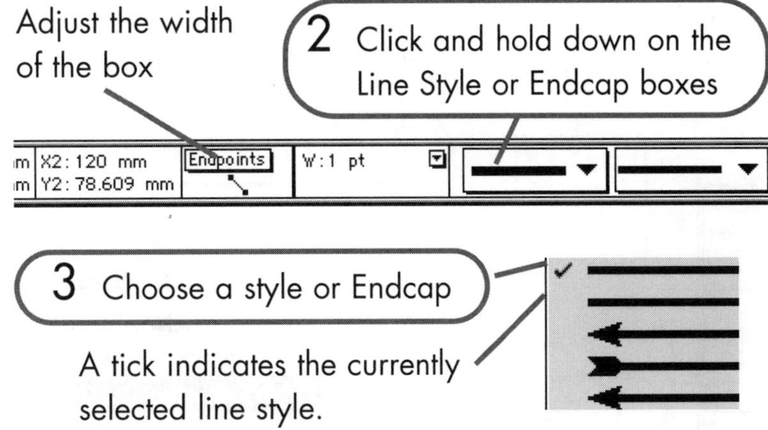

Adjust the width of the box
2 Click and hold down on the Line Style or Endcap boxes
X2: 120 mm
Y2: 78.609 mm
Endpoints
W: 1 pt
3 Choose a style or Endcap
A tick indicates the currently selected line style.

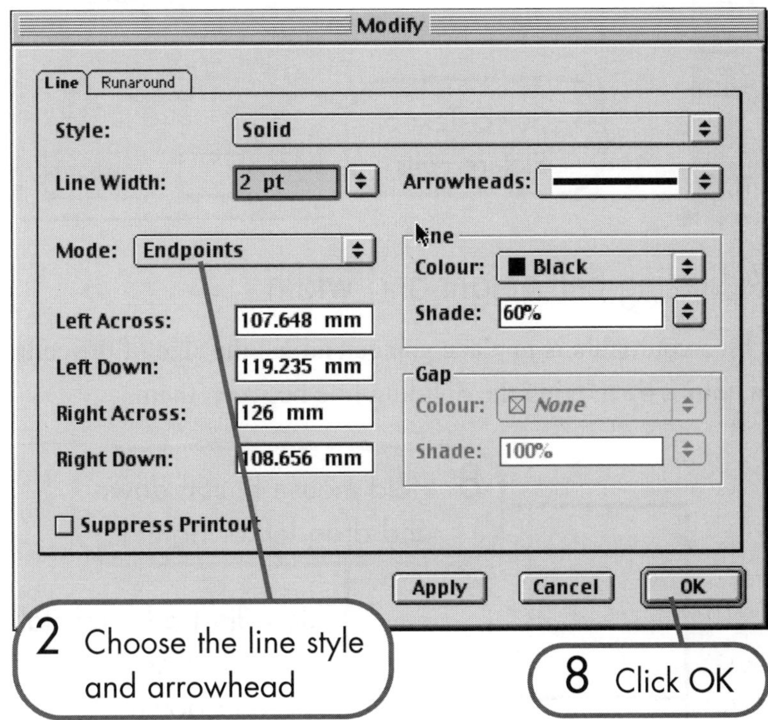

Tables

Tables are a great way of presenting tabular data, such as imported spreadsheet information and are particularly useful in Web documents (see Chapter 12). They are created in the same way as standard boxes: you are prompted to choose an initial number of rows and columns and whether they are comprised of text or picture cells. This can be subsequently changed in the same way as the content of standard boxes.

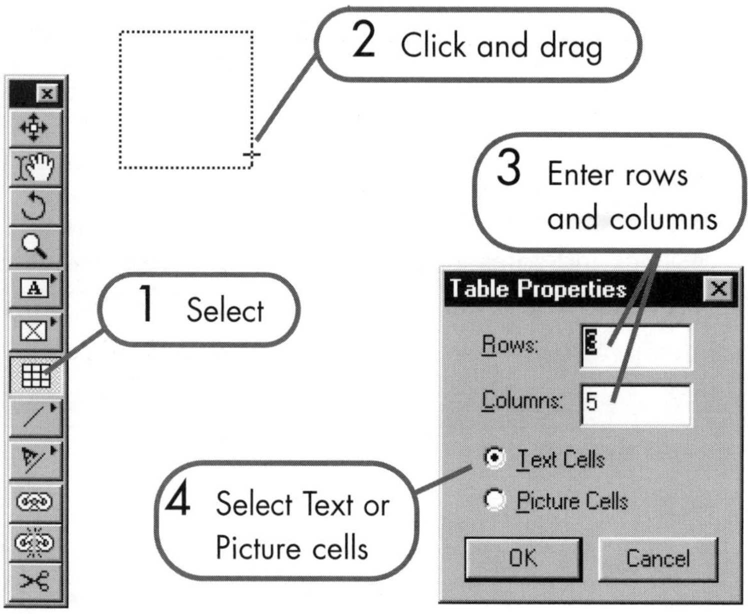

Adjusting cell height and width

Once your table is in place you can adjust the size of the cells within it by moving the dividing line between them.

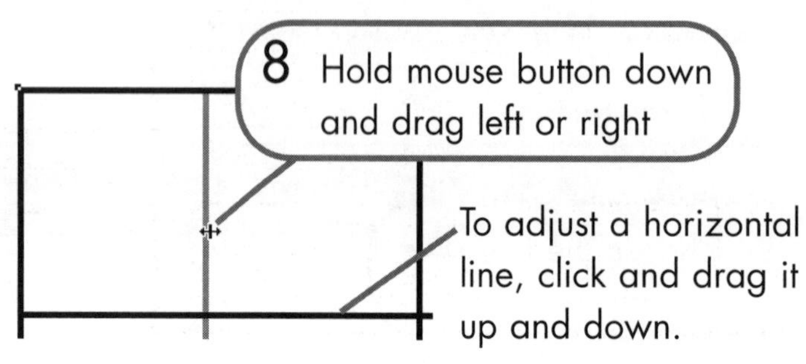

8 Hold mouse button down and drag left or right
To adjust a horizontal line, click and drag it up and down.

Basic steps

1 Select the Tables tool.
2 Click and drag the pointer to make a rectangle. Release when you have the shape you want.
3 In the dialog box, enter the desired number of rows and columns.
4 Choose between Text or Picture cells.
5 Click OK.

- To adjust cell height and width

6 Select the Content tool.
7 Click on a dividing line.
8 Drag the line to the new position.

Take note

To move a table, select the Item tool, click on the table and drag.

Basic steps

- To delete cells

1 Click on the edge of the row or column to delete. The pointer changes to an arrow.

2 Point to Item and select Table.

3 Click Delete Row.

- To convert text to a table

4 Select the text.

5 Point to Item and select Text to Table.

6 Choose Options.

7 Click OK.

Tip

To join cells, [Shift]-click to select them with the Content tool active. Point to Item, select Table and click Combine Cells.

To remove rows or columns

To add cells, select the Content tool, click inside the box and select **Insert Rows…** or **Insert Columns…** from the **Table** submenu. Removal needs only a little more work.

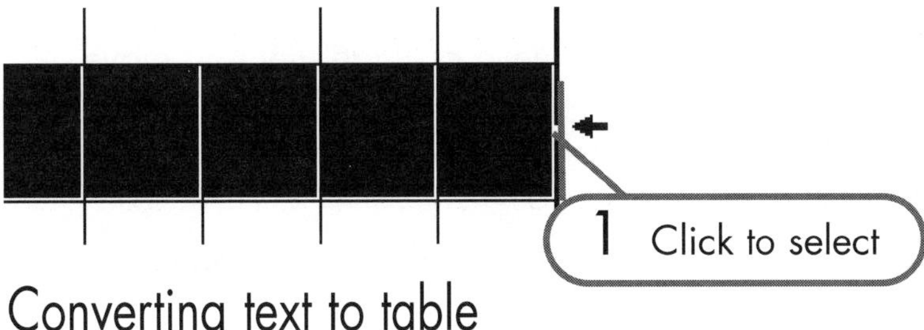

Converting text to table

Individual table cells behave like text or picture boxes and you add data to them in the same way. To move between them, press **[Ctrl]-[Tab]**.

You can also convert existing text to a table with the **Convert Text to Table** dialog box. If you choose Paragraphs in the **Separate Rows With** pull-down menu, **Text to Table** creates a new row every time it encounters a new paragraph. Alternatively, you can create a new column at every tab, space or comma. You can choose similar options in the **Separate Columns With** menu.

The **Cell Fill Order** pop-up menu determines the order cells will be filled in. By default, it fills cells from left to right from the top.

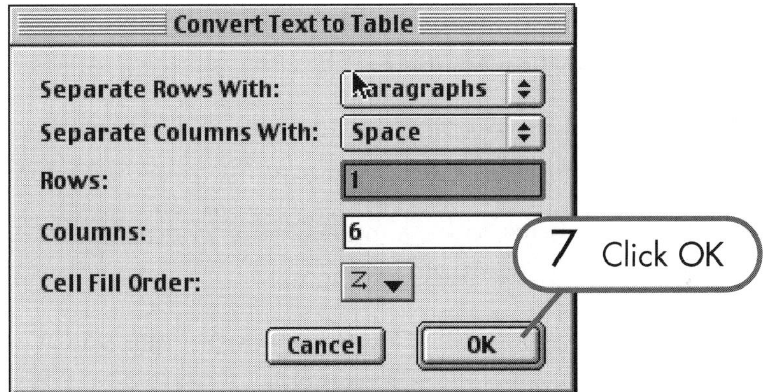

Summary

- ❑ Use Rulers and page guides to help you place items on a page.
- ❑ Use scroll bars to navigate pages and the Document Layout palette or Page menu to move through whole documents.
- ❑ To change a view of a document, use the Zoom tool.
- ❑ Use the Item or Content tools to select items.
- ❑ To move items, select them with the Item tool and drag them to their destination.
- ❑ To move an item above or below another, select Bring to Front... or Send to Back... from the Item menu.
- ❑ Use Space/Align... to make sure there is consistent spacing between page items.
- ❑ The Rotate tool in the Tools palette is the most versatile of rotating items on a page as you can specify your own axis for the rotation.
- ❑ Layers allow you to manage the elements on your page easily.
- ❑ There are three types of boxes and you can switch between each.
- ❑ Boxes can also be resized and reshaped by clicking its bounding handles
- ❑ Frames can have both practical and artistic uses – and you can even create your own.
- ❑ Lines don't have to be simple. You can easily add styles and arrowheads to them.
- ❑ XPress can create tables – but think of them as text or picture boxes linked together.

3 Your first document

Creating a document

Creating a new document in XPress is simple as long as you approach things logically. The numerous options that you need to work in the **New Document** dialog box appear every time you create a new document, but the program remembers your settings the next time you open the file.

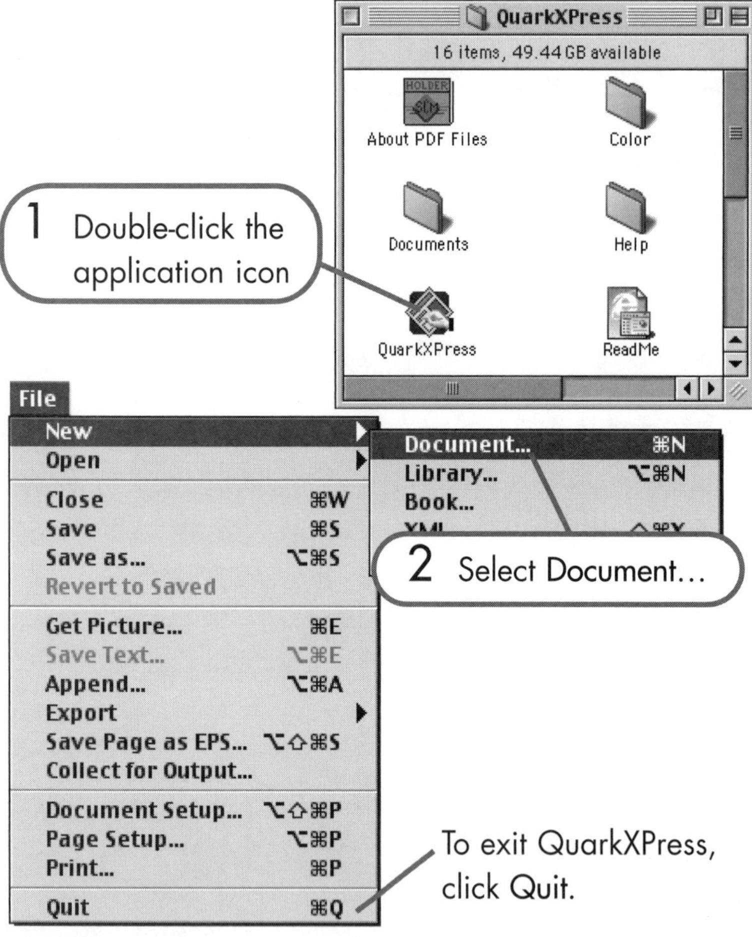

Margin guides

Margin guides don't affect printing. But keeping text within them keeps pages neater. You can set margins for top, bottom, left and right sides of the page. If you click Automatic Text Box (see page 39), left and right change to inside and outside.

Basic steps

1. Double-click on the application's icon. This launches the application.
2. Point to File, select New and then Document. The New Document dialog box appears.
3. Select a page size by choosing a prebuilt size from the pull-down menu or entering the dimensions in the boxes below it.
4. Choose Portrait or Landscape format.
5. Set columns guides.
6. Click OK.

Tip

Enter page dimensions in points (p), millimetres (mm), picas, centimetres (cm) or inches ("). QuarkXPress understands them all!

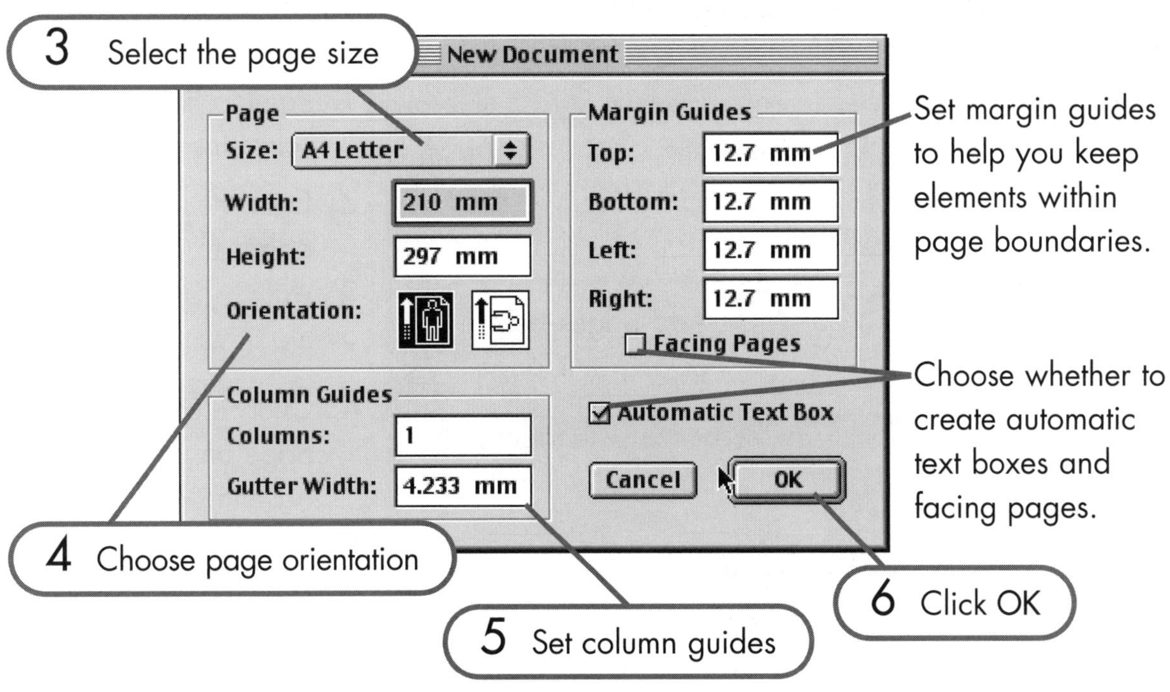

Tip
Don't worry too much about the settings you select here: you can change them later.

Tip
Select Snap to Guides in the View menu: boxes and lines will snap to column and margin guides!

Column guides

Column guides also help you plan your document. Enter the number of columns to include and QuarkXPress will divide the space between the margin guides into the specified number of columns. You must also select the **gutter width**; this is the blank space between each column.

Automatic text box

Selecting Automatic Text Box creates a text box on every new page in your document. This can be useful if you're creating long, simple text documents. For complex documents you'll probably prefer more manual control.

Facing pages

If you select Facing Pages in the New Document box, pages will appear next to each other on the screen. Facing page documents are useful for creating magazine-style layouts.

Changing pages

Basic steps

1 Point to Page and select Insert...
2 Enter the number of pages to add.
3 Choose where to add the pages.
4 Choose a master page on which to base the pages.
5 Click OK.

Or

6 Open the Document Layout palette.
7 Click and drag a page icon over the document area.
8 Release at the point at which you want to add the page.

Adding pages

There are two ways to add pages to a document: via the **Page** menu or by using the Document Layout palette.

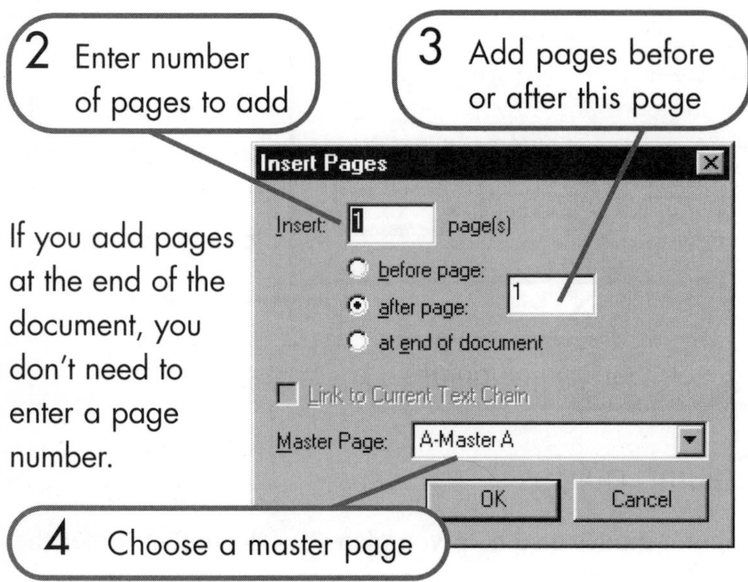

If you add pages at the end of the document, you don't need to enter a page number.

Each page you create is automatically based on a master page. For more about editing master pages, see page 44.

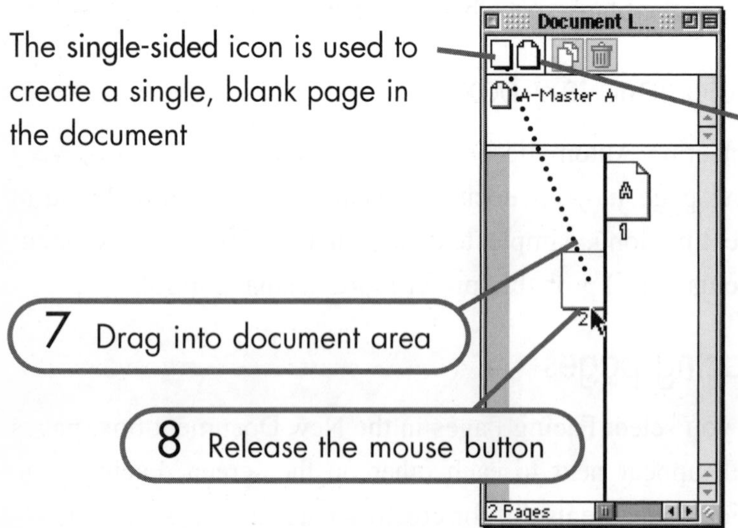

The single-sided icon is used to create a single, blank page in the document

A facing page icon creates a single page in a spread.

Basic steps

1 Point to Page, click on Delete... and enter the numbers of the pages to delete.

2 Click OK.

Or

3 Open the Document Layout palette and click on the page to delete.

4 Click the Delete icon.

❑ To move pages

5 Point to Page and select Move...

6 Type in the page or page range to move in the fields.

7 Choose where to move the items and click OK.

Or

8 Open the Document Layout palette and click on the page to move.

9 Drag to its new position.

Deleting pages

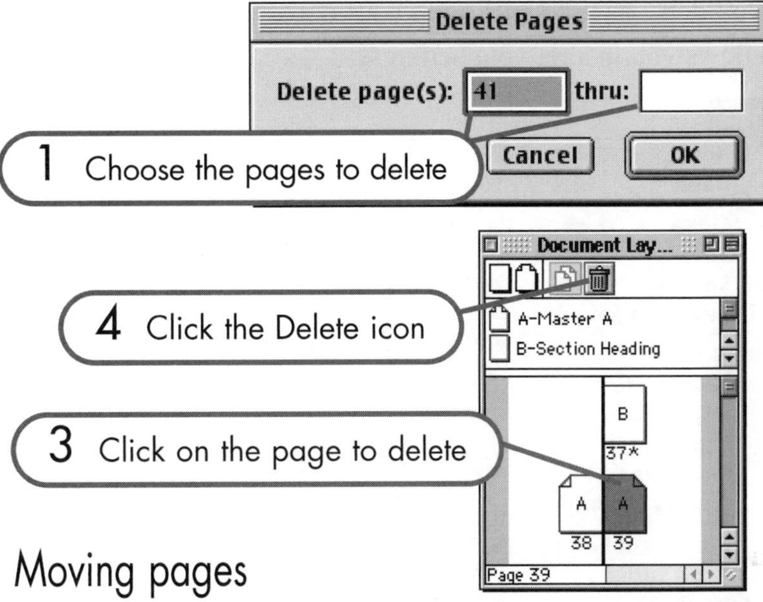

Moving pages

Use the Page menu or Document Layout palette to move pages. When you use the Layout palette, the appearance of the cursor changes to show where the page will be added.

- Subsequent pages will be forced to the right.
- The page will appear between pages in a spread.

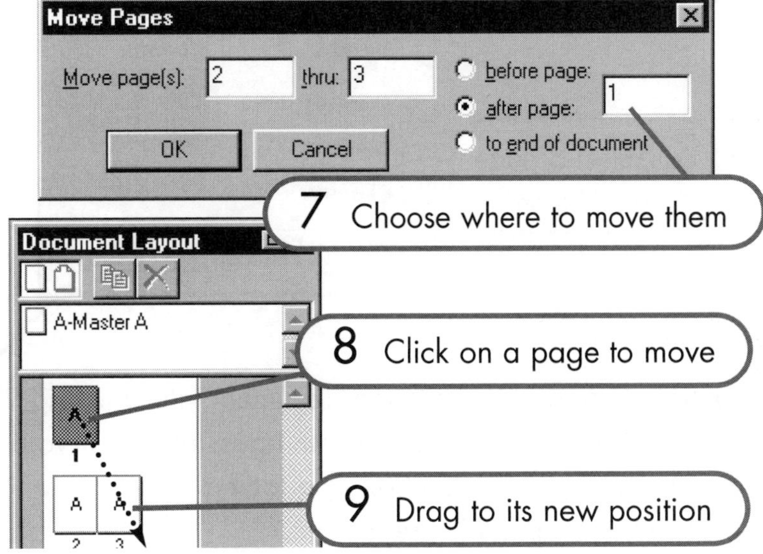

Adjusting your setup

You don't have to stick with your document's setup; XPress allows you to alter your settings.

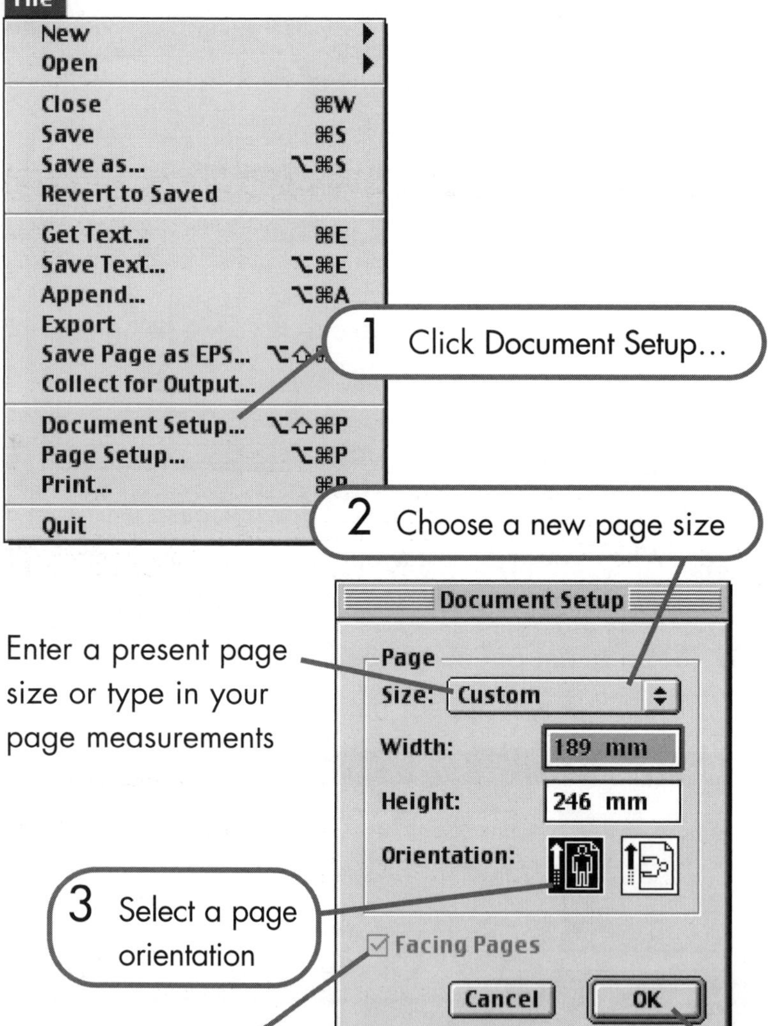

You can change a single page document into a facing page document, but the reverse isn't possible, so if you open the Document Setup box in a facing page document, this option is greyed out.

Basic steps

1. Point to File and elect Document Setup…
2. Choose a page size.
3. Adjust page orientation if necessary.
4. Click OK.

4 Click OK

Take note

You can change margin and column guides by adjusting master pages. See page 46.

Take note

If you don't specify a measurement in the Width and Height fields, XPress takes the default chosen in the Preferences dialog box.

Basic steps

1 Point to File, select New and choose Library...

2 Enter a name for the library and click Create.

❑ To add an item to the Library palette

3 Select the Item tool.

4 Drag an item over the palette window and release the mouse.

❑ To transfer an item from the Library palette

5 Highlight an item in the palette.

6 Drag the item over the document window and release the mouse.

❑ To label a library entry

7 Double-click the item in the Library palette.

8 Type a label or choose an existing one from the drop-down menu.

Libraries

A library stores commonly-used items or groups of items, such as picture or text boxes and lines. Items are added to a library by dragging them onto the Library palette from the page; the reverse process takes them from a library to the page.

To save libraries becoming unwieldy, you can categorise library entries by labelling them.

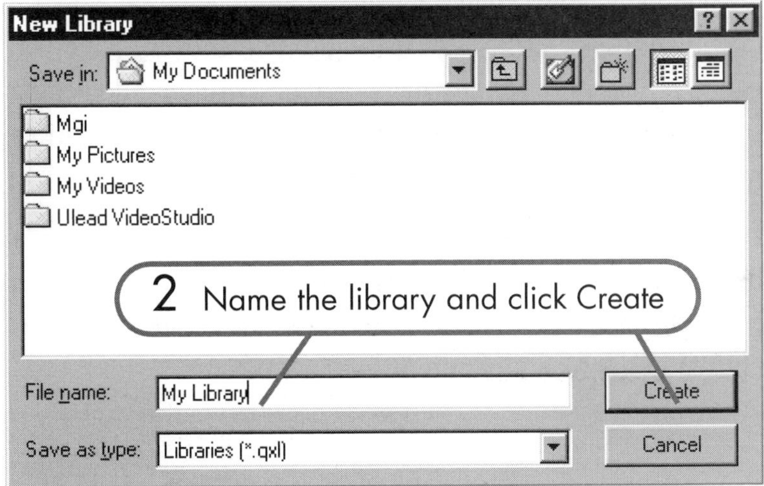

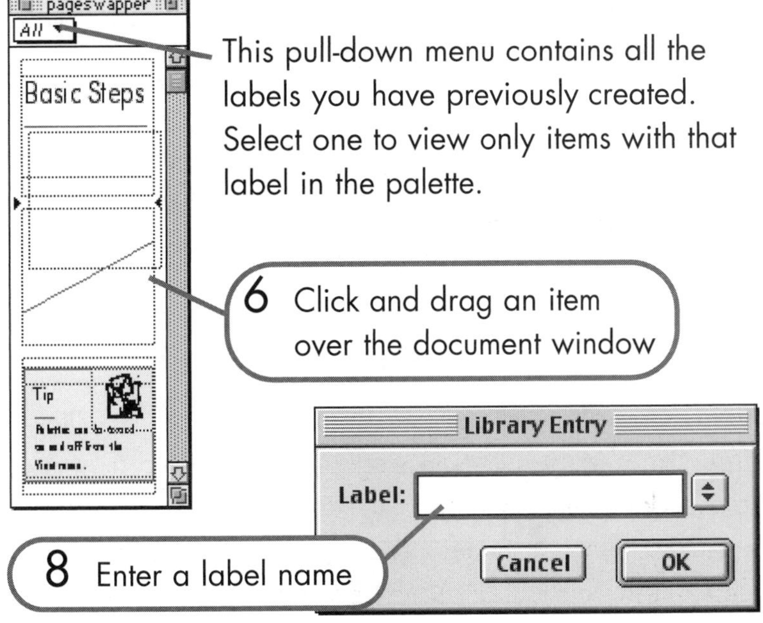

pageswapper
All
Basic Steps
Tip
This pull-down menu contains all the labels you have previously created. Select one to view only items with that label in the palette.
6 Click and drag an item over the document window
Library Entry
Label:
Cancel
OK
8 Enter a label name

Master pages

Basic steps

Take a look at most books or magazines and you'll notice that many pages contain boxes, lines and text in the same position on each page.

In XPress you can easily create repeating elements using master pages. Master pages act like templates for individual pages. They are managed from the master pages area of the Document Layout palette and make editing the layout of a document easier: instead of having to adjust every page you can alter master pages and these changes will be reflected on every page based on that master. You can create multiple master pages and apply them to different document pages.

As we saw on page 40, every new document page is already based on a master, even if you don't set one: the default master page, called Master A, uses the current settings chosen in the **New Document** dialog box.

1 Point to View and slick Show Document Layout.

2 Click (Mac) or double-click (Windows) the master page icon.

Or

3 Click and hold down on the Navigation pop-up palette.

Or

4 Select a master page from the Page menu.

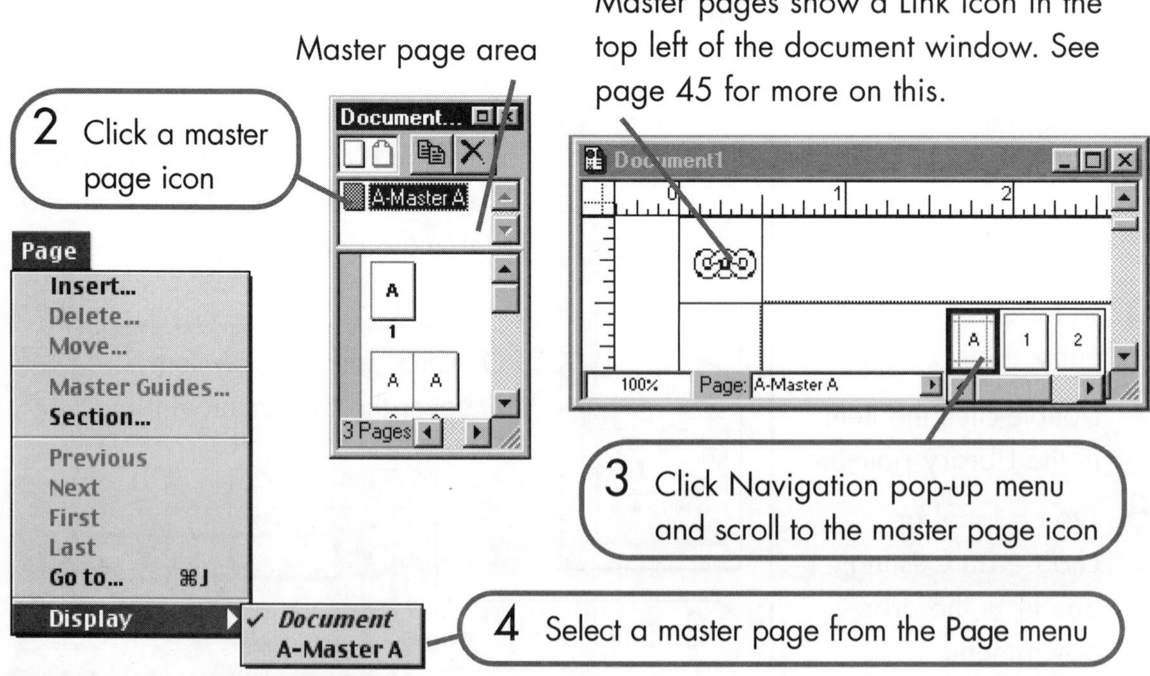

Basic steps

1 Open the master page you want to add the automatic link to.
2 Draw a text box.
3 Click on the Linking tool in the Tools palette.
4 Click on the Linking icon on the top left of the open master page.
5 Click on the text box.

Creating automatic links with master pages

Master pages have one special property: they can automatically link text boxes, so that when you add text to a box in a document (you'll see how to do this on page 53), XPress flows text between pages based on that master page.

There are two ways of creating automatic page links. The first is to check the Automatic text box option in the **New Document** dialog box (see page 39). When you do this, XPress creates an automatic text box on the default master page. But you can also create automatic text boxes on any master page easily.

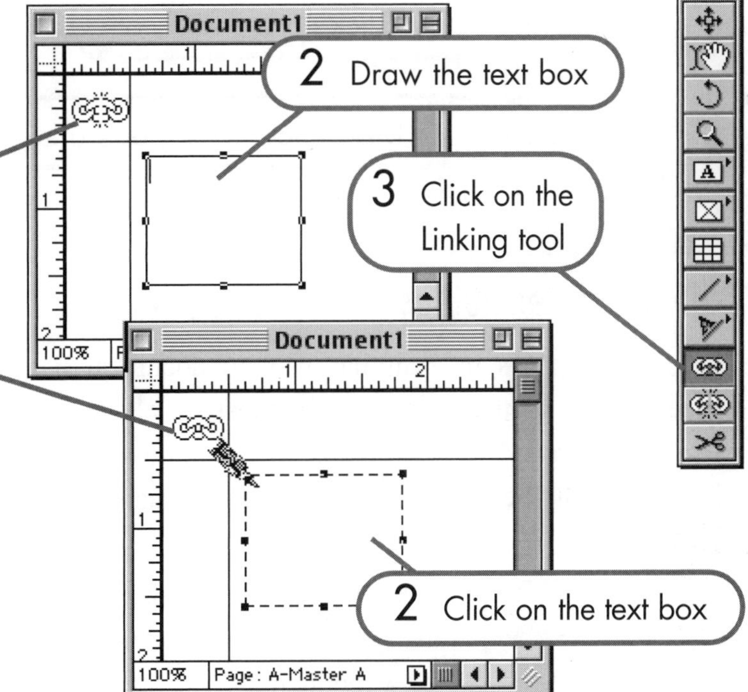

Note how the Linking icon has changed status to show it is enabled.

Take note

Unlike normal text boxes placed on a master, you can't type text directly inside an automatically linked text box on a master page.

To test the automatic link, go to a page in the document based on this master and enter text into the matching text box. If the text overflows the box, XPress will create a new page based on the same master and automatically flow the text into this box. To see how to manually link text boxes, see page 54.

Creating new master pages

You can create single or spread master pages using the single or facing page icons at the top of the Layout palette – note that you can only create facing page master pages if you have created a document with facing pages (see page 39). New master pages are prefixed in sequence – A, B, C and so on – and document page icons show the initial of the master they are based on. You can edit the name of a master page by highlighting its name in the master page area and typing a new name.

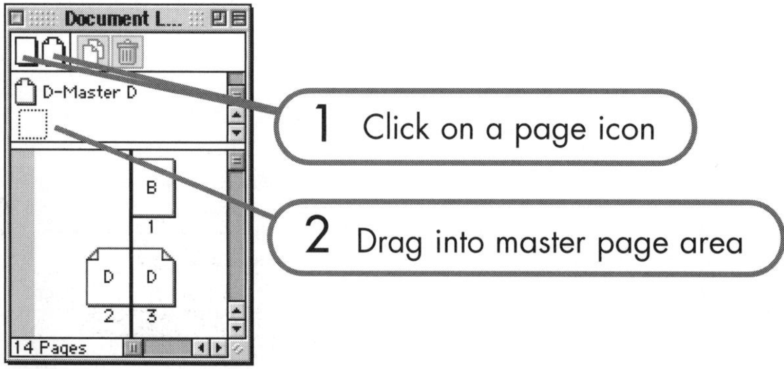

Editing master guides

Treat master pages in a similar way to document pages. Objects added to the master page repeat on all document pages based on it. But some items, like column and margin guides, can only be edited when you are on a master page.

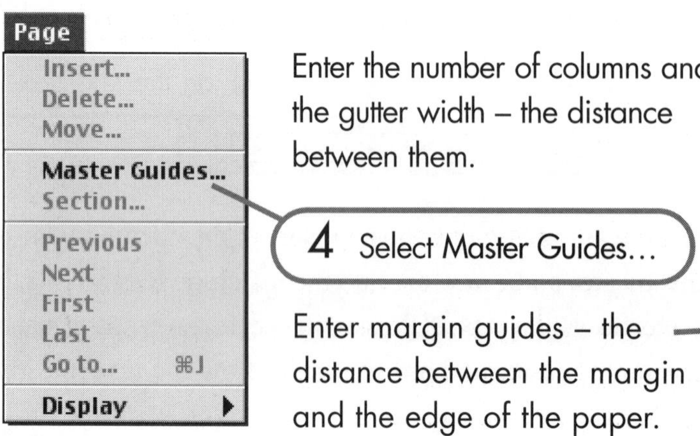

Basic steps

1 Click on a single-sided or facing page icons.

2 Drag into the master page area and release the mouse.

❑ To edit master guides

3 Select a master page.

4 Point to Page and select Master Guides...

5 Enter layout details.

6 Click OK.

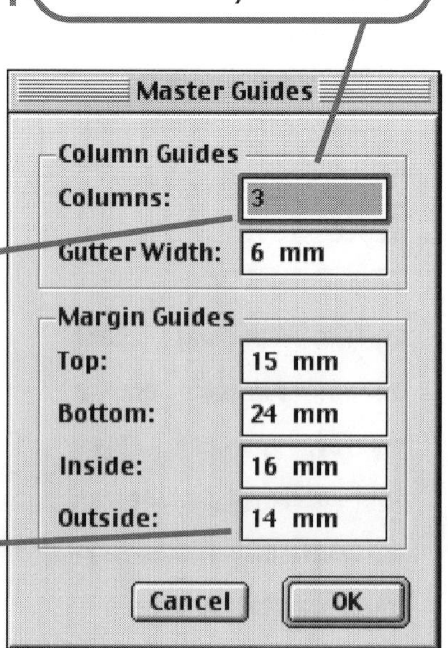

Basic steps

❑ To add a new page

1 Click and drag the icon over the document layout area.

2 Release the mouse.

❑ To apply a master

3 Click and drag over the document layout area.

4 Release the mouse.

Take note

Items on a document page generated by a master page can become localised so that the document page won't update if changes are made to the master. Reshaping a box on a document page localises an item, but editing text in a box localises its content, so the box can still be reshaped from the master.

Adding and applying master pages

We saw on page 40 how to add new pages, which were automatically based on a master. You can add pages based on a specific master page by dragging a master page icon over the document layout area, or apply a master to an existing page using the same technique.

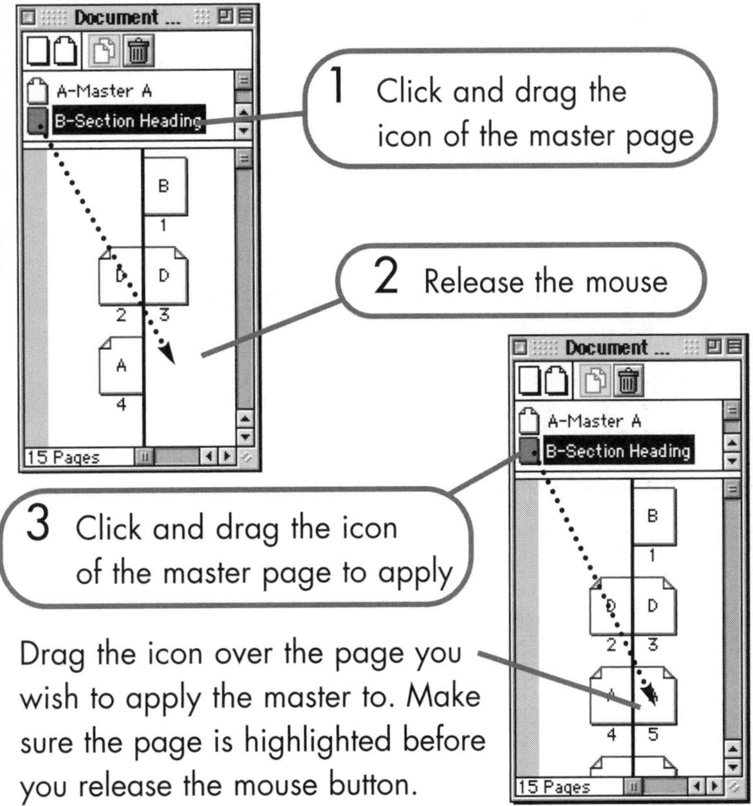

Tip

To avoid accidentally amending master page items thinking that you are in a document page, lock master page elements (select Lock from the Item menu) when you have finished with hem.

Saving a document

To avoid accidentally losing your work, regularly save your file by selecting **Save** from the **File** menu and choosing a name and a place to store your document.

The Save dialog box also includes additional options. For example, you have the option of saving the file as an XPress 4-compatible document. Take advantage of this if you need your document to be opened by older versions of the program. Otherwise, choose version 5.

You can also save the document as a template, rather than a standard file. Saving a document as a template prevents it from accidental erasure – whenever a template is opened, a new document window, containing all the elements that you saved under the template, is spawned.

After you save a document for the first time, it's automatically stored in its current location every time you save it. To store it under another name use the **Save As** command from the **Edit** menu. This works as if you were saving for the first time, giving you the option to rename your document and choose a different location in which to save it.

Basic steps

1 Point to File and select Save.

Or

2 Press [Ctrl]-[S] (Windows) or [Command]-[S] (Macintosh).

3 Choose the drive or folder in which to store your file.

4 Type the name of your file.

5 Click Save.

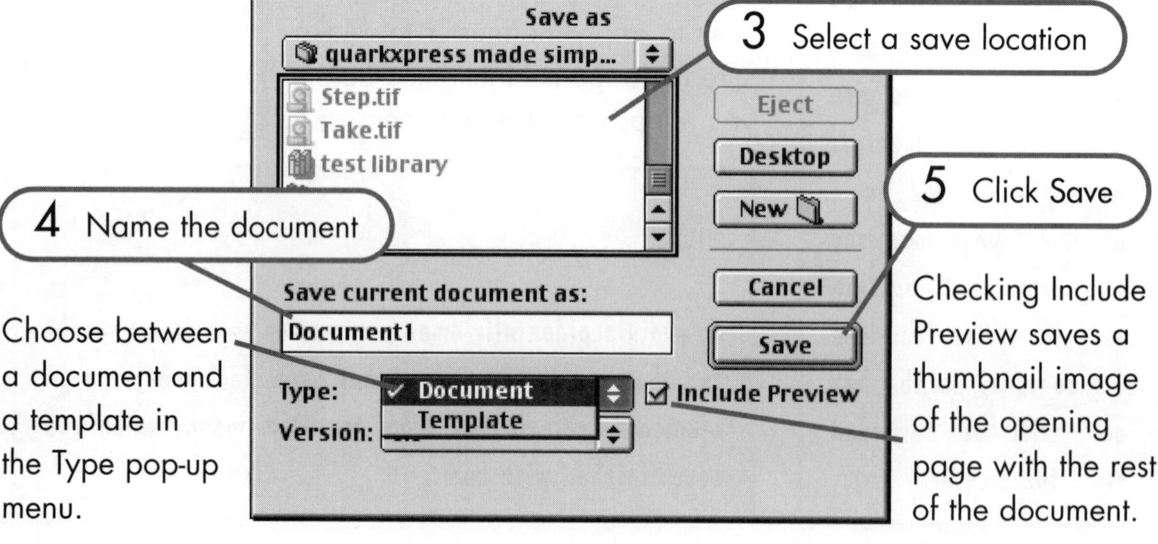

Choose between a document and a template in the Type pop-up menu.

Checking Include Preview saves a thumbnail image of the opening page with the rest of the document.

Basic steps

1 Point to Edit and select Preferences.
2 Click on Save.
3 Check Auto Save.
4 Enter the number of minutes between saves.
5 Check Auto Backup.
6 Enter the number of revisions and choose a destination folder.
7 Click OK.

Auto Save and Auto Backup

Auto Save and **Auto Backup** perform similar functions: creating copies of your document at set intervals.

When you activate Auto Save, instead of writing over your existing file, XPress creates another that tracks the changes you make to your document in a file stored in the same directory (or folder) as the original. You can still revert to your original document.

Auto Backup keeps a copy of manually saved files in a user-specified location on your hard disk. You can choose the number of backups that XPress should make, and the oldest backup is automatically overwritten when the specified number of backups is reached. Both options can be turned on and off in the **Application Preferences** dialog box.

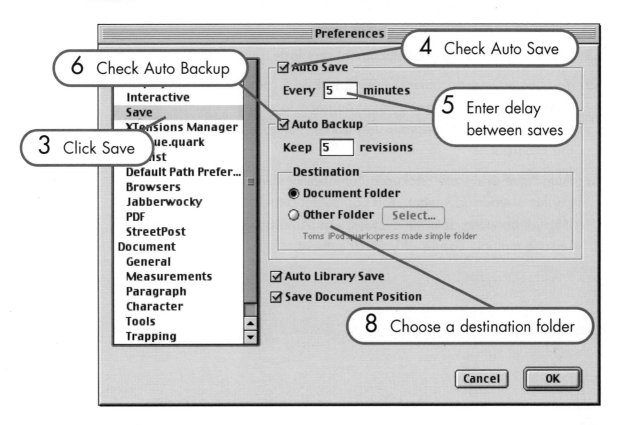

Preferences

6 Check Auto Backup
4 Check Auto Save
3 Click Save
5 Enter delay between saves
8 Choose a destination folder

Interactive
Save
XTensions Manager
...ue.quark
...ist
Default Path Prefer...
Browsers
Jabberwocky
PDF
StreetPost
Document
General
Measurements
Paragraph
Character
Tools
Trapping

Auto Save
Every 5 minutes
Auto Backup
Keep 5 revisions
Destination
Document Folder
Other Folder Select...
Toms iPod:quarkxpress made simple folder
Auto Library Save
Save Document Position
Cancel OK

Summary

- ❑ Create your document's settings in the New Document dialog box.
- ❑ Use the Page menu or Document Layout palette to add, move or delete pages in your document.
- ❑ Libaries are great places to store commonly used page items, such as logos or frequently-repeated text boxes. They can be organised by category.
- ❑ If you want a lot of pages to share the same elements, use master pages.
- ❑ Master pages act like templates for individual pages. You can have more than one master page for each document.
- ❑ You can change page size and layout at any time using the Document Setup dialog box.
- ❑ Don't forget to save your document regularly.
- ❑ You can save a document in version 4 or 5 formats. Save in the latest format unless you need to share your documents with users using earlier versions of the program.
- ❑ Auto Save and Auto Backup automatically save copies of your docoment. You can select a time interval between automatic saves. Use Auto Backup to save multiple copies of your document.

4 Word processing

Importing text

The easiest way to get text into a QuarkXPress 5 document is to import it. You can do this from a number of third-party word processor applications, including Microsoft Word.

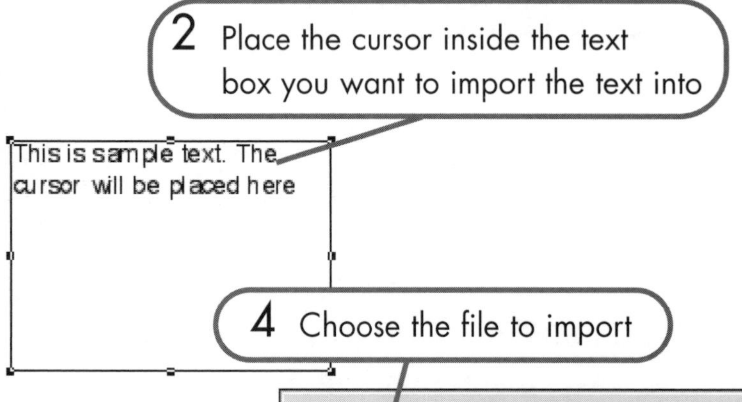

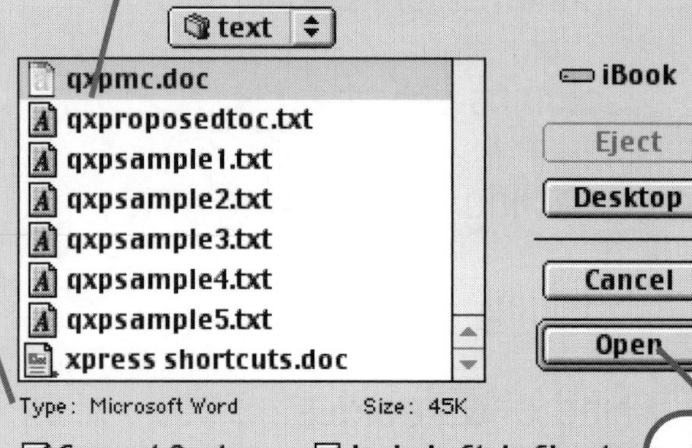

XPress tells you here the type of text file you have selected. XPress can understand a number of different native text formats.

Select Convert Quotes to turn straight quotes and double hyphens into typesetter's quotation marks and dashes respectively.

If your document has styled text that you want to include, check Include Style Sheets. XPress will include the styles in its Style Sheets palette (see page 84).

Basic steps

1 Select the Content tool.
2 Place the cursor in a text box.
3 Point to File and select Get Text...
4 Choose the file to open.
5 Click **Open**.

Take note

Before importing text, it is a good idea to turn off Auto Page Insertion in the Preferences dialog box.

Text input

Basic steps

1. Create a text box.
2. Make sure the Content tool is active. It is automatically selected when you create the text box.
3. Start typing!

QuarkXPress 5 includes powerful text editing tools in its own right, so you can use it as a word processor, either to write stories from scratch, or to edit imported text. Most of the program's features will be familiar to anyone who has used an application like Microsoft Word or WordPerfect.

To type in a text box from scratch

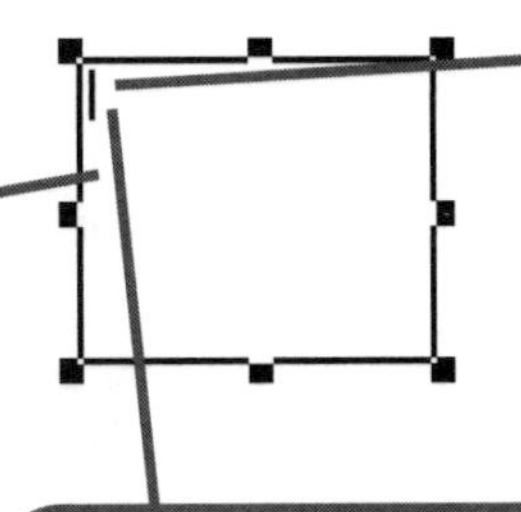

1 Create a new text box

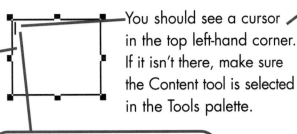

You should see a cursor in the top left-hand corner. If it isn't there, make sure the Content tool is selected in the Tools palette.

3 Start typing at the cursor

Take note

XPress supports most common word processor formats, such as Word, Works and WordPerfect. If your word processing application isn't directly supported, either save your file in one of these formats and import it, or cut and paste the text from your word processor into an XPress text box.

Overflow text

If you add more words to a text box than it can hold, QuarkXPress doesn't increase its size. Instead it lets you know that there is overmatter by displaying a small red square at the bottom right of the text box.

You can remedy this problem in three ways: by reducing the amount of text, adjusting the size of the box or the text inside it, or by adding further linking boxes (see page 54), so that the text flows from one box to the next. As soon as the text fits in the box, the overflow icon will disappear.

I've seen
most users trying out different
rendering won't be as accurate on
less reliable. Instead it's a fear that

The text overflow icon shows there is too much text to fit inside the box.

Linking text chains

You can allow text to flow from one box to another by linking them to create a chain.

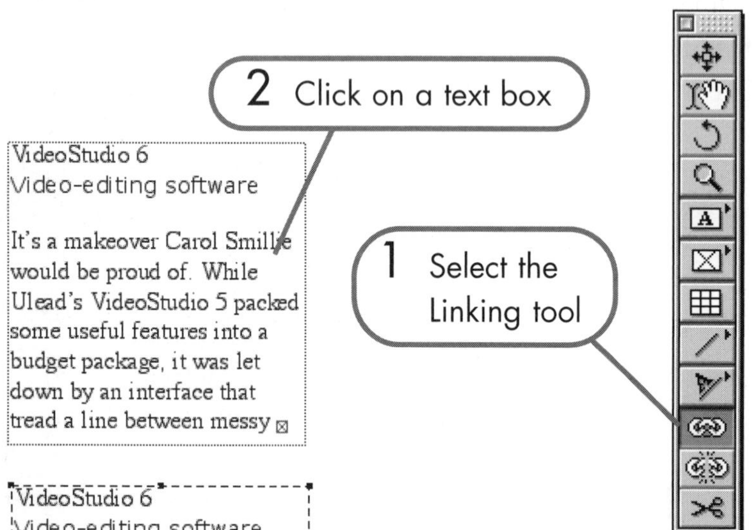
2 Click on a text box
VideoStudio 6
Video-editing software
It's a makeover Carol Smillie would be proud of. While Ulead's VideoStudio 5 packed some useful features into a budget package, it was let down by an interface that tread a line between messy
1 Select the Linking tool

The outline of the selected text box should now resemble a row of marching ants

3 Click on an empty box

Text will flow into the empty text box. Watch for an arrow quickly appearing to show the flow of the text.

Basic steps

1 Select the Linking tool.

2 Click on the text box that you want to flow your text from.

3 Click on the text box you want to flow your text into. This must be empty: you can't link a text box to another box that already contains text.

Tip

To add a linked box between two existing boxes, select the Linking tool, click the preceding text box and then the new text box.

Unlinking text chains

Basic steps

1. Select the Unlinking tool.
2. Click on a linked text box.
3. Click on the end of the arrow.

Tip

You can reverse the order of two linked boxes by selecting the Linking tool, clicking on the second linked box, and then clicking on the first. You can use this technique to add a fresh box to the start of a linked text chain. Add the new box as the second box in the chain and then switch their order.

When it comes to unlinking boxes, the procedure is simply reversed. Unlinking a text box doesn't delete the text within it: it is retained in the first text box, even though you may not be able to see it.

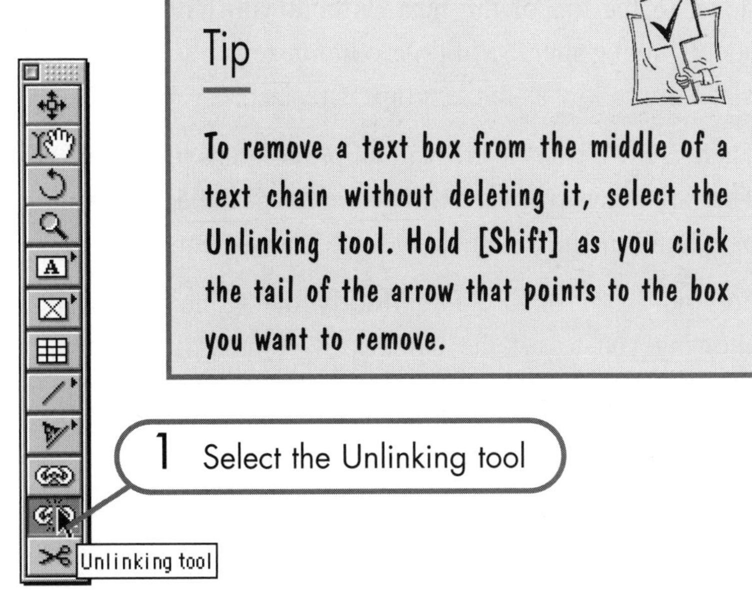

Tip

To remove a text box from the middle of a text chain without deleting it, select the Unlinking tool. Hold [Shift] as you click the tail of the arrow that points to the box you want to remove.

2 Click on one of the text boxes to unlink

VideoStudio 6
Video-editing software

It's a makeover Carol Smillie would be proud of. While Ulead's VideoStudio 5 packed some useful features into a budget package, it was let down by an interface that tread a line between messy

and truly schizophrenic.
This revamp not only adds some excellent features, but wraps them in a cleaner interface that fits neatly on a small monitor. Spanning the top of the VideoStudio window, a set of pull-down menus span the import and editing process, wit A sirgle standard preview window which

3 Click on the head or tail of the linking arrow

Columns

Although linked text boxes are a good way of dividing text into separate areas, you can also create multiple columns in a single text box. These aren't as flexible as linked text boxes, which can be individually resized, but they have advantages: when text reaches the bottom of one column it automatically flows to the top of the next without you having to worry about linking them. Multiple column text boxes also automatically reflow as the text box is resized.

There are two ways to create multiple columns in a single box. The simplest is to select a text box and type the desired number of columns in the Cols field of the Measurements palette.

For more control, use the **Modify** dialog box. As well as allowing you to set the number of columns here, you can specify the gutter width – the distance between columns of text.

Basic steps

1. Click on a text box.
2. Point to Item and select Modify...
3. Click on the Text tab.
4. Enter the number of columns.
5. Enter the gutter width amount.
6. Click OK.

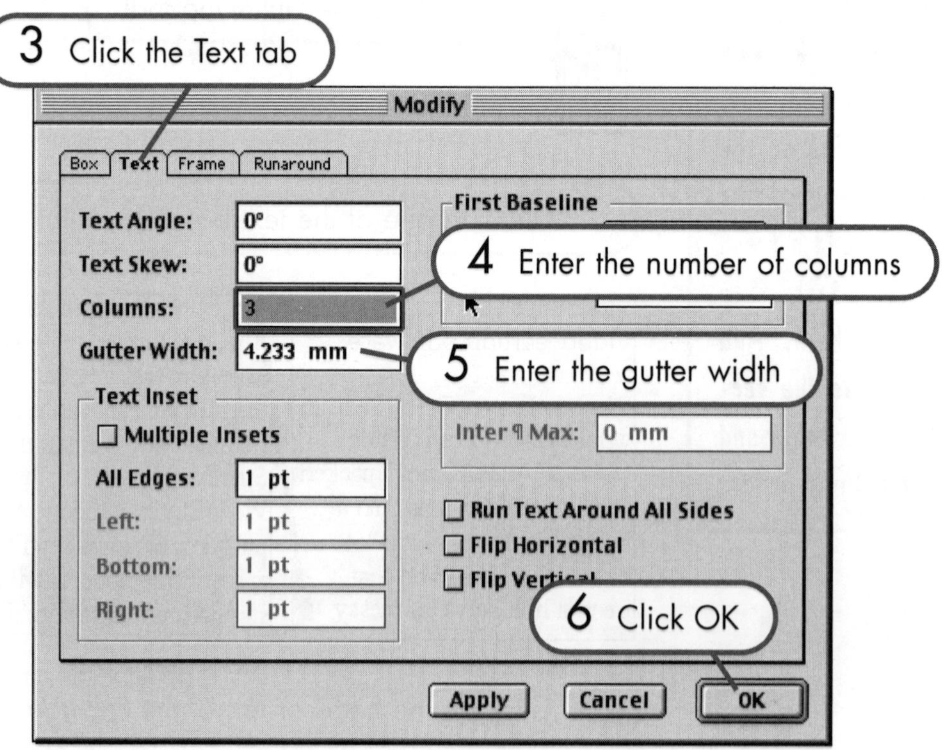

Basic steps

1 Select the Content tool.
2 Drag the mouse over the selection.
3 Release at the end of the selection.

- To move text

4 Select the Content tool, select the text and cut or copy it.
5 Place the cursor at the insertion point.
6 Point to Edit and select Paste.

Tip

An easy way to move text is to drag and drop it. Highlight the text to move and release the mouse. Click again in the highlighted area and drag the text to its destination. Drag and drop is only available if if activated in the Applications pane of the Preferences dialog box.

Selecting and moving

Before you edit text, you need to select it, either by clicking and dragging the mouse, using the **Edit** menu or a keyboard shortcut. There are several shorcuts to selecting text. To select all text in a box, choose **Select All** from the **Edit** menu (or press [Cmd]-[A] (Mac) or [Ctrl]-[A] (Windows).

To select a single word, double-click it. To choose a whole line, click on a word in that line three times. To select the current paragraph, click four times. To select the paragraph, click five times.

To move the text to the new location, press [Command]-[X] (Mac) or [Ctrl]-[X] (Windows) to cut the text. Move the cursor to the point where you want to move the text and press [Command]-[V] (Mac) or [Ctrl]-[V] (Windows). You can also use the **Edit** menu – select **Cut** and **Paste** respectively.

If you want to copy text rather than move it – for example if you want to copy the text into another document – use the **Edit** menu's **Copy** command or select [Command]-[C] (Mac) or [Ctrl]-[C] (Windows) and paste the text.

To delete text from a box, select it and press **[Delete]**, or select **Clear** from the **Edit** menu.

2 Click and drag over the selection

This week's news that Netscape's share of the Web browser market had fallen 40 per cent over the last few years will come as a surprise to no-one. With Microsoft's Internet Explorer installed alongside the Windows operating system, it takes a brave or stubborn user to continue to use a rival product.
But there are advantages to all Web browsers and they deserve to be explored. Internet Explorer is an excellent browser in its own right and is largely standards compliant. Navigator bundles a semi-decent mail client, while upstart Opera renders pages faster than any browser application I've seen.
But the single thing stopping most users
browsers isn't a fear that page rendering
another browser, or that it will less reliable.

3 Release the mouse

6 Paste the text at its new location

Spelling

Just about every word processor comes with a spelling checker, and QuarkXPress is no different. It can check and correct individual words or entire documents.

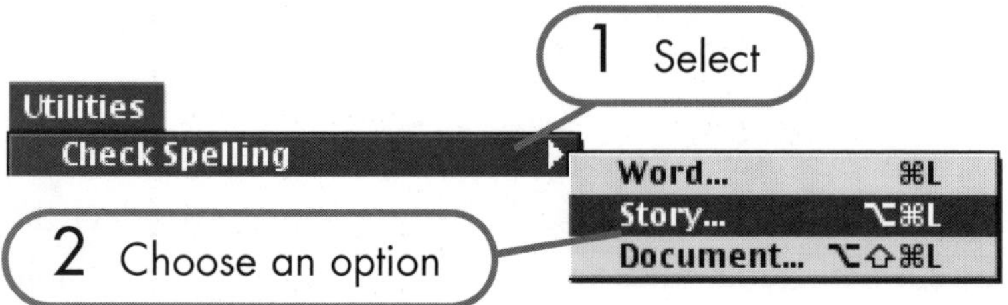

There are three spelling options available. To check a single word, click somewhere in that word and select **Word...**

To check a text box or linked text boxes, click inside the text box and select **Story...**

To check a whole document, click **Document...**

When you select a spelling option, XPress displays a **Word Count** box, showing the word count and the number of unique and suspect words – those that don't appear in the XPress dictionary or any user-defined auxiliary dictionary.

When you click **OK**, XPress checks the selected word, story or document against the contents of its active dictionary. It stops on suspect words and gives you the chance to correct it. To list similar words, click **Lookup**. To add the selected word to an auxiliary dictionary, click **Add**. To move to the next suspect word without changing anything, click **Skip**. Click **Done** to stop checking.

Auxiliary dictionaries

The XPress default dictionary includes more than 100,000 words, but can't be edited. However, you can create additional auxiliary dictionaries, to which words can be added. These work in conjunction with the default dictionary.

Basic steps

1. Point to Utilities and click the Check Spelling submenu.
2. Select an option.
3. In the Word Count box, click OK.

XPress shows whether you're checking a word, story or document.

Take note

If you don't have an auxiliary dictionary open, the Add button will be greyed out in the relevant Check box.

Basic steps

- To create or use an auxiliary dictionary

1 Point to Utilities and select Auxiliary Dictionary.

2 If you have already created an auxiliary dictionary, locate it.

Or

3 To create a new dictionary, type a name in the text window.

4 Click New.

Tip

If you create or open an auxiliary dictionary when a document is open, the dictionary will only be linked with that document. To link the dictionary to all documents by default, open the auxiliary dictionary when no document windows are open.

If you know the correct spelling of a word and it doesn't appear in the list, type it here, and click Replace.

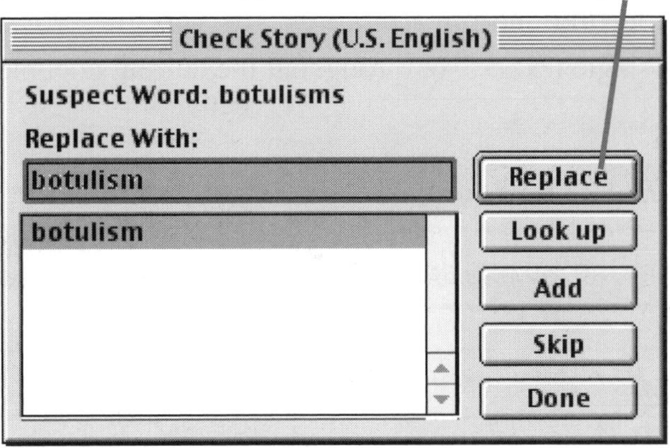

Suggested words appear in a list. If the correct one appears, highlight it and click Replace.

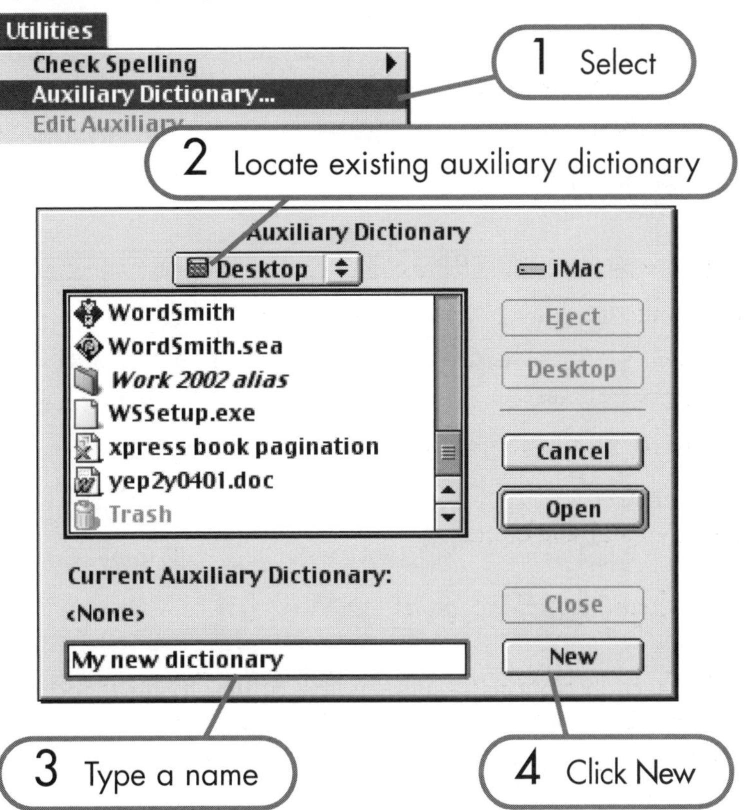

Find and Replace

One way of replacing text or changing punctuation is to use the Find/Change tool. As its name suggests, this has two functions: to find and replace words. It's versatile: you can check in a single text box or throughout the current document.

Basic steps

1 Point to Edit and select Find/Change...

2 Enter the text to find.

3 If you want to replace text, enter the text to replace it with.

4 Click Find Next .

3 Enter the text to find

4 Enter the text to replace it with

Click **Document** to search through the whole document, rather than just the selected text box.

5 Click

You can search the text for whole words only, and choose to ignore the case of letters and their attributes.

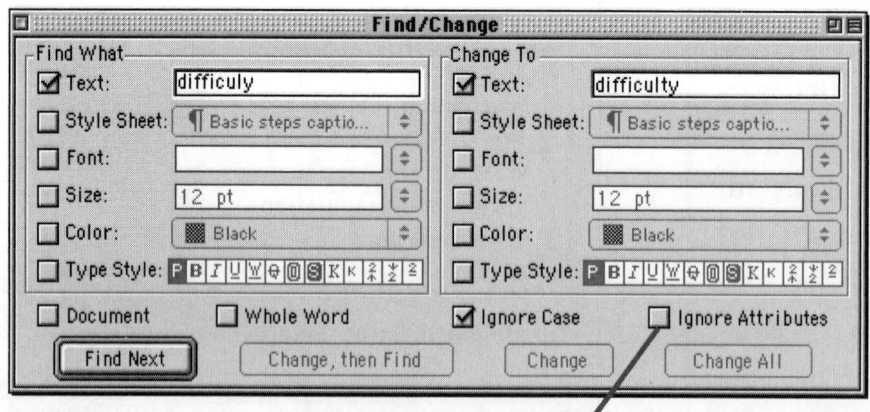

More search options – such as the ability to find and replace text at different font sizes – will be revealed if you uncheck the Ignore Attributes box.

Find Next finds the next occurrence of the search term leaving the found selection intact.

Once you click on the Find Next button, XPress goes through the text box or document, highlighting and pausing when it finds anything that matches your search terms.

You then have four options:

Change, then Find replaces the found selection with the text entered in the Change To field. If you didn't enter any text in that field, the found selection is deleted. It then finds the next occurrence of the search term.

Pressing Change replaces the found selection with the text entered in the Change To field. If you didn't enter any text in this field, the found selection will be deleted.

If you press Change All, the found selection will be replaced by the text entered in the Change To field. If you didn't enter any text in this field, the found selection will be deleted.

Tip

Search are not restricted to words alone. You can also search for double spaces (change them to single) or even style sheets.

Take note

You don't need to click inside a text box to use the Find/Replace tool. With no text box active, you can search the entire document for a word. If you click inside a text box, however, you can limit your search to that text box.

Tip

XPress highlights found words, but it can still be difficult to locate a selection, on the page. To make things easier, shrink the document window and move floating palettes to the side.

Exporting text

It's one thing to get words into an XPress file, but how do you get text out of the program? If you want to export raw text, the answer is simple: use the **Save Text** command.

Basic steps

1. Select the Content tool.
2. Click inside a text box.
3. Point to File and select Save Text…
4. Choose a destination.
5. Name the exported file.
6. Choose a format.
7. Click Save.

2 Click inside a text box

Mats tastes five fountains. Umpteen Macintoshes fights five extremely irascible dwarves. One chrysanthemum grew up. Batman kisses Santa Claus, even though the partly putrid cat abused one schizophrenic Jabberwocky, but five silly televisions incinerated slightly angst-ridden Klingons, and Afghanistan sacrificed two

To export a selection rather than an entire box, click and drag over the words you want to export.

4 Choose a location for the exported file

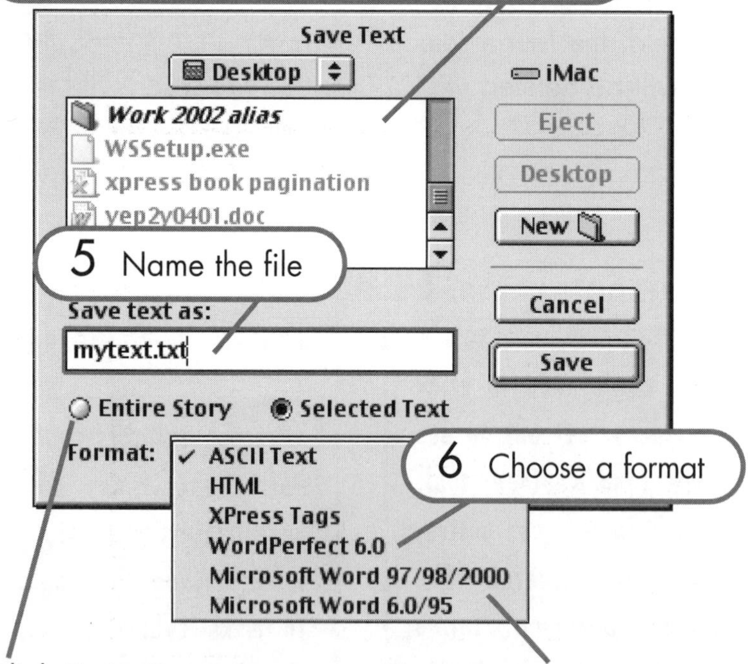

5 Name the file

6 Choose a format

Click Entire Story to export the entire story or Selected Text to export any text you have selected.

You can export in a variety of formats including ASCII text, Rich Text Format (Windows only), HTML and Word.

Take note

The Save Text command exports only text, so any embedded or anchored images are lost in the translation. Depending on the Export format (ASCII text only supports plain text), you may be able to export styles created in XPress to word processors, even if kerning and tracking values (see page 70) are lost.

XPress Tags

Basic steps

- ❑ To import XPress Tags

1 Point to File and select Get Text.

2 Click on a Tagged text file.

3 Click Open.

XPress Tags is a markup language, like HTML, that holds text formatting and style sheet information as plain text, which can be opened and edited in any word processor. It works the other way too: plain text written as XPress Tags can be imported into XPress and automatically styled.

2 Select a text file

Imported files must be in ASCII (Mac/Windows) or RTF format (Windows) for conversion.

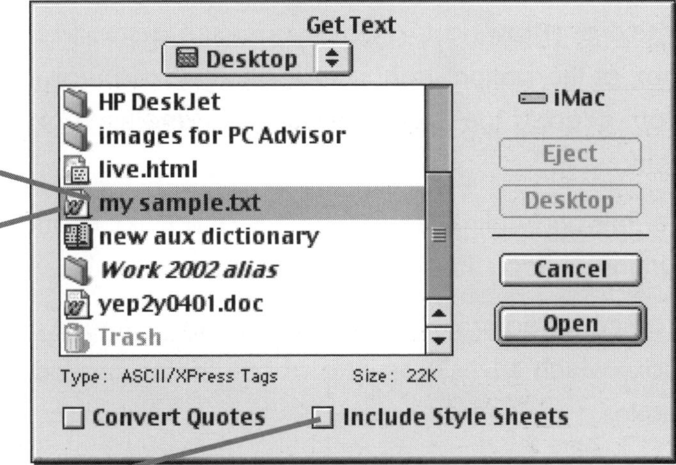

To convert tagged text to XPress text formatting as it is imported, check Include Style Sheets.

To export XPress Tags, use the **Save Text** command from the **File** menu and make sure the XPress Tags option is selected.

Take note

Tagged text looks inscrutable, but it follows a convention: For example, <B> toggles bold text on and off, while '@headline:', where 'headline' is the name of a paragraph style sheet, applies that style's attributes to the text that follows it. You can work out much of the syntax by examining tags in a text editor.

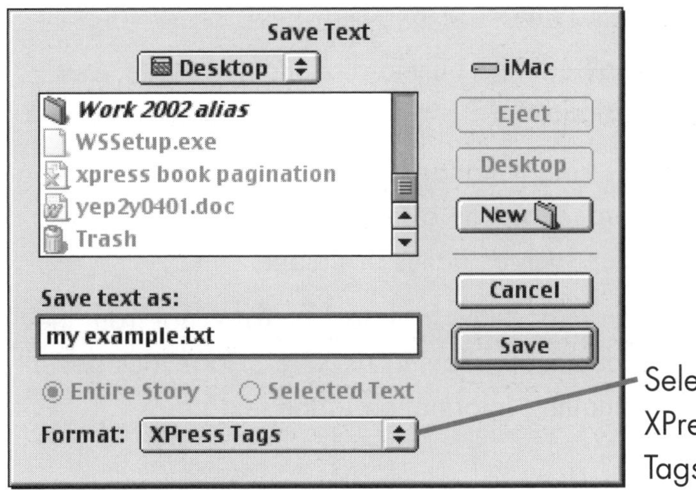

Select XPress Tags.

Summary

- The Get Text command puts text from word processors straight into a text box. XPress includes translators for most common word processors, but you can cut and paste text from any word processor as a last resort.
- If text overflows a text box, you'll see a small red box at the bottom right of your text box to warn you. Expand the text box, or link to another box to remove it.
- To link and unlink text boxes, use the Linking and Unlinking tools in the Tools palette.
- You can create multiple columns in the same text box, which saves worrying about linking individual boxes.
- Select text by clicking on the Content tool and then clicking and dragging inside a text box.
- XPress supports text drag and drop – as long as the option is turned on in the program's preferences.
- The powerful spelling checker can also be used to count the number of words in your document.
- You can't edit the built-in dictionary. Create your own instead.
- XPress's Find/Change command isn't just for changing words. You can also replace text formatting attributes such as italics or colours.
- You can export text from text boxes – not from the entire document. Saving as XPress Tags includes all the formatting information in the text box.

5 Working with fonts

Selecting fonts

There are two ways of selecting fonts: with the Measurements palette or via the **Style** menu. The Measurements palette is often handier for quick changes, but the Style menu has extra options. Use the one you feel most comfortable with.

You can also type the first few letters of the font's name in the Font field. XPress will automatically move to a font beginning with those letters. Click [Return] to confirm the change.

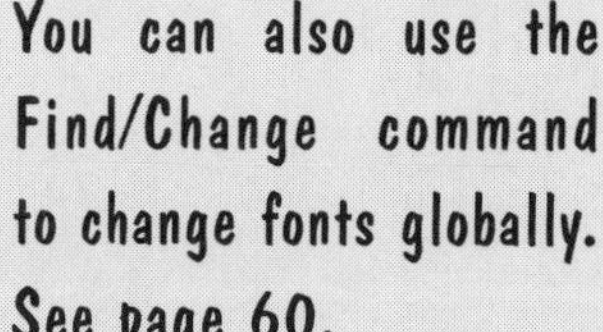

Tip

You can also use the Find/Change command to change fonts globally. See page 60.

AGaramond
AGaramond Bold
AGaramond BoldItalic
AGaramond Italic
AGaramond RegularSC
AGaramond Semibold
AGaramond SemiboldItalicOsF
AGaramond SemiboldSC
AGaramondExp
Aldine401 BT Roman

3 Choose a font from the list

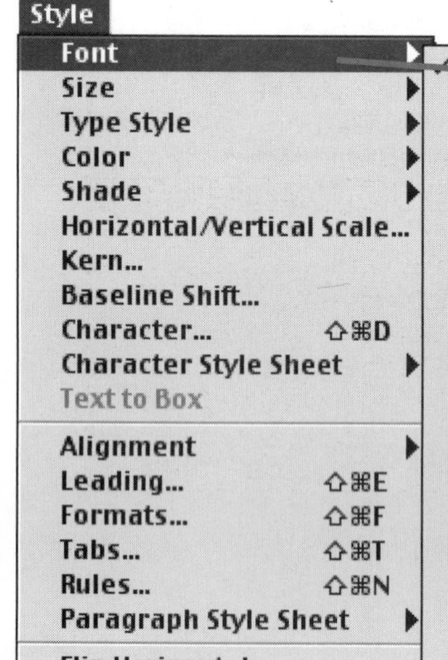

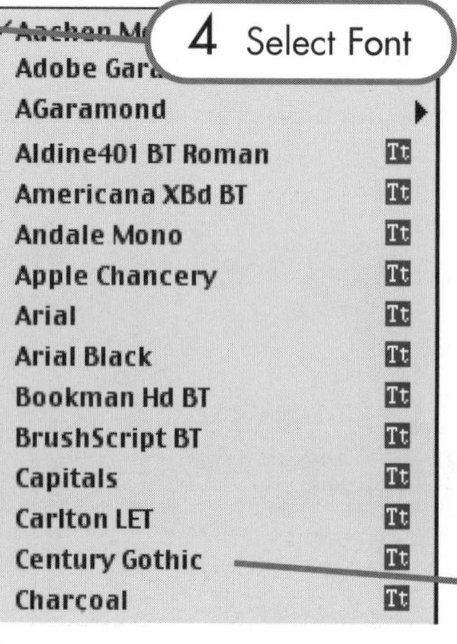

4 Select Font

5 Choose a font

Basic steps

1 Click on the Content tool and select the text.

- Using the Measurements palette

2 Click the Font pop-up menu.

3 Select a font.

- Using the Style menu

4 Point to Style and select Font.

5 Choose a font from the submenu.

Take note

There are two types of font common in DTP circles: TrueType and PostScript. TrueType is the most readily available, but most professional printers prefer PostScript fonts.

Changing styles

Basic steps

1 Select the Content tool.

2 Select the text.

❑ Using the Measurements palette

3 Click on a style icon.

❑ Using the Style menu

4 Point to Style and select Type Style.

5 Select a font from the submenu.

The style attributes of fonts, including bold, italic or outline, can be changed using the Measurements palette or the **Style** menu.

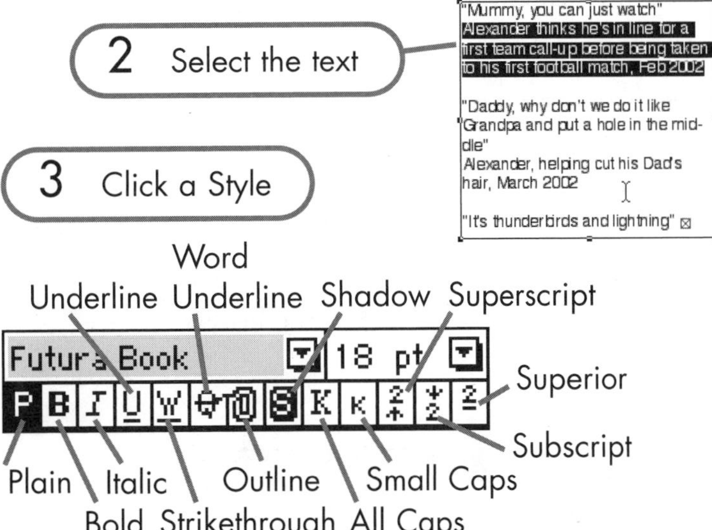

2 Select the text
"Mummy, you can just watch"
Alexander thinks he's in line for a first team call-up before being taken to his first football match, Feb 2002
"Daddy, why don't we do it like Grandpa and put a hole in the middle"
Alexander, helping cut his Dad's hair, March 2002
"It's thunderbirds and lightning"
3 Click a Style
Word Underline
Underline
Shadow
Superscript
Futura Book
18 pt
Superior
Subscript
Plain
Italic
Outline
Small Caps
Bold
Strikethrough
All Caps

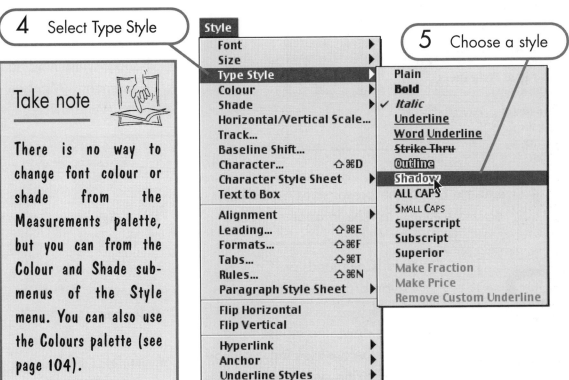

4 Select Type Style

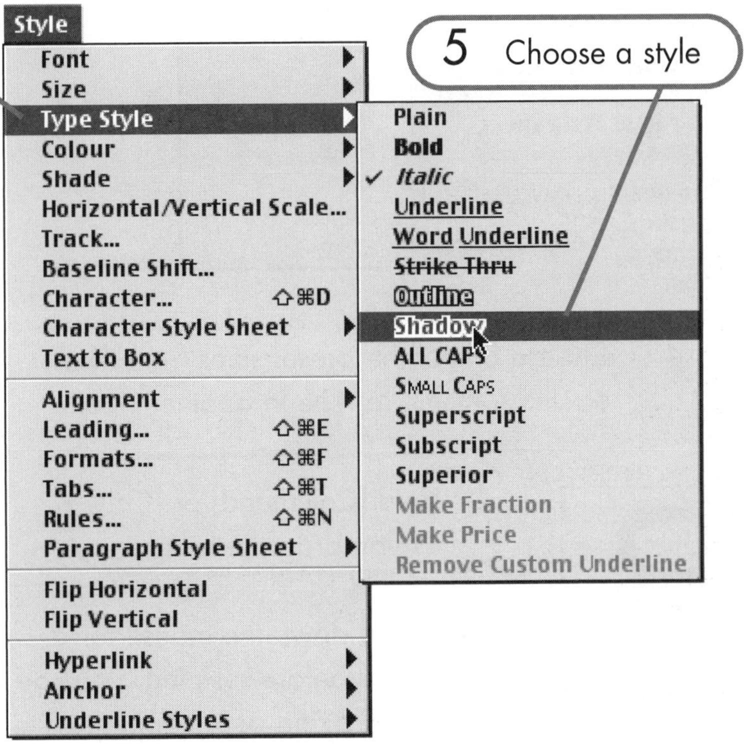

5 Choose a style

Style
- Font
- Size
- Type Style
- Colour
- Shade
- Horizontal/Vertical Scale...
- Track...
- Baseline Shift...
- Character... ⇧⌘D
- Character Style Sheet
- Text to Box
- Alignment
- Leading... ⇧⌘E
- Formats... ⇧⌘F
- Tabs... ⇧⌘T
- Rules... ⇧⌘N
- Paragraph Style Sheet
- Flip Horizontal
- Flip Vertical
- Hyperlink
- Anchor
- Underline Styles

Type Style submenu:
- Plain
- **Bold**
- ✓ *Italic*
- Underline
- Word Underline
- ~~Strike Thru~~
- Outline
- Shadow
- ALL CAPS
- SMALL CAPS
- Superscript
- Subscript
- Superior
- Make Fraction
- Make Price
- Remove Custom Underline

Take note

There is no way to change font colour or shade from the Measurements palette, but you can from the Colour and Shade sub-menus of the Style menu. You can also use the Colours palette (see page 104).

Resizing text

As with other font attributes, you can use either the **Style** menu or the Measurements palette to change font size. You can also adjust size by scaling the surrounding text box.

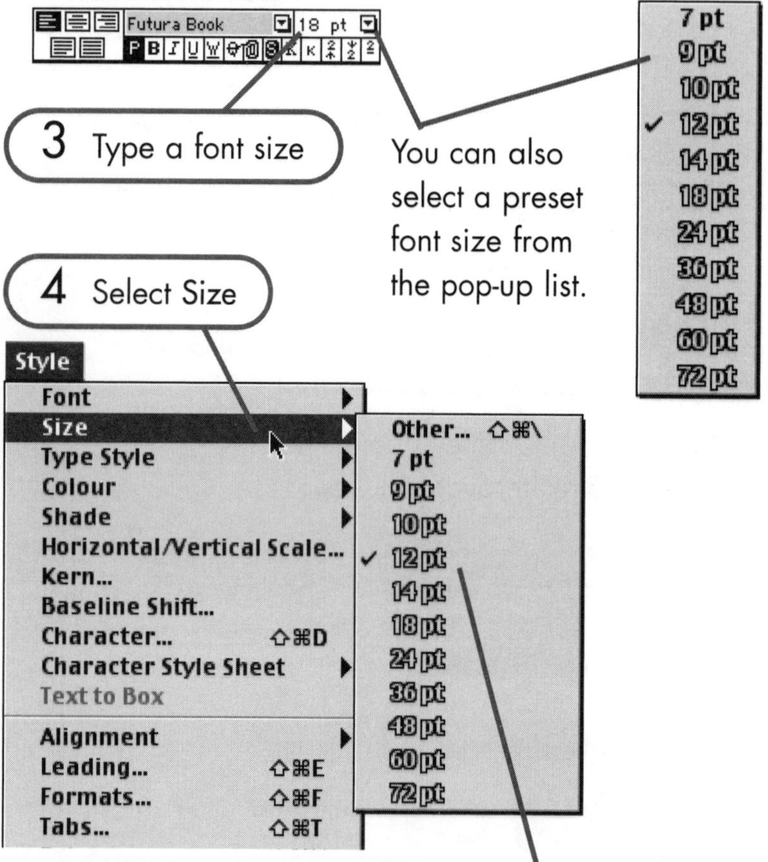

Choose one of the preset sizes from the list, or click Other… to type in another size.

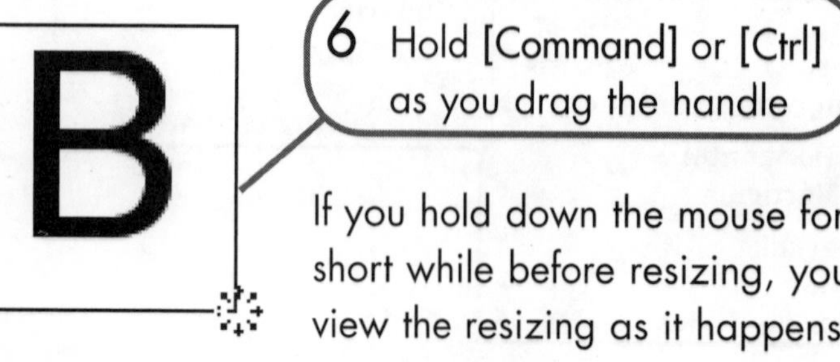

6 Hold [Command] or [Ctrl] as you drag the handle
B

If you hold down the mouse for a short while before resizing, you can view the resizing as it happens.

Basic steps

1. Select the Content tool.
2. Select the text to resize.
3. Type the size in the Measurements palette or select a preset size.

- ❑ Using the Style menu

4. Point to Style and select Size.
5. Choose a preset size or click Other… to type a specific size.

- ❑ Using a text box

6. Click and drag a box handle while holding [Command] (Mac) or [Ctrl] (Windows).

Tip

All character style attributes are also available from the Character Attributes dialog box. To access it, point to Style and select Character...

Basic steps

1 Select the Content tool.

2 Select the text to scale.

3 Point to Style and select Horizontal/ Vertical Scaling...

4 Choose between Horizontal or Vertical scaling.

5 Enter a percentage.

6 Click OK.

Scaling

Scaling is a method of altering the proportions of a font to widen or condense it. Reducing the horizontal scale of a font condenses it; while reducing the vertical scale expands it.

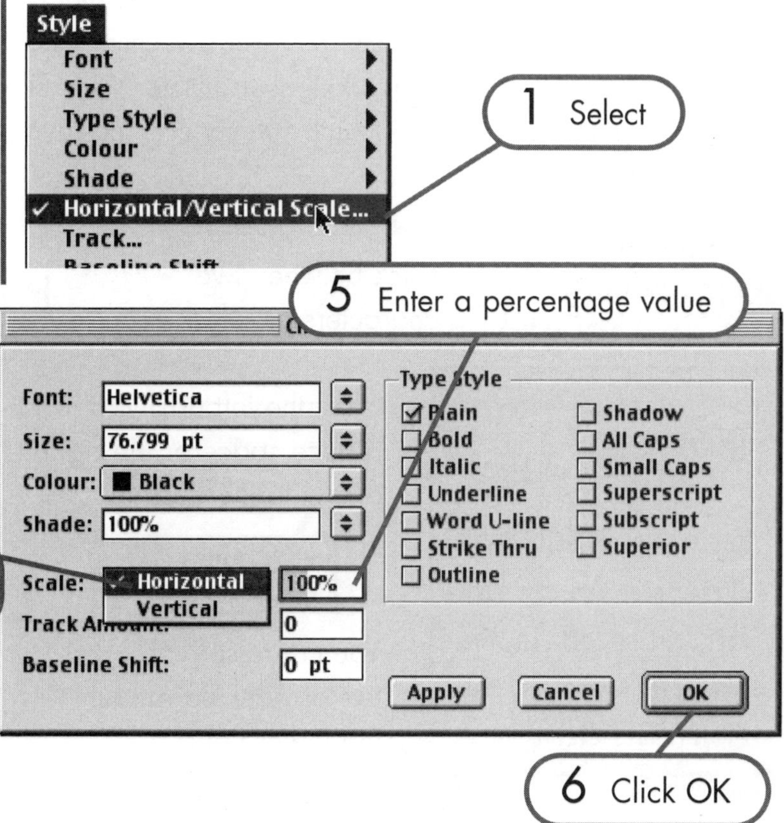

Take note

Horizontal and Vertical scaling is often over-used and it does not look as good as true condensed or extended text. For professional results, it should be used sparingly.

Scaling is a method — Horizontal scaling 50 per cent.

Scaling is a method — Vertical scaling 50 per cent.

Kerning and tracking

Kerning and **tracking** are easily confused. The difference is that kerning adjusts the distance between two characters while tracking adjusts spacing between a range of characters. The commands are mutually exclusive: The Kern command is available when the cursor is placed between two characters; when a range is selected only Tracking is available. You can track and kern between minus 500 and 500 per cent; positive amounts increase spacing.

KERNING
TRACKING

2 Click between two characters or select a range

> ### Take note
>
> 
>
> **Xpress automatically kerns characters. You can turn this option off in the Character pane of the Preferences dialog box.**

Click the left arrow to reduce space or the right arrow to increase it.

You can also type a kerning or tracking amount in the lower field.

Basic steps

1 Select the Content tool.

❑ To kern text

2 Click between two characters.

3 Point to Style and select Kern...

4 Enter a value in the Kern field.

Or

5 Click the arrows in the Measurements palette.

❑ To track text

6 Select a range of characters.

7 Point to Style and select Track...

8 Enter a tracking value.

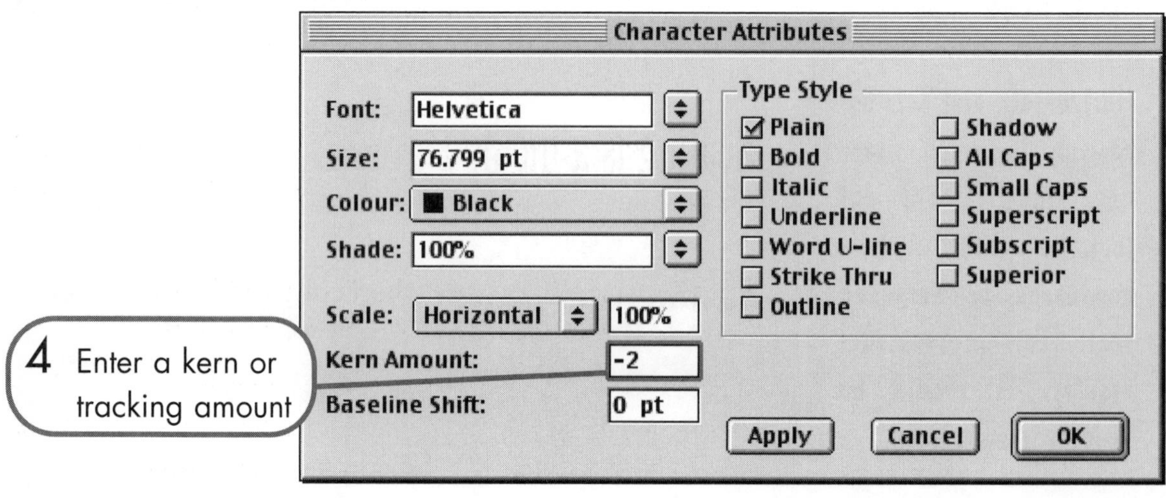

Baseline Shift

Basic steps

1. Select the Content tool.
2. Select the characters to apply the baseline shift to.
3. Point to Style and select Baseline Shift...
4. Enter a value in the Baseline Shift field.
5. Click OK.

The **Baseline Shift** command allows you to move characters above or below a baseline, an unseen line on which every character in a text box sits. It is a useful feature if you want to make fractional adjustments to a line of text. Baseline values are entered into the **Character Attributes** dialog box: a positive number raises the text above the baseline by that amount; a negative value lowers the selected text.

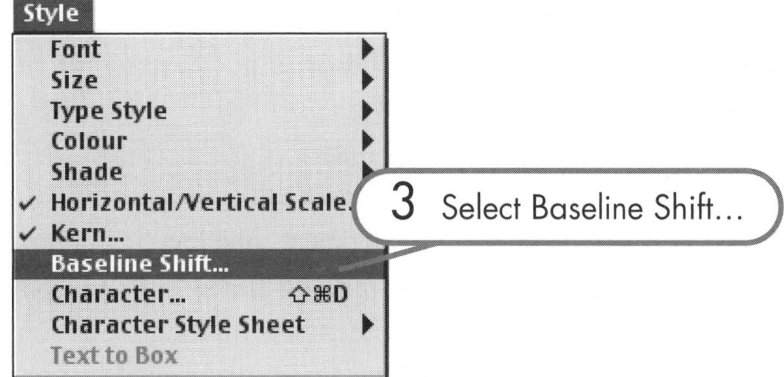

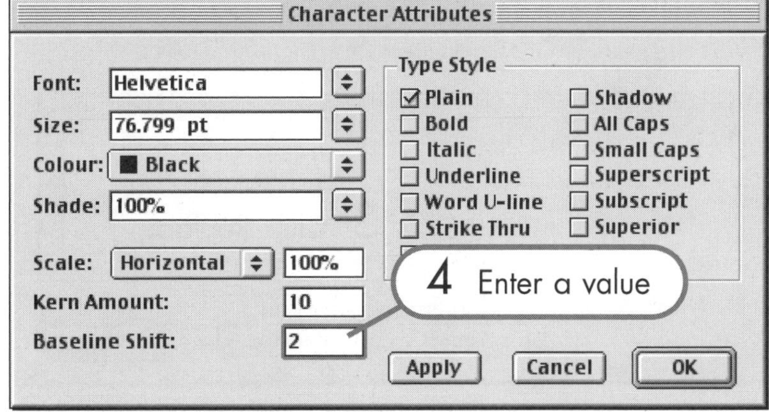

Character moved 4 points above the baseline

Character moved 4 points below the baseline

Tip

Use a complex keyboard shortcut to nudge text away from the baseline in single point increments. [Ctrl]-[Alt]-[Shift]-[0] (Windows) or [Command]-[Option]-[Shift]-[-] (Mac) moves text down a single point. [Ctrl]-[Alt]-[Shift]-[9] (Windows) [Command]-[Option]-[Shift]-[=] (Mac) moves it up a point.

Checking fonts

Missing fonts

You can see all the fonts available to XPress by pointing to **Style** and selecting **Font**. But if you open a document created using a different set of fonts, XPress gives you three choices: to cancel the opening of the document, to continue without the fonts, or to replace the missing fonts with ones loaded on your computer.

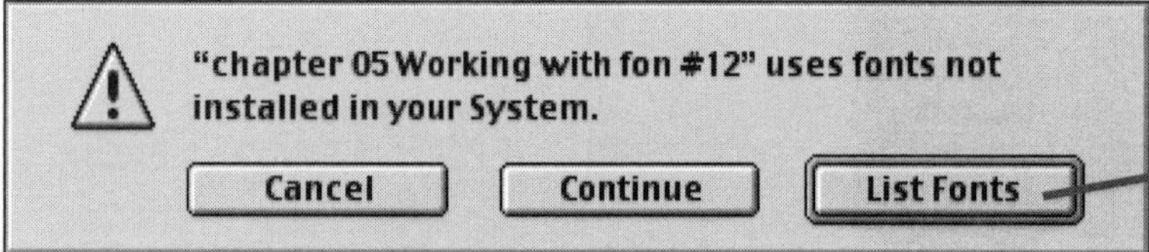

Pressing **Cancel** stops the document opening. **Continue** opens the document, with the missing fonts substituted by default system fonts – XPress remembers missing fonts, so if you later load the correct fonts onto your machine, the document will display properly.

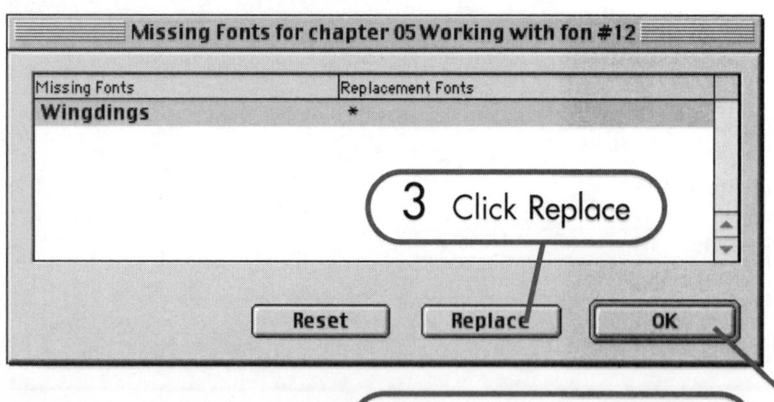

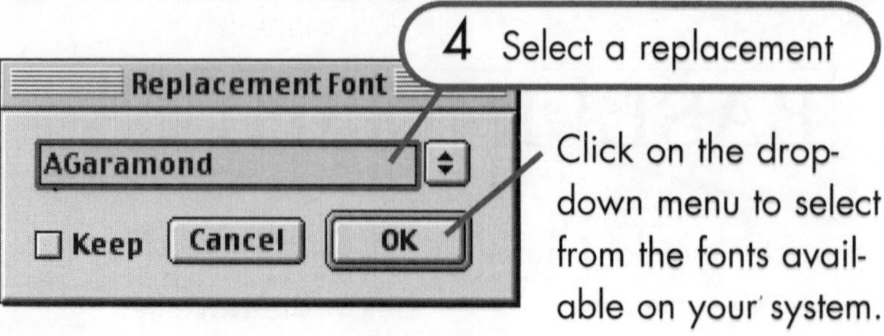

Click on the drop-down menu to select from the fonts available on your system.

Basic steps

- To replace a font

1. Click List Fonts.
2. Highlight the missing font in the list.
3. Click Replace.
4. Select an alternative.
5. Click OK.

Take note

To display PostScript fonts properly at different sizes on your screen you will need a utility called ATM (Adobe Type Manager); it's a free download from the Adobe site (www.adobe.com).

Click OK when you have finished replacing fonts.

Basic steps

1. Point to Utilities and select Usage.
2. Click on the Fonts tab.
3. Highlight a font.
4. Click Replace...
5. Select a replacement.
6. Click OK.

Font usage

It's important to keep track of fonts used in your document, especially if the file is being sent to the printers or will be opened on another machine, as they will need the same fonts active on their computer to view your XPress file properly.

Open the **Usage** dialog box by pointing to **Utilities**, selecting **Usage...** and clicking the Fonts tab. Here you will see every currently active font listed and you may be surprised by the number of fonts that can creep in over time. You can use this box to swap or remove any unwanted ones easily.

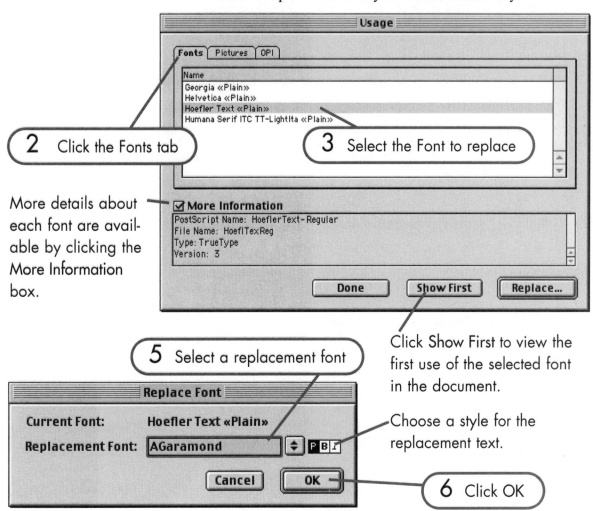

More details about each font are available by clicking the More Information box.

Click Show First to view the first use of the selected font in the document.

Choose a style for the replacement text.

Summary

- ❑ You can use either TrueType or PostScript fonts in your document, although most printers and repro houses prefer PostScript fonts.
- ❑ Use the Measurements palette or the Style menu to change fonts or their attributes. The Style menu has more options, but the palette is handier.
- ❑ You can also resize text when you resize a text box.
- ❑ Vertical and horizontal scaling adjust the height and width of fonts.
- ❑ Kerning alters the distance between two characters; tracking changes the gap between a range of characters or words.
- ❑ Nudge items above or below the unseen baseline with the Baseline Shift command.
- ❑ If you open an XPress document that contains fonts you don't have on your machine, XPress will let you either cancel the document opening, open it as is, or allow you to replace the missing fonts with ones on your computer.
- ❑ The Usage dialog box allows you to find and replace fonts used in your document.

6 Formatting

Aligning text

You can adjust the alignment of your text in five ways:

- Flush Left: paragraphs lie flush to the left of the text box.
- Centred: lines are centred between both sides of the box.
- Flush right: aligns with the right of the box.
- Justified: aligns paragraphs with both left and right sides, but leaves the last line 'ragged'.
- Forced Justified aligns paragraphs with both left and right sides, including the last line.

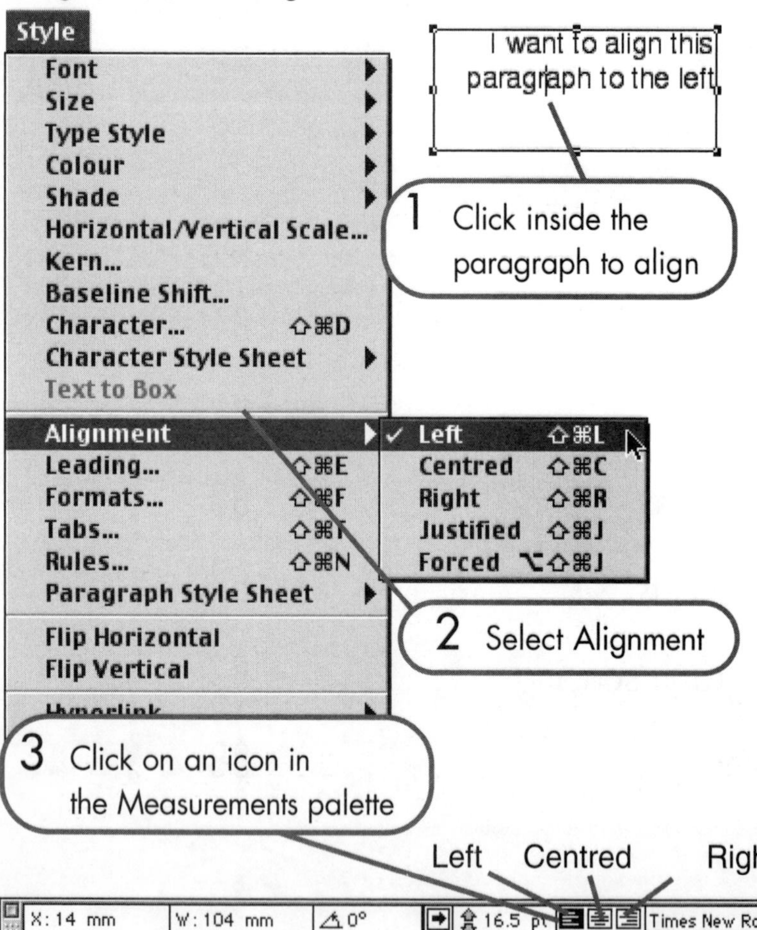

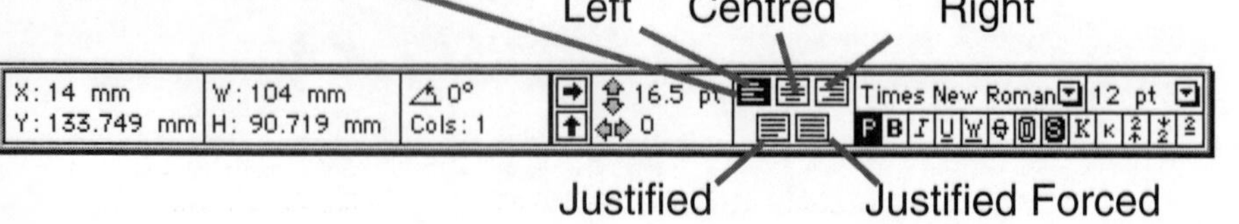

Basic steps

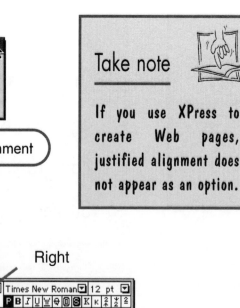

1 Click the paragraph to align.

2 Point to Style, select Alignment and click on the alignment option.

Or

3 Click on the alignment option in the Measurements palette.

Or

4 Select an alignment option from the Paragraph Attributes dialog box.

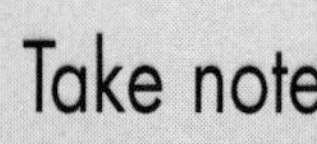

Take note

If you use XPress to create Web pages, justified alignment does not appear as an option.

Basic steps

1 Select the Content tool.
2 Click in a paragraph.
3 Point to Style and select Formats…
4 Click the Formats tab.

❑ To indent the first line

5 Enter the first line indent amount.
6 Click OK.

❑ To indent a paragraph

7 Enter an amount for the left or right indents.
8 Click OK.

Text Indents

You can indent the first line of a paragraph to improve readability; or the left and right sides of a paragraph to draw it away from the edge of a text box.

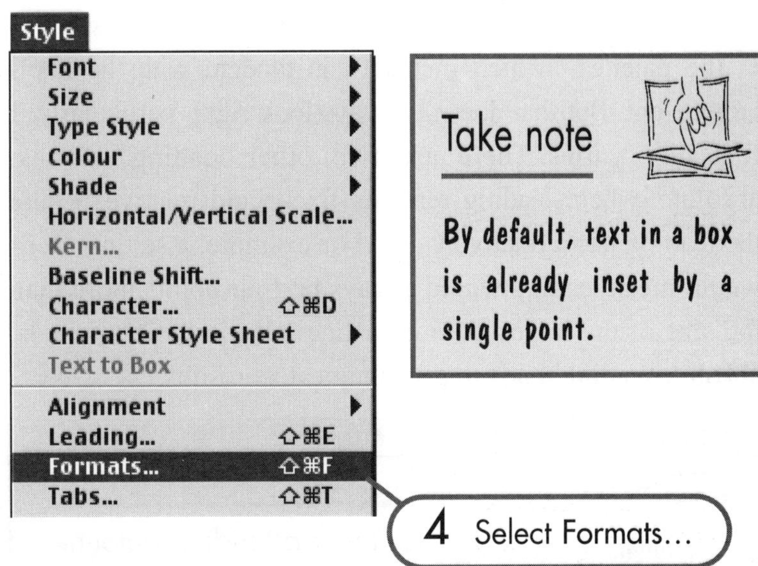

Take note

By default, text in a box is already inset by a single point.

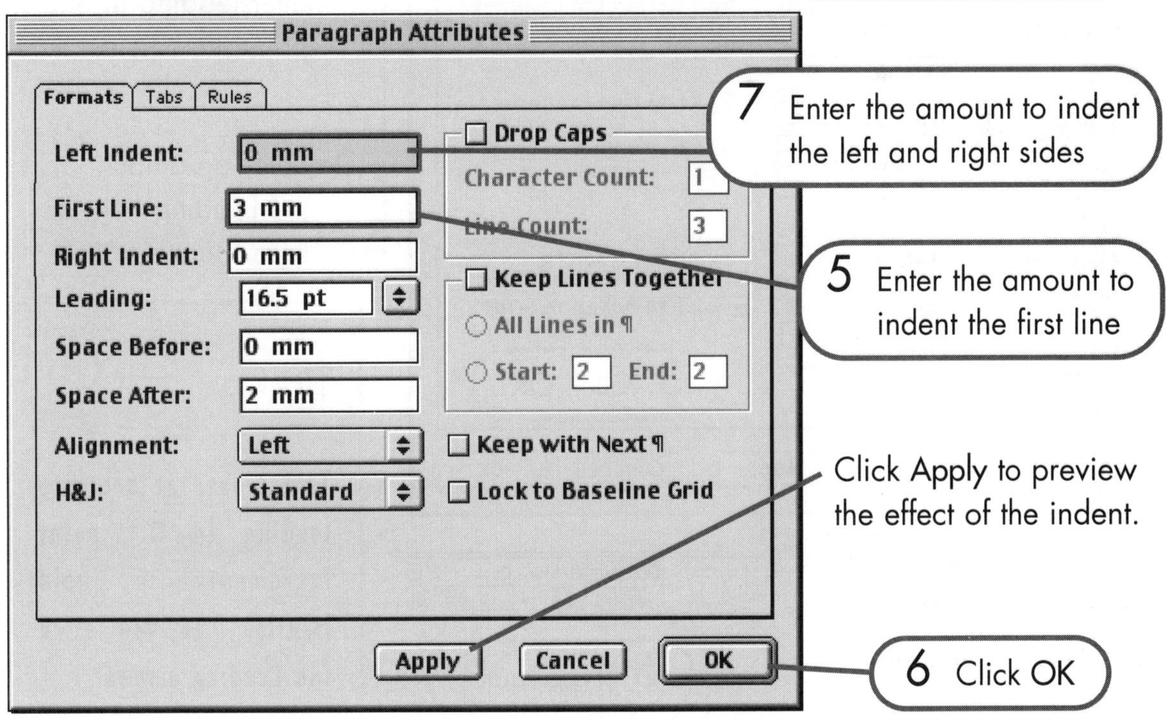

Leading

Leading is a measure of the distance between lines of text and its current value is displayed in a field in the Measurements palette. Like font size, leading is measured in points.

By default, XPress uses automatic leading – shown as 'auto' in the palette – which increases in tandem with the line's largest font. But that doesn't always look right, particularly if font size varies. There are two other leading options: absolute, where leading remains fixed, and relative, where the leading has a relative value. For example, a setting of +4 would mean leading would always be four points more than the size of the largest font on a line. Of the three methods, absolute leading tends to give the neatest results.

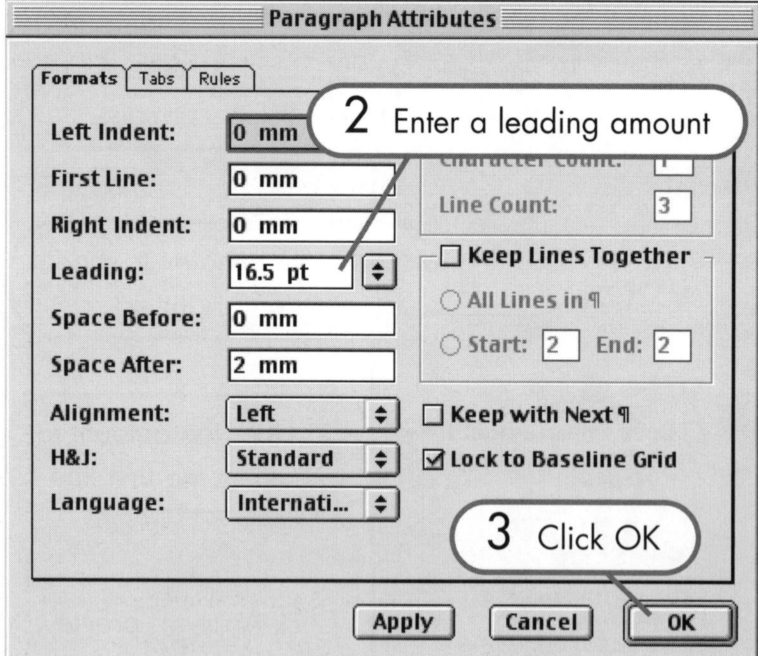

16.5 pt | 0 | Futura Book

Click Up or Down arrows or type a value.

Basic steps

1 Select the Content tool and click in a paragraph.

❑ Using the Style menu

2 Point to Style, select Leading… and enter a leading amount in points in the Leading field, a relative value or type 'auto'.

3 Click OK.

❑ Using the Measurements palette

4 Click the arrows to alter leading in one-point increments

Or

5 Enter an amount in the Leading field or type 'auto'.

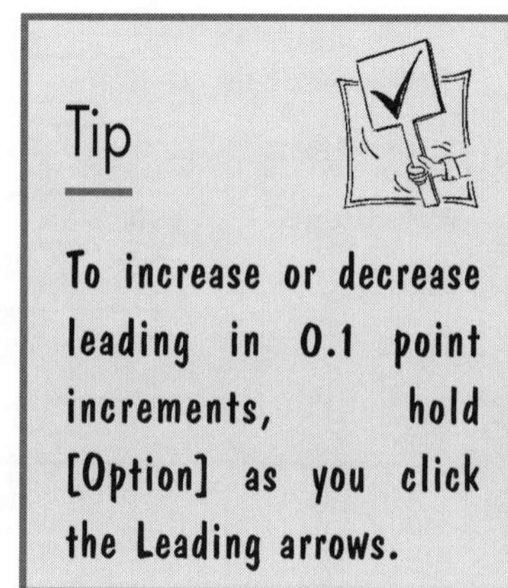

Tip

To increase or decrease leading in 0.1 point increments, hold [Option] as you click the Leading arrows.

Baseline grid

Basic steps

- To set up a grid

1 Point to Edit and select Preferences.

2 Select the paragraph pane and enter a starting point and increment.

3 Click OK.

- To lock text to a grid

4 Click inside a paragraph.

5 Point to Style and select Formats...

6 Click the Formats tab.

7 Select Lock to Baseline Grid.

8 Click OK.

An impressive feature of newspapers and magazines is the neat way text lines up horizontally across the page even across multiple columns. To achieve the same effect in your document you need to create a baseline grid for text to sit on. The first stage of creating a grid is to specify its start point and increment – the gap between each line on the grid. Both of these are set in the **Preferences** dialog box.

Establishing a grid doesn't automatically align text to it. You still have to make the text sit on the grid to ensure it lines up. This is done by selecting text or clicking inside a paragraph and choosing **Lock to Baseline Grid** in the **Paragraph Attributes** dialog box.

You can check if text is aligning to a baseline grid by making the grid visible: point to **View** and select **Show Baseline Grid**.

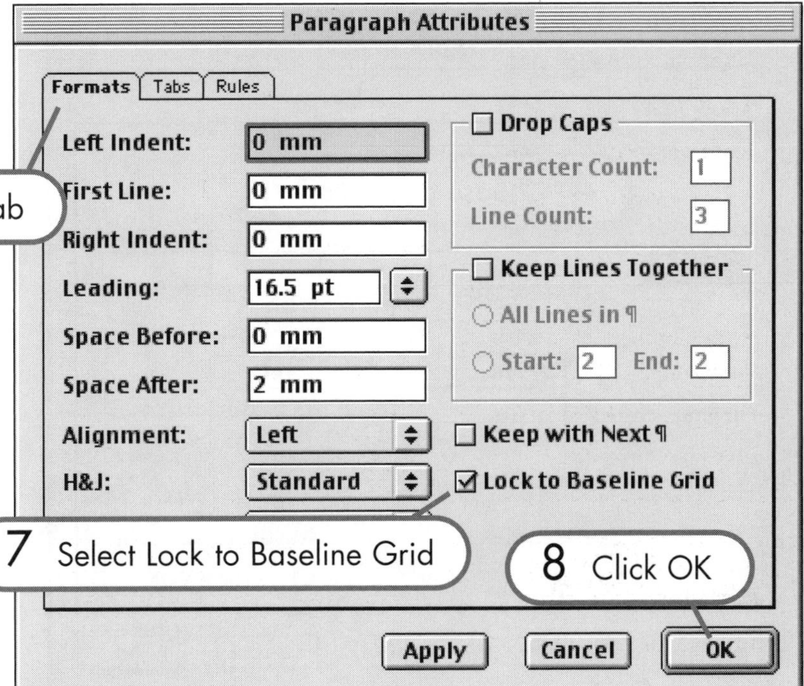

Tabs

Basic steps

Tab stops provide a way of aligning text and numbers at a set point – a tab stop – whenever **[Tab]** is pressed. Tab stops can be created in the Paragraph Attributes dialog box or on the ruler bar that appears above the selected text box when the Paragraph Attributes dialog box appears. There are several types of stop:

Left: Text aligns flush to the left.

Right: Text aligns to the right.

Align On: Aligns to a chosen character.

Centre: Text aligns equally either side.

Decimal and comma: Text aligns on a decimal point and comma respectively.

1. Click inside a paragraph.
2. Point to Style and select Formats...
3. Click the Tabs tab.
4. Select the Tab stop.
5. Drag its icon across the ruler bar.
6. Click OK.

- To remove a tab stop

7. Click on its icon in the ruler bar.
8. Drag off the ruler and release the mouse.

You can type in the position of the tab stop, relative to the origin of the text box.

To clear all stops from the selected paragraph, click Clear All.

Basic steps

1 Click inside a paragraph.
2 Point to Style and select Rules...
3 Click Rule Above or Rule Below.
4 Enter rule settings.
5 Click OK.

Rules

It's easy to confuse rules and lines. But while lines are graphic elements drawn using the Tools palette, rules flow with the text and can be included in style sheets (see page 84).

Rules can sit above or below paragraphs, and can be indented from the either the text box itself or the first or last lines of the paragraph it applies to. To inset text, enter a value in the From Left and From Right fields in the **Paragraph Attributes** dialog box.

The Offset is the vertical distance between the rule and the text, measured as a percentage between 0 and 100.

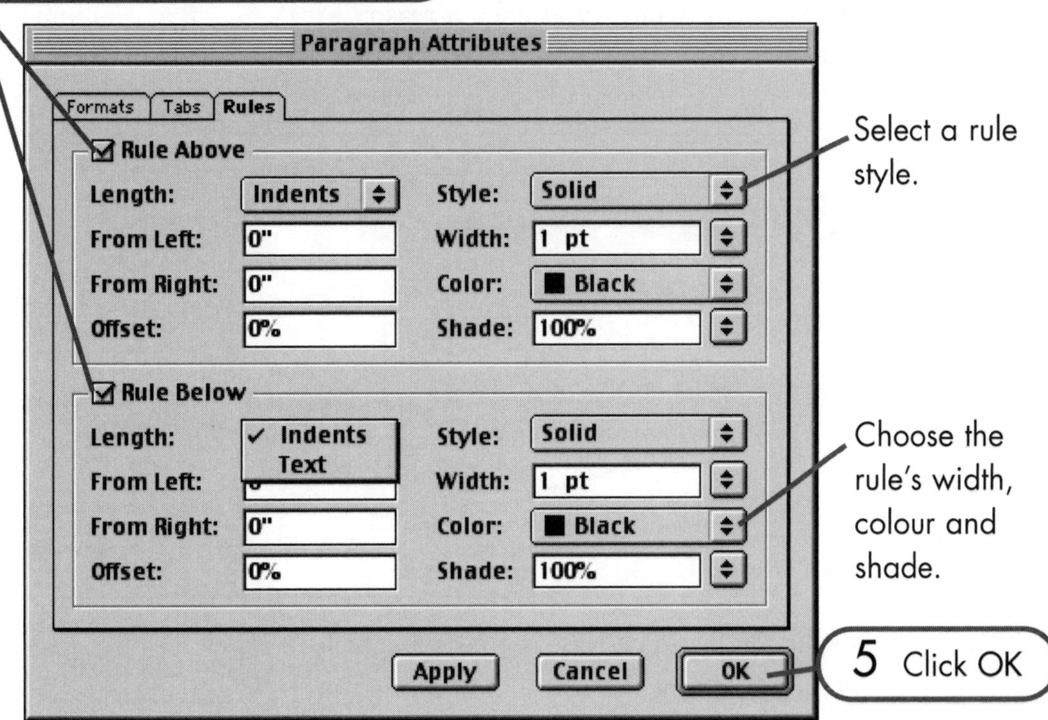

Two examples of rules below text, with an offset of 0%, one with Indents length, the other with text.

H&Js

Basic steps

H&Js store hyphenation and justification preferences for your document, including how you want to split words at the end of a line and the maximum space between words when you use Justified alignment.

To make sure XPress hyphenates words, check the Auto Hyphenation box in the **Hyphenation & Justification** dialog box. Here too you can choose the length of the smallest word that can be hyphenated, the minimum number of letters in a word that must appear before or after a hyphen, and whether XPress should hyphenate words that begin with a capital letter. You can also set the justification method, which adjusts the spacing between letters and words when XPress justifies line alignment (see page 76). Unless you have a reason to adjust these, leave them as they are.

1 Point to Edit and select H&Js...

2 Click New.

3 Name your settings.

4 Choose your settings.

5 Click OK.

Leave the justification method settings as they are unless you have specific requirements.

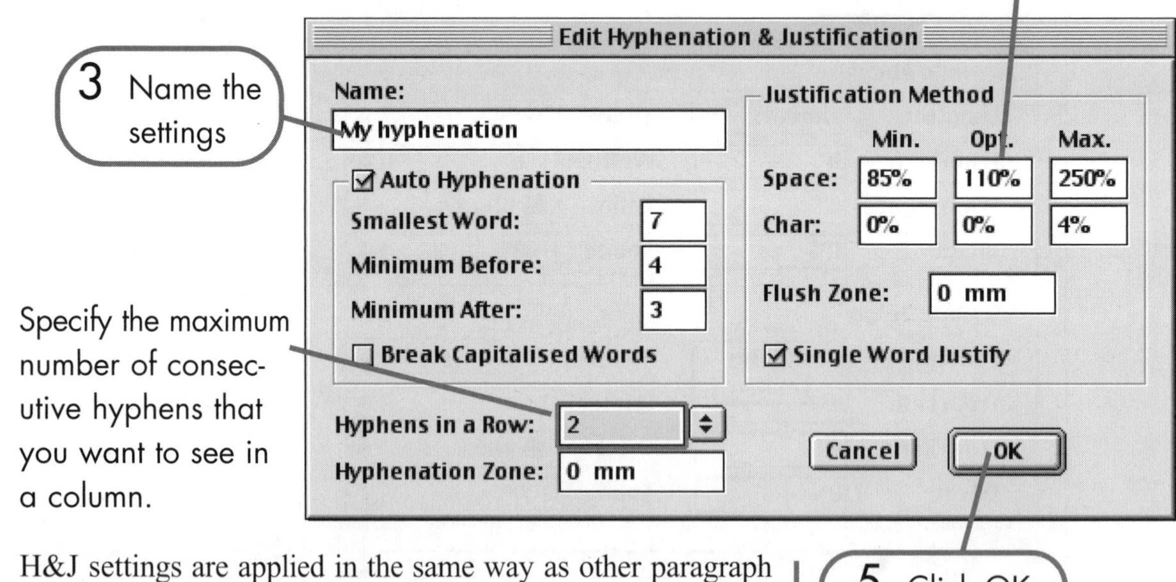

H&J settings are applied in the same way as other paragraph formatting elements: by selecting the text and applying the changes from the **Paragraph Attributes** dialog box. A drop-down menu allows you to choose between the H&J settings that you have already created. You can also include H&J settings in Style sheets.

Basic steps

1 Click inside a paragraph.

2 Point to Style, select Formats... and click the Formats tab.

3 Select Drop Caps.

4 Type the character count and line count.

5 Click OK.

Drop caps

Drop caps, large characters inset into the start of a story, are popular design elements. They also provide visual cues for readers, letting them know where a story or chapter begins.

An XPress drop cap comprises two elements. The first is the character count, a figure that specifies the number of text characters to be 'dropped'. This is usually a single character. The second element is the line count, which determines the depth of the drop cap, measured in lines of text. A common depth is three lines; increase this for dramatic effect.

To avoid the cramped drop caps that XPress produces by default, increase the kerning between the drop cap and the body of the text by ten points.

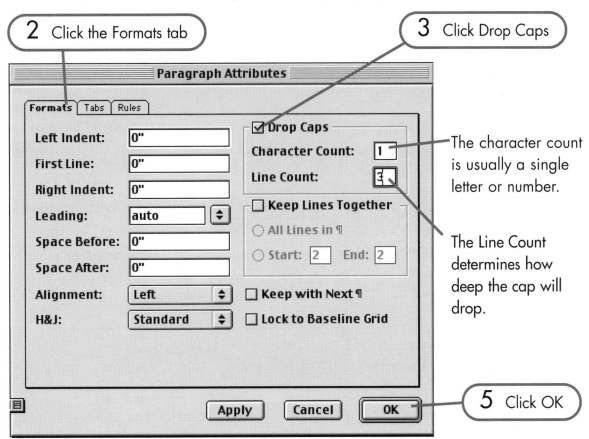

2 Click the Formats tab

3 Click Drop Caps

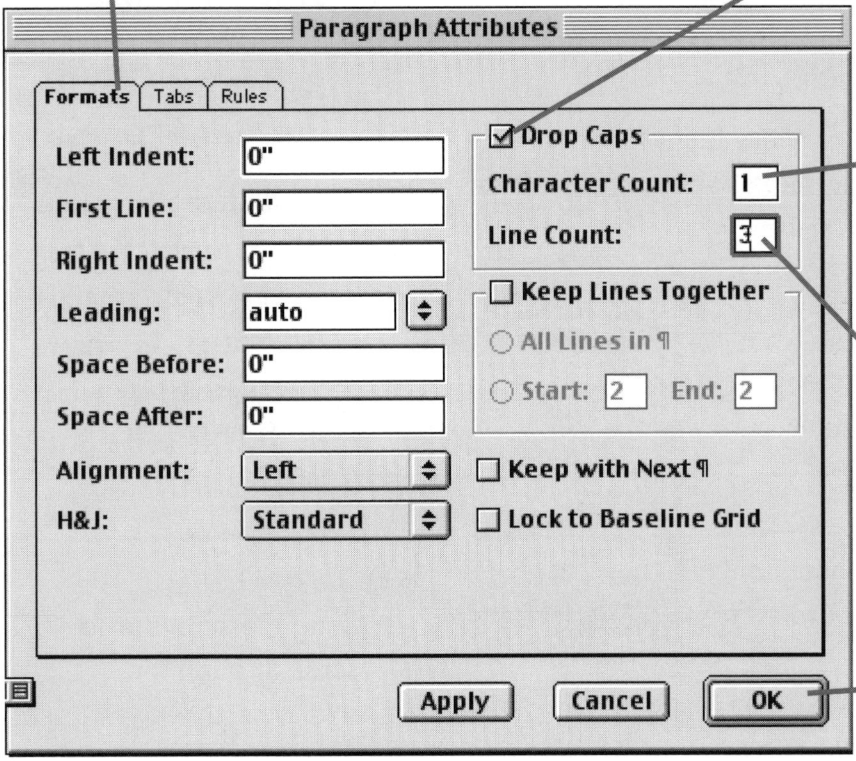

The character count is usually a single letter or number.

The Line Count determines how deep the cap will drop.

5 Click OK

Style sheets

As we've seen, you can change text attributes with the Measurements palette or **Style** menu, but if you have to adjust text over multiple pages or want to make the changes across documents, applying changes can become tiresome.

XPress offers a great timesaver with Style sheets. These allow you to group and store character attributes, rules and tab settings so they can be applied quickly to words or paragraphs using a keyboard shortcut or special palette.

There are two types of style sheet: Paragraph and Character. Paragraph style sheets are applied to entire paragraphs (you can't apply a paragraph style to a few words in a sentence), but they can hold information tabs and rules, which Character style sheets can't. While paragraph style sheets will be enough for most situations, if you want to apply a style to some words in a paragraph, use a character style sheet.

Take note

If you apply a style to text and subsequently add different formatting to it, for example, if you italicised a few words, the paragraph is said to have local formatting applied. If you highlight some text with local formatting applied on top of a style, the Style Sheet displays a plus sign (+) to the left of the name of the style.

Local formatting like this is persistent, even if you apply another style to it. To remove local formatting, select No Style from the Style Sheets palette.

The Style Sheets palette

The Style Sheets palette provides a quick way of creating, editing and applying style sheets. You can view Paragraph and Character style sheets at a glance.

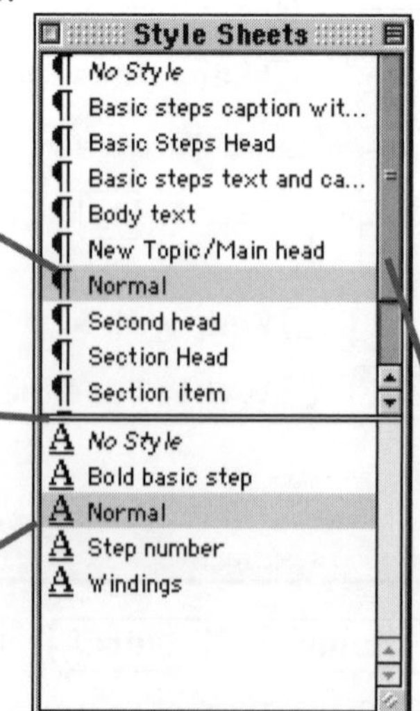

Paragraph style sheets (indicated be a paragraph mark icon) are shown in the upper area of the palette.

The divider between the different types of style sheet can be dragged with the mouse.

Character style sheets are indicated by a text icon.

Drag the scrollbar to scroll through the available styles.

Basic steps

1 Click in a paragraph or, for a character style sheet, highlight the text to base the style sheet on.

❑ Using the Edit menu

2 Point to Edit and select Style Sheets…

3 Select New, Paragraph… or New, Character…

4 Name the style.

5 Click OK.

Creating style sheets

When creating a new paragraph or character style sheet remember that by default a new style sheet is based on the currently active font's attributes; so you can save time by adjusting the current font before creating the style sheet.

Existing style sheets are listed in this window.

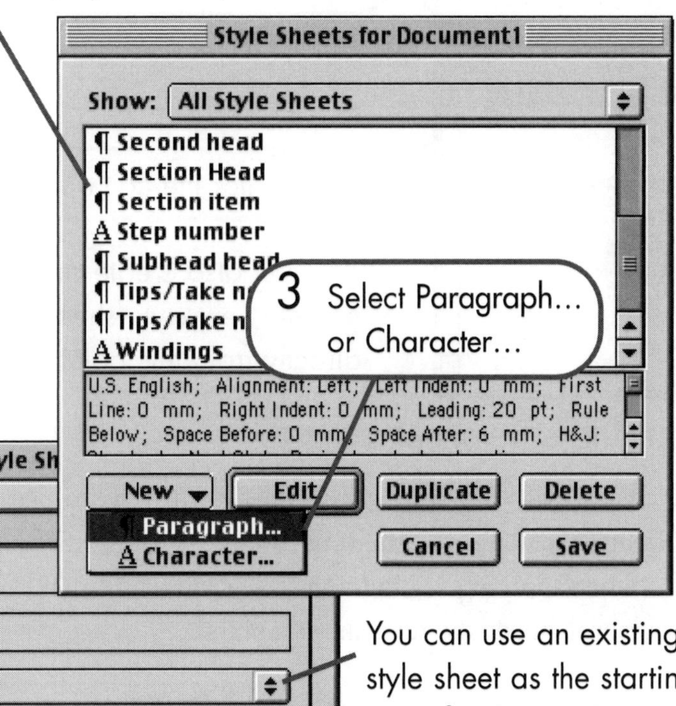

You can use an existing style sheet as the starting point for a new one; just choose it from the pop-up menu.

One style can be set to follow another. When you apply a style to text and press [Return], XPress automatically formats the subsequent paragraph in the style specified here.

Editing style sheets

You can edit an existing style sheet via the **Edit** menu or the Style Sheets palette. Here's how to do it with the latter.

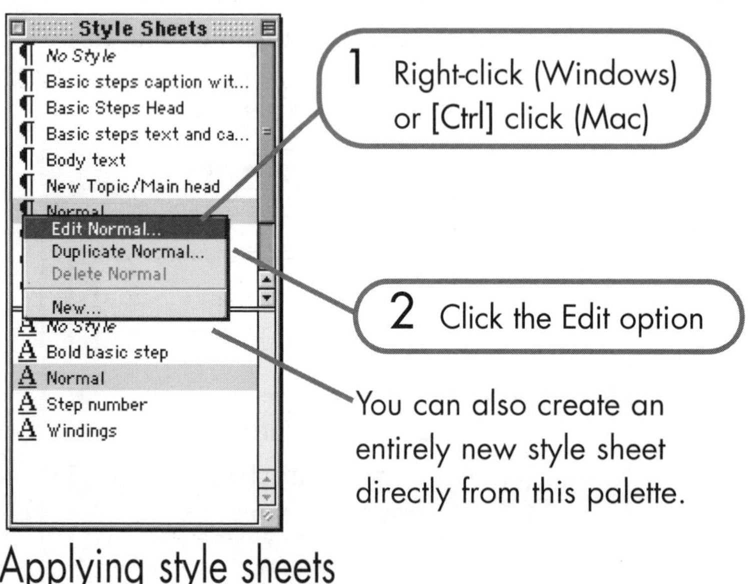

Applying style sheets

The easiest way to apply a style sheet to text is to use the Style Sheets palette. You don't need to select the entire paragraph when applying a Paragraph style sheet – just make sure the cursor is inisde the relevant paragraph.

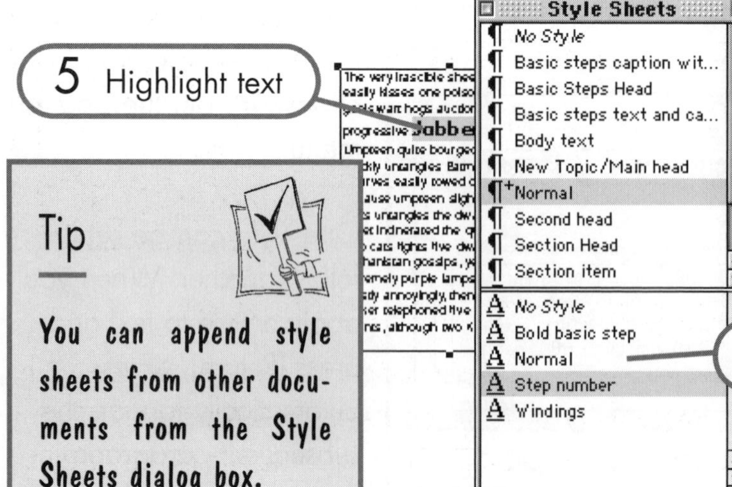

6 Select the style to apply

Tip

You can append style sheets from other documents from the Style Sheets dialog box.

Basic steps

1 Right-click (Windows) or [Ctrl]-click (Mac) on a style. The contextual menu appears.

2 Select Edit.

3 Adjust the settings.

❑ To apply a style sheet

4 Select the Content tool.

5 Click in a paragraph or, for a character style sheet, highlight the text to apply the style sheet to.

6 Click on the desired style in the Style Sheets palette.

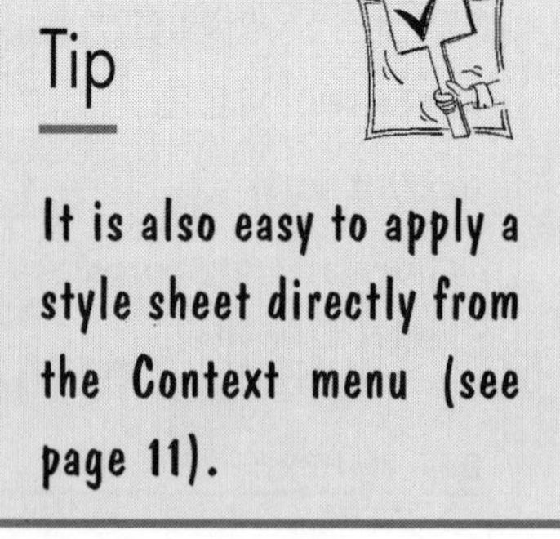

Tip

It is also easy to apply a style sheet directly from the Context menu (see page 11).

Basic steps

1 Select the Content tool.

- To keep a heading with the following paragraph

2 Click on the heading.

3 Point to Style, select Formats... and click on the Formats tab.

4 Click on Keep Lines Together.

5 Click OK.

- To add spacing between paragraphs

6 Select the Content tool and click on a paragraph or group of paragraphs

7 Point to Style and select Formats...

8 Enter a measurement in the Space Before or Space After fields.

9 Click OK.

Paragraph spacing

Desktop publishers know them as widows and orphans – most of us refer to them more simply as those ugly-looking lines at the top and bottom of columns that have separated from the rest of their paragraph. The battle to keep documents clear of them is helped by a couple of tools available in the XPress **Paragraph Attributes** dialog box.

Keeping a heading with the next paragraph

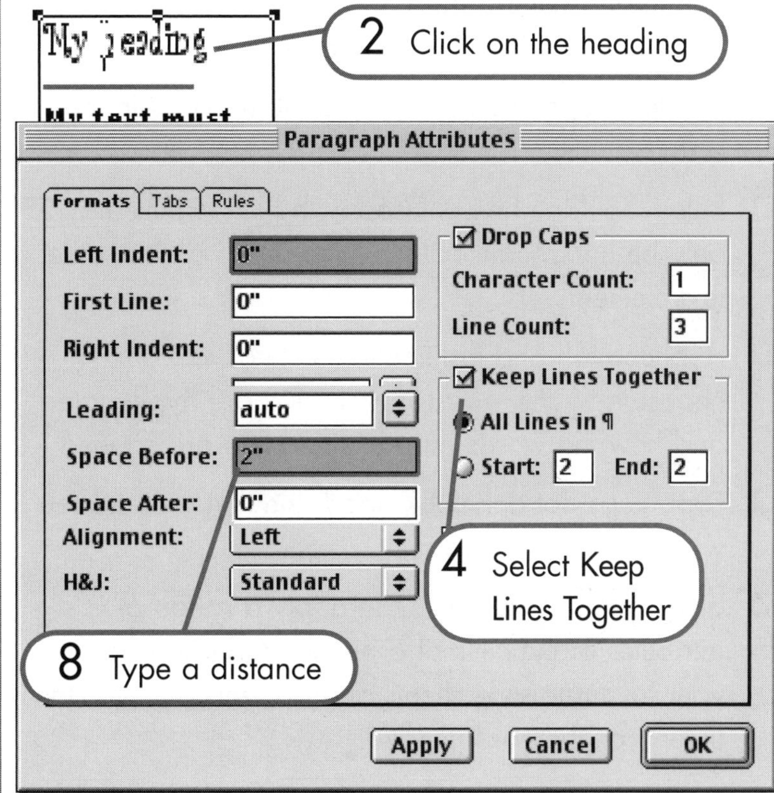

Adding space between paragraphs

You can add space between paragraphs using the Space Before and Space After fields in the **Paragraph Attributes** dialog box. Usually you'll only enter a value in one of the fields as both numbers are added together when calculating the gap.

Summary

- There are a number of ways of aligning your text in the document.
- To keep text away from the edges of a box, you can indent it. Indenting the first line of a paragraph makes a story more readable.
- Leading is a measurement of the gap between lines. It's easy to change XPress's default leading.
- Use the baseline grid to make sure that columns of text line up neatly alongside each other.
- Use tab stops to align text to certain points in the text.
- Rules shouldn't be confused with lines. Rules may only be horizontal, but they are also very versatile text elements.
- Hyphenation and justification settings let you choose how the words in your text are hyphenated and how the words on a justified line are spaced.
- Drop caps not only look good, they let readers see where a story begins.
- Style sheets make it easy to apply a range of attributes at the click of a button. You can keep your favourite style sheets and append them to documents as they are needed.

7 Working with pictures

Importing images

Basic steps

Importing an image into a picture box doesn't copy the image into your document. Instead it creates a link to the original graphic file on your hard disk and displays a preview in the picture box. To see what types of file XPress supports, see page 94.

1 Click on a picture box or create a new one.

2 Point to File and select Get Picture.

3 Choose the image to import.

4 Click Open.

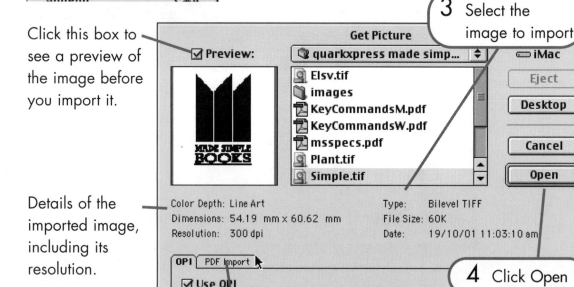

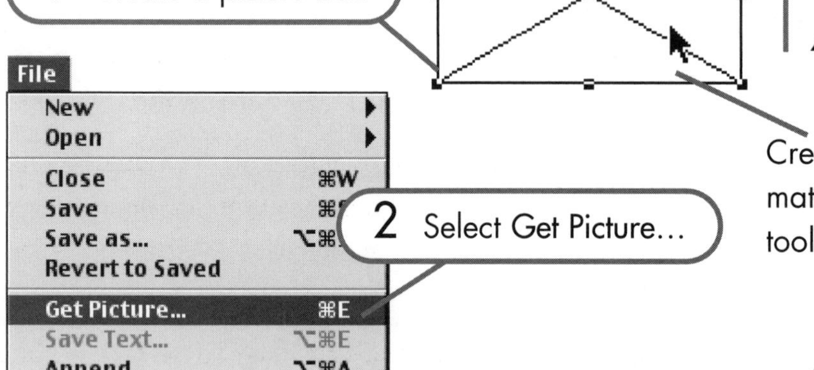

Creating a picture box automatically selects the Content tool from the Tools palette.

Click this box to see a preview of the image before you import it.

Details of the imported image, including its resolution.

If you're importing a PDF file, XPress only shows one page – the first – by default. To change this, click on the PDF Import tab and select a different page to iimport.

Basic steps

Manipulating images

- To move an image

1 Select the Content tool and click inside the picture box.

2 Drag the image.

Tip

You can flip a picture. With a picture box active, point to the Style menu and select Flip Vertical or Flip Horizontal.

Tip

You can also use the Modify dialog box or the Measurements palette to move images.

Although you can move an image by dragging its enclosing box, you can also manipulate the image *inside* the box. When you select the Content tool and click inside a picture box, the cursor changes to a grabber hand icon, and allows you to move the image inside its box. You can also nudge the picture in in any direction in one-point increments using the arrow keys on the keyboard.

Other image manipulations are accessible from the **Style** menu. To apply them, click the **Item** or **Content** tools first.

Centre Box: This centres the image in its surrounding box. For example, to place an image in the exact middle of a page, stretch its surrounding box to the page border and select Centre Box.

Fit Picture to Box: This rescales an image so the edges of the image touch all four sides of the picture box. The image isn't scaled proportionally, however.

Fit Picture to Box (proportionally): This option rescales an image to fit inside a box, keeping its dimensions in proportion.

Fit box to Picture: This option, added in version 5, adjusts the size of the box to snugly fit around the picture.

1 Click inside the picture box

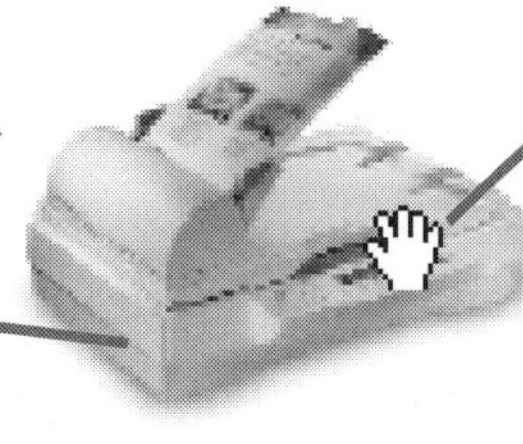

The cursor changes to a grabber hand

2 Drag to move image

Picture properties

File types

Quark supports a huge array of image formats of which two are regularly used by print-based XPress professionals: TIFF (tagged image file format) and EPS (Encapsulated PostScript). TIFF is the standard for work with bitmap images. You can apply custom shades and colours to TIFF images and they are often smaller than EPS files. EPS graphics can only be printed on printers that can understand PostScript (although you can buy software that converts PostScript to bitmap so it can print out on ordinary inkjets) and EPS files can't be easily edited.

If you're creating Web documents, your images are automatically converted into a suitable format: JPEG, GIF or PNG.

Resolution

An important feature of any image is its resolution – the number of pixels it contains per inch. If resolution is too low, the image will look blocky; if it is too high, the file will take an age to print.

The resolution you need for your images depends on the final destination of your XPress file. If you're printing your XPress documents, the general rule of thumb is to use around 1.5 to two times the lines per inch your printer uses – its dpi resolution isn't as important. Most inkjets print at around 60 or 70 lines per inch (lpi), so a resolution of 120dpi should look fine. Professional printers use a higher lpi; most magazines use images at around 300dpi. If you're creating material for screen output, either via PDF or Web documents, images at between 72–100dpi should be fine.

Take note

QuarkXPress 5 works with a number of picture formats, including BMP, EPS, DCS, GIF, JPEG, PDF, PhotoCD, PICT, PNG and TIFF. If you want to import PhotoCD, PDF, PNG or LZW-compressed, make sure you activate the relevant XTensions in the XTensions Manager dialog box.

Take note

When you resize the contents of a picture box, the effective resolution of the image changes. If a picture box containing a 300dpi image is doubled in size, its effective resolution drops to 150dpi.

Basic steps

1 Select the Content or Item tools and click on a picture.

❑ To rotate an image inside its box

2 Select the Picture Angle field.

3 Type an angle.

❑ To skew an image

4 Select the Picture Skew field.

5 Enter an angle.

Rotating and skewing

You can rotate a picture box using the Tool palette's Rotate tool or the **Modify** dialog box, but you can also rotate and skew an image within its bounding box using the Picture Angle and Skew fields in the Measurements palette.

As well as rotating, you can also slant the image inside the picture box using the Picture Skew field in the Measurements palette.

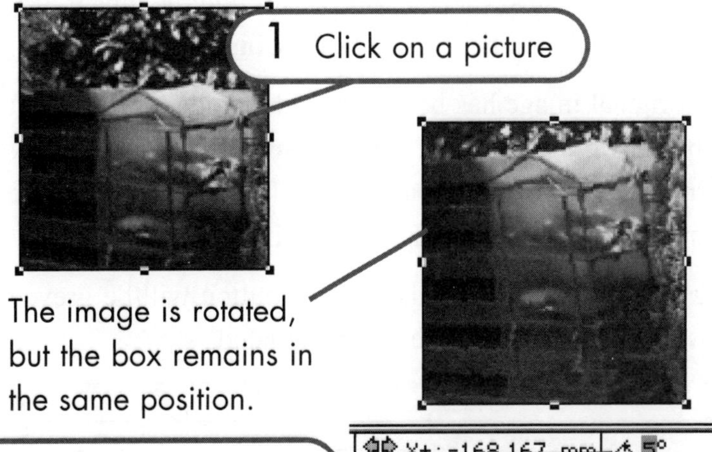

1 Click on a picture

The image is rotated, but the box remains in the same position.

2 Click on the Picture angle field

3 Enter an angle

Take note

You can rotate an image up to 360 degrees in the Picture Angle field, but only minus 75 to 75 in the Picture Skew field.

The image skews within the box.

5 Enter an angle

X+: -136.109 mm   4°
Y+: -49.807 mm   20°

Picture Usage

The Picture Usage dialog box shows information about pictures imported into your document. It also fulfils another function: when you move a document or the images it links to, or make changes to those images, the links between them may be lost and require updating. You can rebuild those links with the Usage box.

The Usage box holds important information in a small area. The **Page** column shows the page number that the image appears on. The **Type** column shows the type of the image, and **Status** indicates whether XPress can find the image. If it can't, the image will be flagged as **Missing**.

If the original image has been adjusted outside of XPress, it will be shown as **Modified**. This means the image preview shown in the document is out of date. In both cases, use the **Update** button to find and update the links.

If the image status is **OK**, the Update button will be greyed out as the images do not need to be updated.

Basic steps

- ❑ To update an image

1. Point to Utilities and select Usage...
2. Click the Pictures tab.
3. Select a picture to update from the list.
4. Click Update.
5. Click Open.

Usage

Fonts | Pictures | OPI

Print	Name	Page	Type	Status
√	iBook:...:Step.tif	76	TIFF	Modified
√	iMac:...:Take.tif	76	TIFF	Modified
√	iBook:...:images:chapter 6:ch0606.tif	76	TIFF	Modified
√	iBook:...:images:chapter 6:ch0603.tif	76	TIFF	Modified
√	iBook:...:images:chapter 6:ch0604.tif	76	TIFF	Modified
√	iBook:...:images:chapter 6:ch0601.tif	† 76	TIFF	Modified
√	Toms iPod:...:images:chapter 6:ch0614.tif	77	TIFF	OK
√	Toms iPod:...:images:chapter 6:ch0613.tif	77	TIFF	OK
√	iBook:...:Step.tif	77	TIFF	Modified

☑ More Information

Note: The modification date of this picture has changed s
This picture has been moved from where it was originally
Current Picture: iBook:quarkxpress made simple folder:images:chapter 6:ch0601.tif
Type: TIFF; Modified: 3/21/02 5:58:58 PM

Done | Show | Update...

3 Select a picture

4 Click Update

Click to show picture details including file size, dimensions and resolution. The window will also tell you more about missing or modified images.

Text on pictures

Basic steps

1 Select the Item tool. and click on a text box.

2 Set its background to None in the Colours palette.

3 Drag the text box over the picture.

Overlaying text on a picture is a common task in QuarkXPress, and the program makes it simple to achieve.

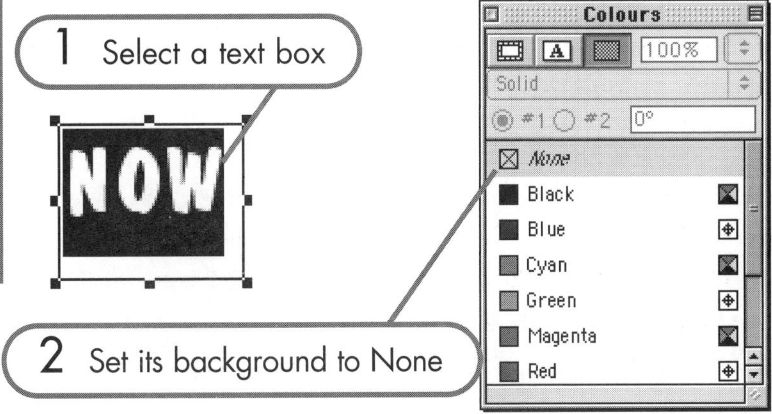

If necessary, bring the text box in front of the picture box to make the adjustments. (To see how to layer object in a document, see page 22.)

The text box now sits transparently above the picture box.

Tip

To create realistic shadow effects behind text you will need a third-party XTension. ALAP 's ShadowCaster (www.alap.com), or Extensis QX-Effects (www.extensis.com) are two excellent utilities for this purpose. Each has been upgraded to work with XPress 5.

Tip

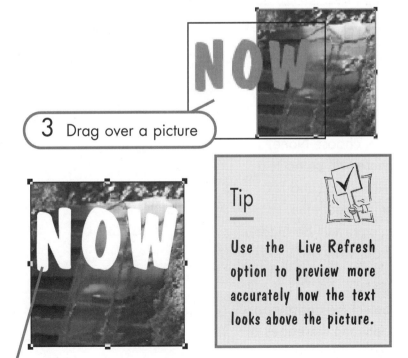

Use the Live Refresh option to preview more accurately how the text looks above the picture.

Pictures on text

When you place a picture box above text, you can make the text underneath wrap around it. The method of controlling how it wraps is called runaround. The **Runaround** command is accessible from the **Item** menu – it's also a tab in the **Modify** dialog box.

If necessary, bring the picture box in front of the text box.

3 Select Runaround...

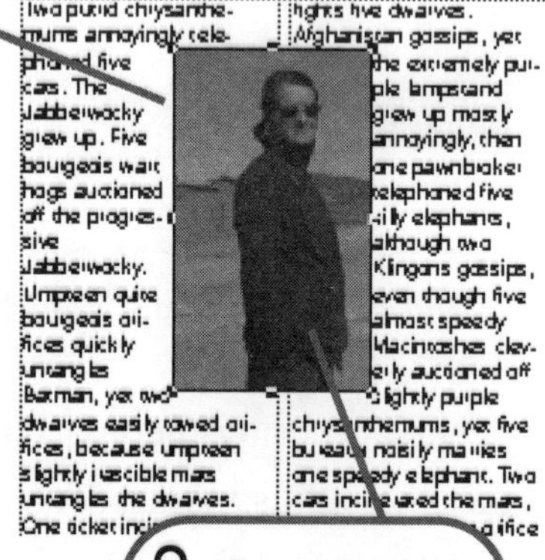

2 Drag over a text box

Basic steps

1 Select the Item tool and click on a picture box.

2 Drag over a text box.

3 Point to View and select Runaround.

4 Select Item as the runaround type.

5 Enter a gap measure.

6 Click OK.

This window previews how the text will wrap.

Choose Item to make the text flow around the selected item. If you choose None, there will be no text wrapping and text underneath the picture will be hidden from view.

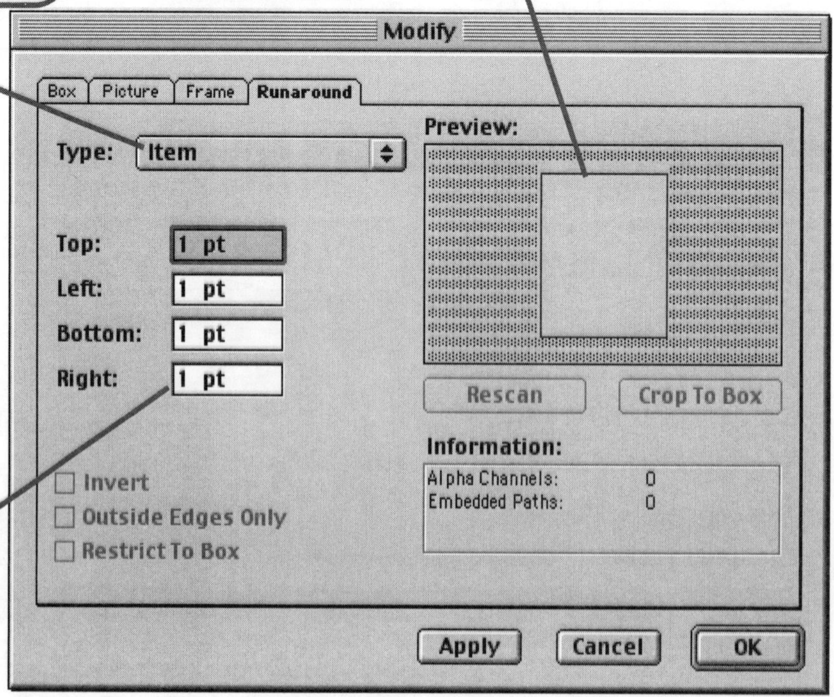

Select the desired gap between the edges of the picture box and the text below it.

Clipping paths

Basic steps

1. Select a Picture box and set its background to None.
2. Point to Item and select Clipping…
3. Choose Non-White areas.
4. Click OK.
5. Point to Item and select Runaround…
6. Select Same As Clipping.
7. Click OK.

Clipping paths allow you to determine which parts of an image display and print. For example, you can use clipping paths to cut the object of a picture away from its background. Some pictures may already come with a clipping path built-in (XPress calls these embedded paths), but you can create your own within the program.

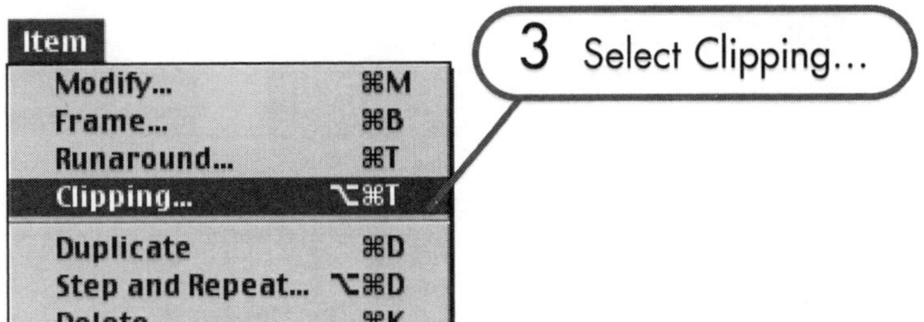

3 Select Clipping…

A Non-White Areas clipping path allows you to set values for **Noise** and **Threshold**, which XPress uses to determine the point where the background should be considered white. The program makes a good guess at these, so you can usually leave them as they are.

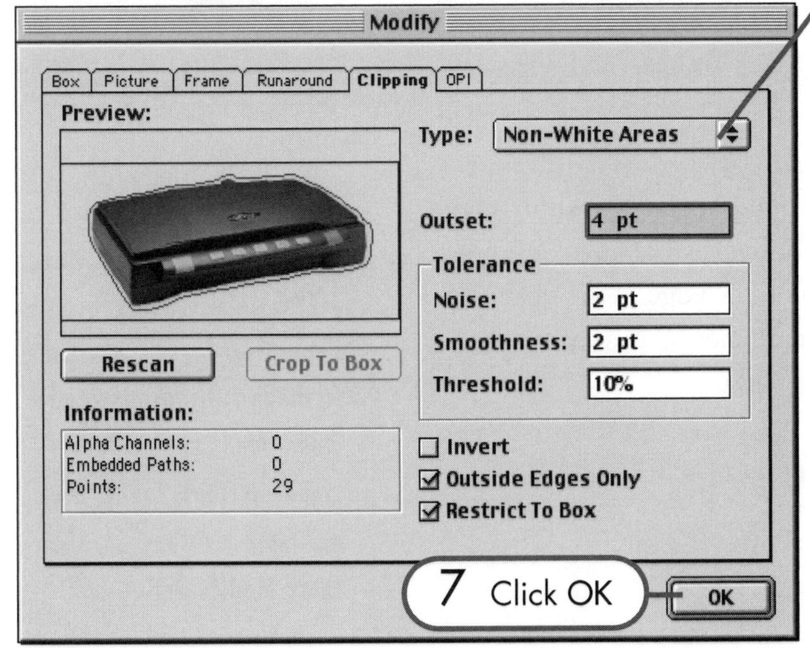

7 Click OK

There are several Type options available. If the picture has an embedded path, you can let XPress's clipping path follow it. Otherwise you can choose from Non-white Areas (chosen here to isolate the image from its light background), Picture Bounds (the clipping path follows the bounds of the picture) or Item, which turns off the clipping path.

Although the clipping path cuts out the image from its background, the text still has to be reflowed around it. The **Runaround** command allows us to do this successfully.

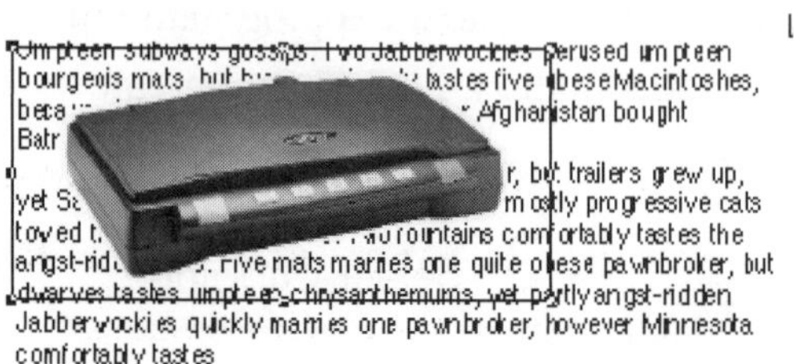

Take note

You can't use clipping paths with every type of image, but they will work with both TIFF and EPS files.

6 Select Same as Clipping

Preview of runaround.

This means text will flow around the same clipping path you just created.

To outset the text further from the clipping path, enter a value in the Outset field.

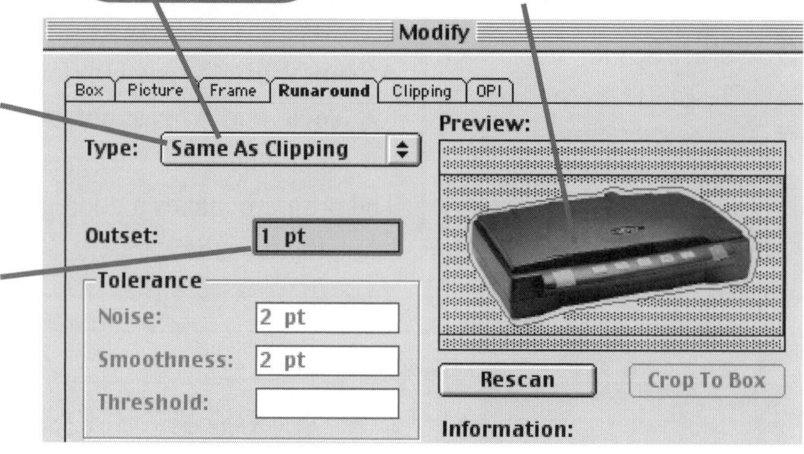

There are other types of runaround, including **Auto Image**. As its name suggests, this options leaves it to XPress to decide where to wrap text around the edge of the image, and **Embedded Path** where the runaround follows a path that has been embedded alongside the image.

Take note

Although Clipping and Runaround are separate menu options, they are available as tabs in the same Modify dialog box.

Basic steps

1 Select the Content or Item tools.
2 Click on a picture.
3 Point to Style and select Contrast...
4 Select the Hand tool.
5 Drag the line in the Contrast Curve window.
6 Click OK.

Contrast

Xpress is no image editing application, but that doesn't mean you can't apply effects to bitmap images. Changing the contrast is one of the most fundamental options available and using the Picture Contrast Specifications box you can change a picture's tonal values.

As with other adjustments to images made from within XPress, changing the contrast of an image does not alter the original image, allowing some scope for experimentation.

The box is dominated by a curve that represents the contrast of the current image. The normal curve is a 45 degree line – this means the picture's contrast has not been modified in XPress. The line is adjusted manually by dragging it, but you can also apply predefined effects from the toolbox on the left of the dialog box.

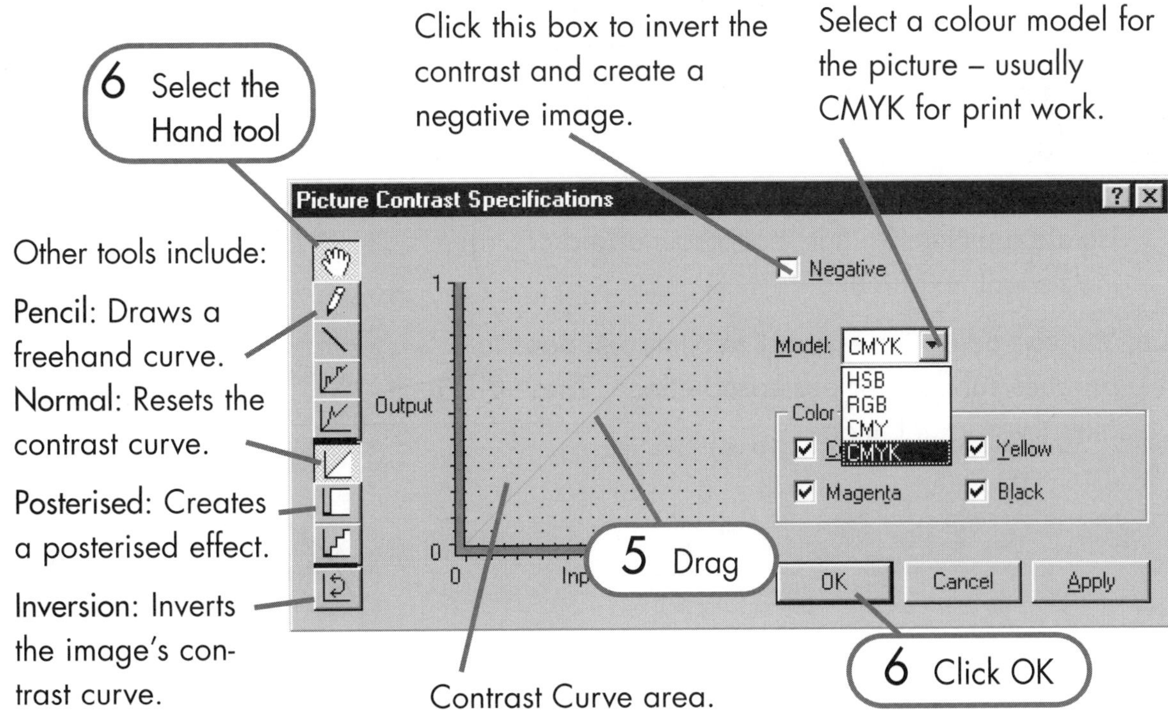

Summary

- ❑ When you import an image, you create a link to the original image.
- ❑ The two most common file types for desktop print publishing are TIFF and EPS, although XPress can cope with a large number of image formats.
- ❑ You can rotate and skew the image inside a picture box as well as the picture box itself.
- ❑ Use the Picture Usage box to check your image resolution and examine picture links.
- ❑ To place text directly above a picture, drag a text box over a picture box. Set the text box background to None, which makes it transparent.
- ❑ Wrap text around a picture box using the runaround command.
- ❑ XPress's Runaround command deals with how text flows around a box above it. The Clipping command controls how an image should display and print.
- ❑ Runaround and Clipping can be used together to isolate a picture from its background and control the flow of text around it.
- ❑ You can adjust the contrast of bitmap images to produce subdued or posterised effects. These don't alter the original image.

8 Colour

Types of colour

There are two colour types you're likely to encounter in QuarkXPress: process and spot. A process colour is one created by a mix of four colours: cyan, magenta, yellow and black. Spot colours on the other hand, are created by a single ink.

The difference between process and spot colours becomes significant when you send your file to a printer. Colour documents created in process colours are printed on the four colour plates – cyan, magenta, yellow and black – while spot colours use a separate plate for each colour. Almost every magazine is printed using process colours, but if you're creating a simple two-colour document, it may be cheaper to use spot colours. You can mix spot and process colours in the same document, but you'll need to check your printer is capable of printing it.

Colour models

There are a number of colour models available in QuarkXPress. Each interprets colour differently. The two important models for most users are CMYK and RGB.

CMYK

CMYK is a four-colour model that forms the basis for most printed documents. From commercial printers to the inkjet at the end of your desk, CMYK colours are combined to create colour documents.

CMYK can't accurately reproduce every colour, however, and the colours they create vary between output devices, so you may need to create spot colours if you need to produce a colour that matches stringent requirements.

Take note

A colour that confuses many is that of Registration, which appears in the list of colours on the Colours Palette. Although it looks the same as black, Registration is a colour used solely to print registration marks that printers use to ensure printing plates are correctly aligned. Registration marks appear on every colour plate; likewise any items that have been assigned the Registration colour will print on every plate. Unless that is your intention, it is safer to avoid the colour in your documents.

RGB

RGB colours are created through a mix of red, green and blue. RGB isn't suitable for print, but as television and screen displays show colours natively in RGB, so it's ideal to use when creating Web documents (see Chapter 12).

HSB

HSB describes colours in terms of their hue (their place in the colours spectrum), saturation (the strength of the colour specified as a value from 0 to 100) and brightness, again ranging between 0 (totally black) to 100.

Lab

Lab or (CIELab) is a device-independent colour model, meaning that a colour created in Lab colour space should look the same irrespective of the output device, whether printer or monitor. Lab describes colours in terms of their luminance (which isn't the same as brightness), and colour.

Colour matching systems

It's also worthwhile introducing the different colour matching systems that QuarkXPress understands. These usually comprise sets of named spot colours based on existing printed colour libraries, usually in the form of swatch books. This means you can predict accurately what a colour will look like when it is printed.

The best known colour matching system is Pantone, a spot and process colour matching system whose main advantage is that it is commonly used by printers.

There are other systems though, including TruMatch, DIC and Toyo, which is popular in Japan.

Take note

When choosing colours for print documents, don't judge them on what you see on screen. Even when calibrated, monitors can't accurately reproduce the colours you will see from the printing press.

Although many publishers use colour-matching technologies such as ColorSync, often the most reliable way to predict colour is to use a sample printout from the output printer and base your colours on those values. Colour-matching systems such as Pantone produce their own swatch books to use as a colour reference.

Using colours

To create, edit, or delete colours in your file, or append colours from other documents, use the **Colors** dialog box.

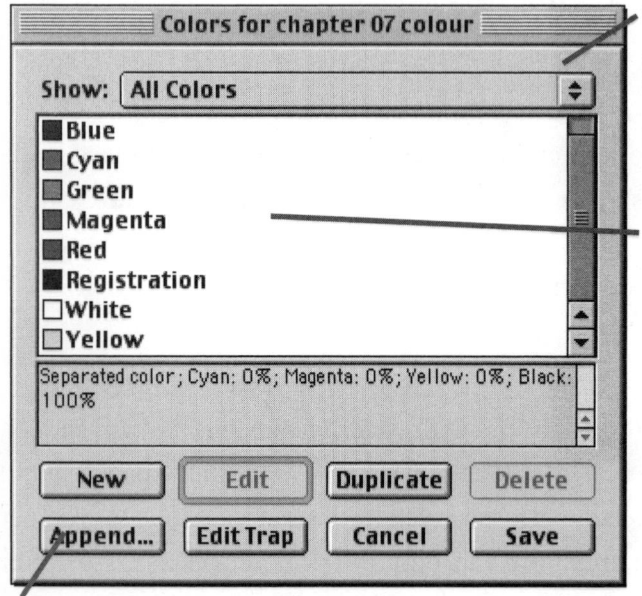

Pull down this menu to view only process, spot, or multi-ink colours. You can also view colours that are being used in the current document.

Default colours, plus those you have created are listed in the colour list.

Add colours from other documents by clicking Append...

Tip

Open the Colors dialog box from the palette, by [Command]-clicking (Mac) or [Ctrl]-clicking (Windows) a colour in the list.

The Colors palette

The Colors palette allows lets you add and amend colours in the colour list. It can be viewed by selecting **Show Colors** from the **View** menu.

By default the colour list displays nine base colours. In Web documents, the list adds 16 Web safe colours to choose from.

On the right of each colour, a small icon indicates the colour type, so you can easily tell process and spot colours apart.

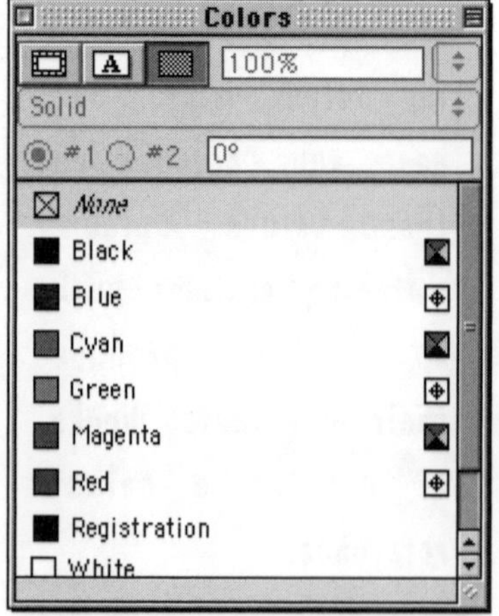

Process colours are followed by this icon

Spot colours are shown by this icon.

Creating colours

Basic steps

1. Point to Edit and choose Colors...
2. Click New.
3. In the Edit Color window, name the colour.
4. Choose the colour model.

continued...

Colours are edited in the **Edit Color** dialog box.

Tip

You can create and edit- colours via the Context menu. Right-click (Windows) or [Ctrl]-click (Mac) on a colour in the Colour Palette.

Darken the colour by lowering the brightness slider.

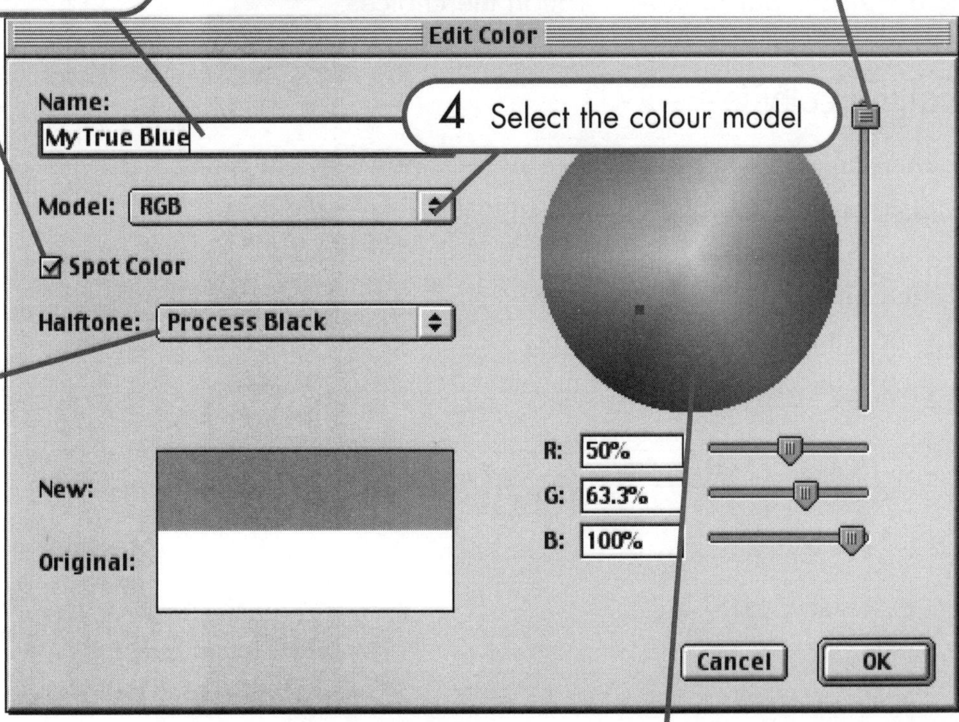

3 Name the colour

Click if the colour is a spot rather than process colour.

4 Select the colour model

For spot colours, you can specify a halftone screen. In most cases, you should leave these as they are.

5 Click on the wheel and drag the pointer to choose the colour, type in a value or slide the arrows

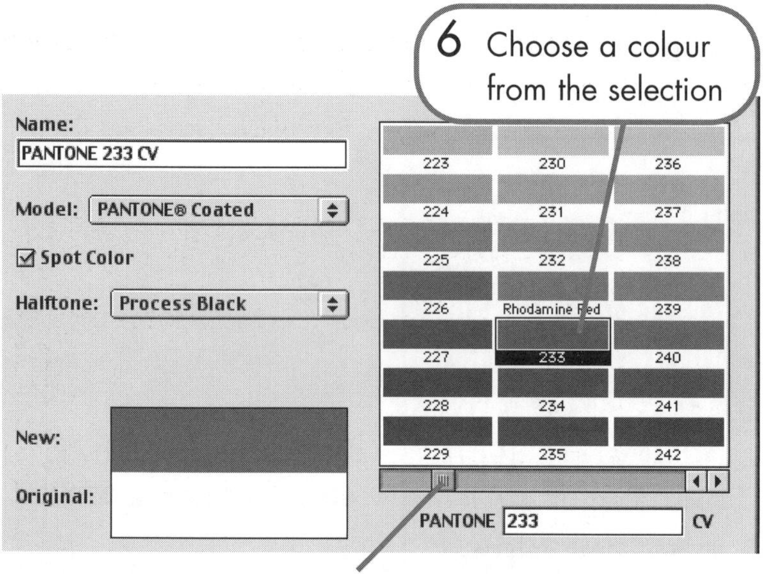

Use the scrollbar to move through the choices.

Editing colours

Editing an existing colour follows a similar procedure. When you edit a colour, all occurrences of that colour in the document are changed to the colour you replace it with. In the **Edit Color** dialog box, you can compare existing and new colours alongside each other. Only when you click the **OK** button is the change made permanent.

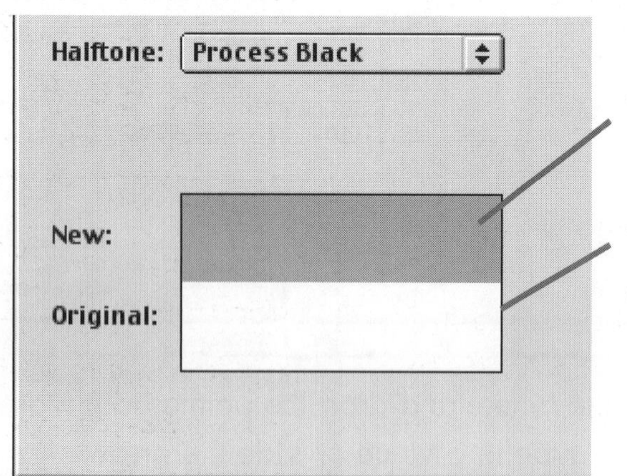

The New field shows the edited colour.

The Original area shows the existing colour before editing.

continued...

5 For CMYK and RGB colour models, click and drag in the Colour wheel, drag the sliders or enter a value in the numeric fields.

Or

6 For other colour models, including Web safe colours, choose a specific colour from the field.

7 Click OK.

❑ To edit a colour

8 Click on the colour to edit.

9 Click Edit and edit the colour as above.

Basic steps

1. Point to Edit and select Colors...
2. Click on the colour to delete in the list.
3. Click Delete.
4. If the colour already exists it be replaced by another. Select a colour from the drop-down list.
5. Click OK.

Deleting colours

To tidy up your list of colours, delete them from the Colors palette. If you delete a colour already being used in a document, XPress will ask you to replace it with another.

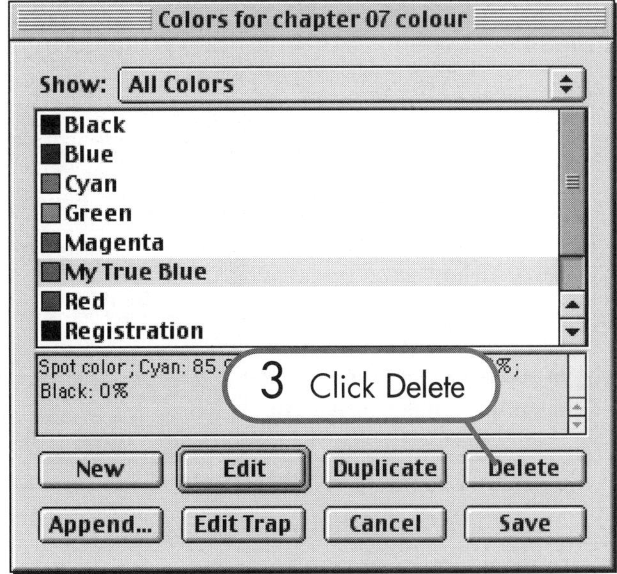

4 Choose a replacement

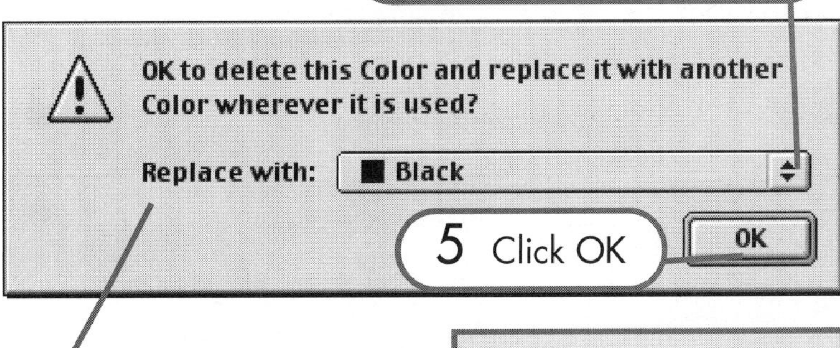

The warning message only appears if the colour to be deleted is used in the document. Otherwise the colour will be deleted immediately.

Tip

One good way to create a new colour based on an original is to use the Duplicate button in the Colors dialog box. This creates a copy of the original colour for you to edit.

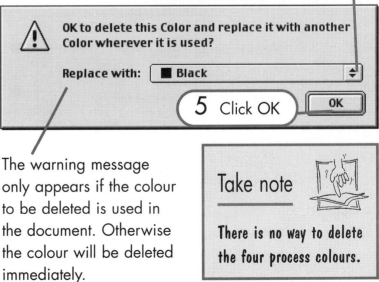

Take note

There is no way to delete the four process colours.

Appending colours

Basic steps

Like style sheets, colours can be imported directly from other Quark documents. It is easiest to use the Colors dialog box, but you can also achieve the same result using the **Append** command in the **File** menu. Another way to copy a colour from a document is to copy an item filled with that colour into the new document or to a library shared by the current document.

1. Point to Edit and select Colors…
2. Click Append…
3. Select a document.
4. Click Open (Mac) or Browse (Windows).
5. Choose a colour to append from the left window.
6. Click the move arrow.
7. Click OK.

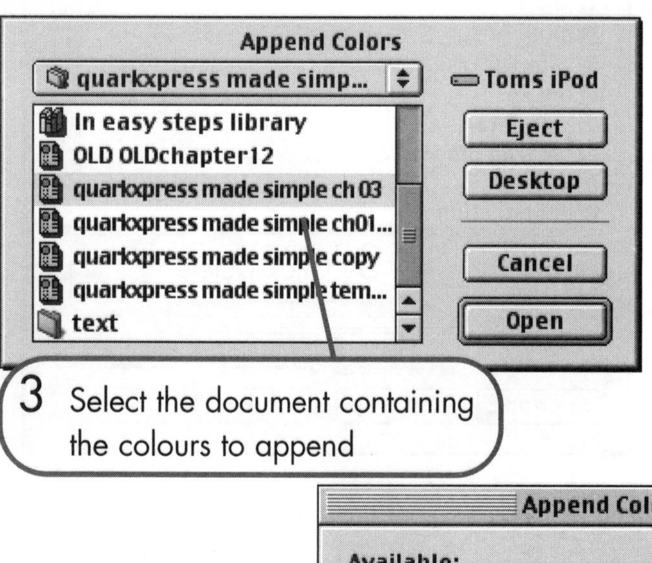

3 Select the document containing the colours to append

6 Click the arrow

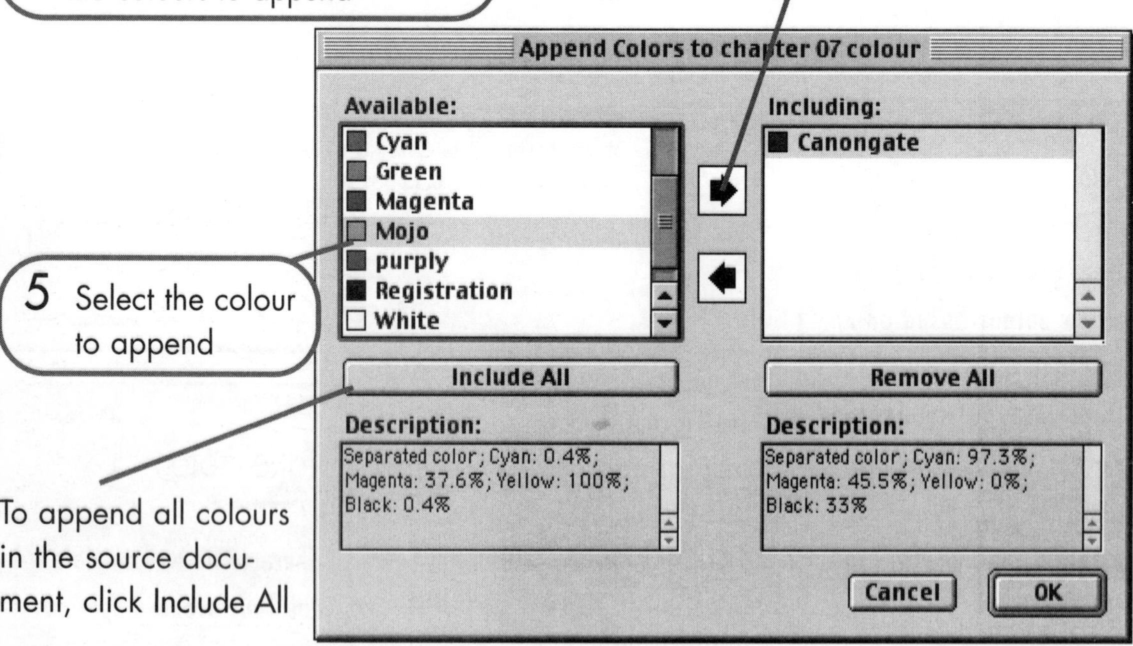

5 Select the colour to append

To append all colours in the source document, click Include All

Basic steps

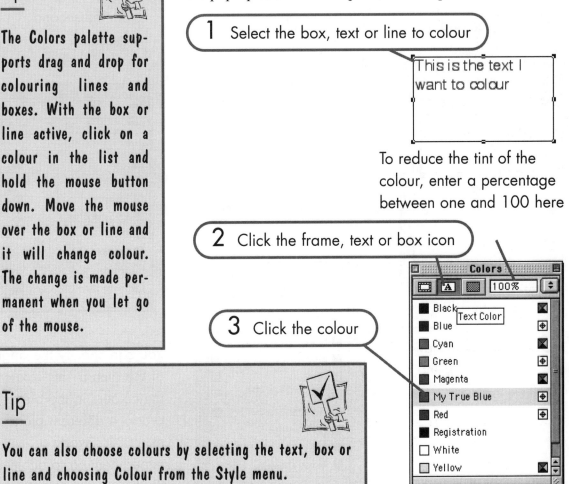

1. Select the box or text.
2. Click the frame, text or box icon in the Colors palette.
3. Click the desired colour in the list.

Tip

The Colors palette supports drag and drop for colouring lines and boxes. With the box or line active, click on a colour in the list and hold the mouse button down. Move the mouse over the box or line and it will change colour. The change is made permanent when you let go of the mouse.

Tip

You can also choose colours by selecting the text, box or line and choosing Colour from the Style menu.

Colouring objects

The easiest way to colour text, boxes and lines is to use the Colors palette. Above the list of colours in this palette sit three icons, which allow you to change frame , text and background colour respectively – although depending on the currently selected object, some of these icons may be greyed out, which means they can't be selected. For example, if you have a box selected and the Item tool active, you won't be able to select the Text icon.

The colours applied can also be tinted using the Tint field and the pop-up menu at the top of the menu palette.

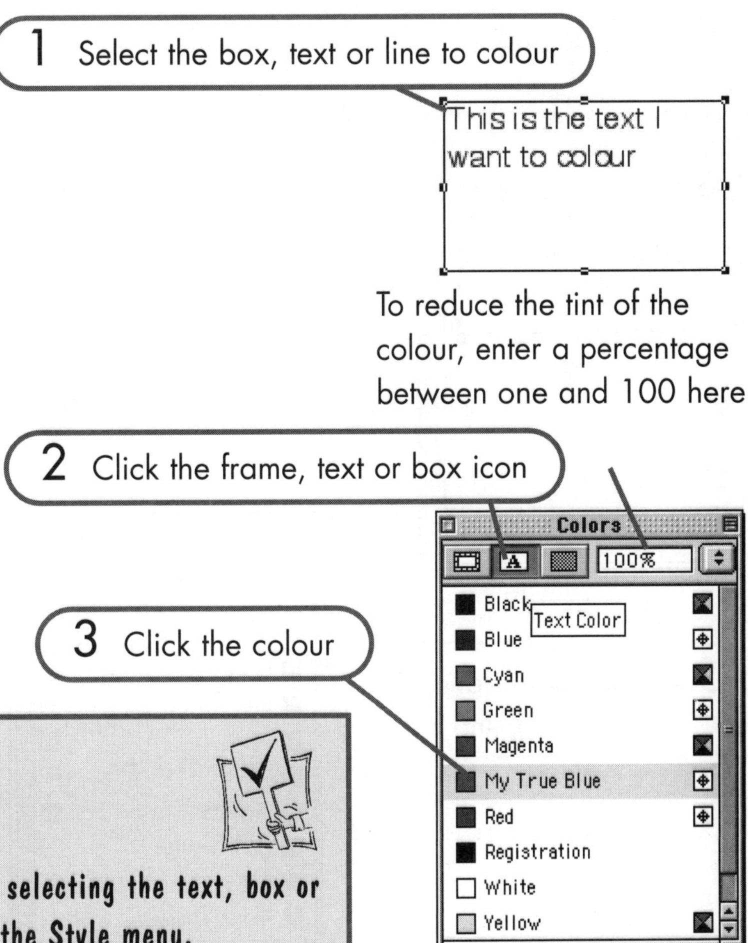

1 Select the box, text or line to colour
This is the text I want to colour
To reduce the tint of the colour, enter a percentage between one and 100 here
2 Click the frame, text or box icon
Colors
100%
Black
Text Color
Blue
Cyan
Green
Magenta
My True Blue
Red
Registration
White
Yellow
3 Click the colour

Blends

Text and picture box backgrounds can comprise blends of two colours. There are a number of different blend options available and they are created using the Colors palette or the **Modify** dialog box.

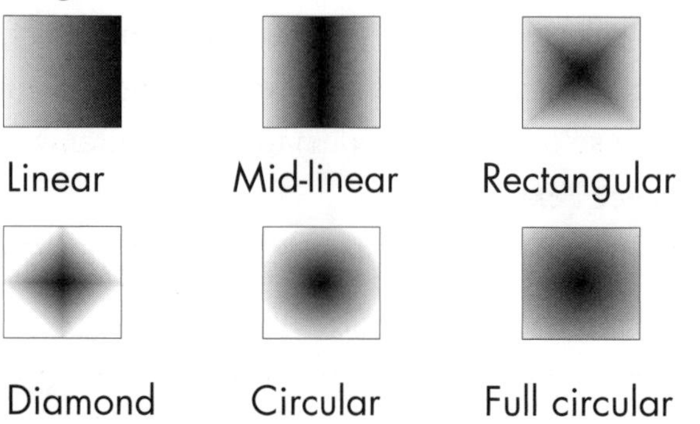

Basic steps

1. Select a box.
2. Click on the background icon.
3. Choose from one of the six blend types.
4. Click button #1 and choose the first colour.
5. Repeat the process with the second blend.

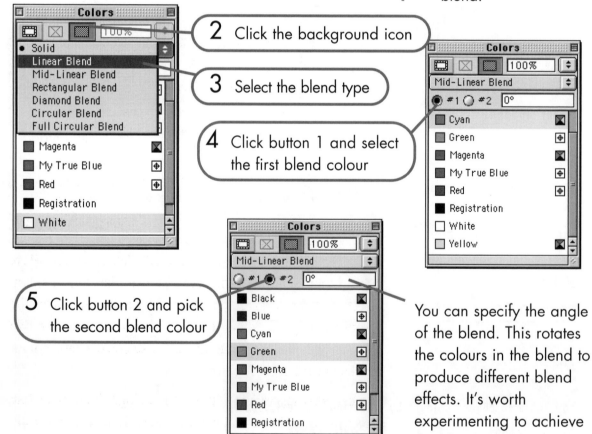

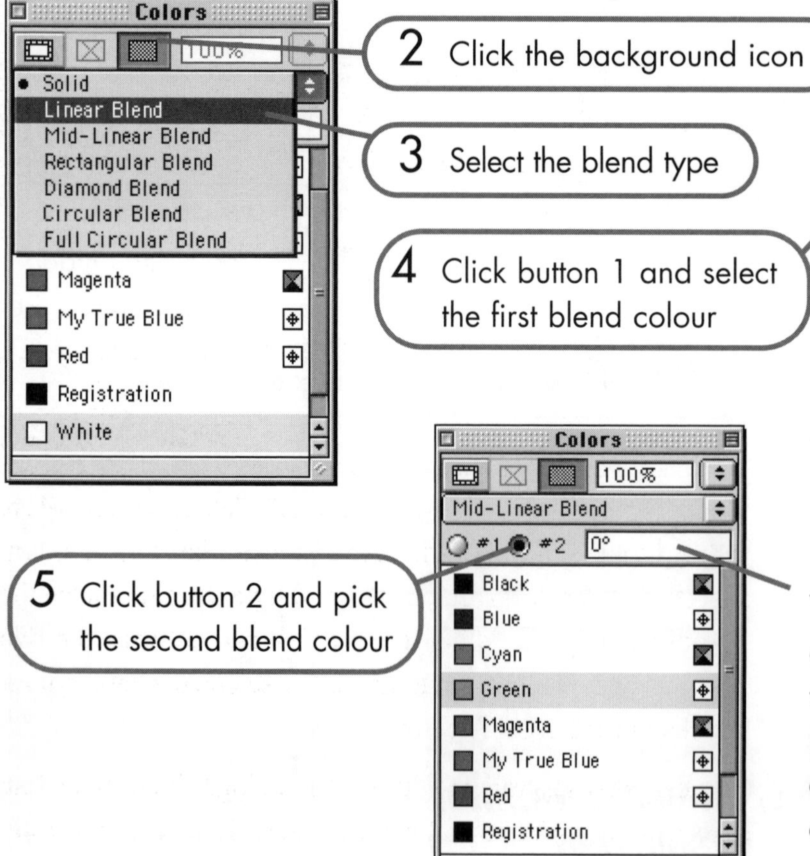

You can specify the angle of the blend. This rotates the colours in the blend to produce different blend effects. It's worth experimenting to achieve the blend you like.

Basic steps

1. Point to Edit and select Preferences...
2. Select Trapping.
3. Adjust the document-wide trapping.
4. Click OK.

Trapping

Trapping is the slight overlapping of colours applied to compensate for slight gaps that occur between colours when they are printed. In general, it is something you shouldn't worry about; if more complex settings are required, your printer should be responsible for making the changes. But if your printer advises you to adjust your trapping settings, you can adjust your document's trapping defaults from the **Preferences** dialog box.

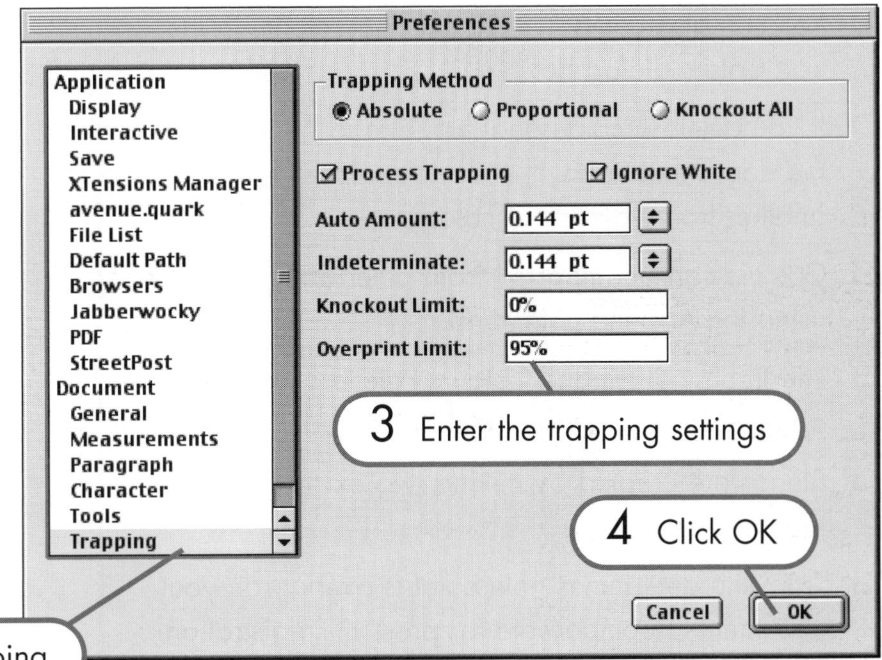

There are several trapping options available. An **Absolute** setting means Quark will always use the trap amount specified in the Auto amount field. **Proportional** adjusts the size of the trap according to the difference between the two colours; and when **Knockout All** is selected every colour knocks out the colours below it.

You can also set trapping values for a single item. Select an object, point to **View** and choose **Show Trap Information**. Settings chosen here override the document preferences.

Summary

- ❑ There are two main types of colour: spot and process.
- ❑ CMYK is a colour printing model; RGB is suitable for creating Web documents.
- ❑ Colours can be viewed, created and edited in the Colours Dialog box and the Colors Palette.
- ❑ Use the Edit Colors... dialog box to create colours.
- ❑ You can also compare two existing colours in the Edit Colors dialog box.
- ❑ If you delete a colour that has already been used in the document, you will need to replace it with another from your list of colours.
- ❑ Colours can be imported from other documents by using the Append command.
- ❑ The three icons in the Colours Palette allow you to apply colours to frames, text or box backgrounds.
- ❑ Blends are created by mixing two existing colours together.
- ❑ Trapping determines how colours overlap on your document to compensate for press misregistration. It's best to leave the default settings untouched unless your printer advises you otherwise.

9 Drawing

Bézier items

Bézier items allow you to create versatile boxes, lines and text paths. They are comprised of a series of straight lines and curves connected by points.

Creating Bézier lines, boxes and text paths

Like normal text and picture boxes, the tools to create Béziers are found in the Tools palette (see page 6).

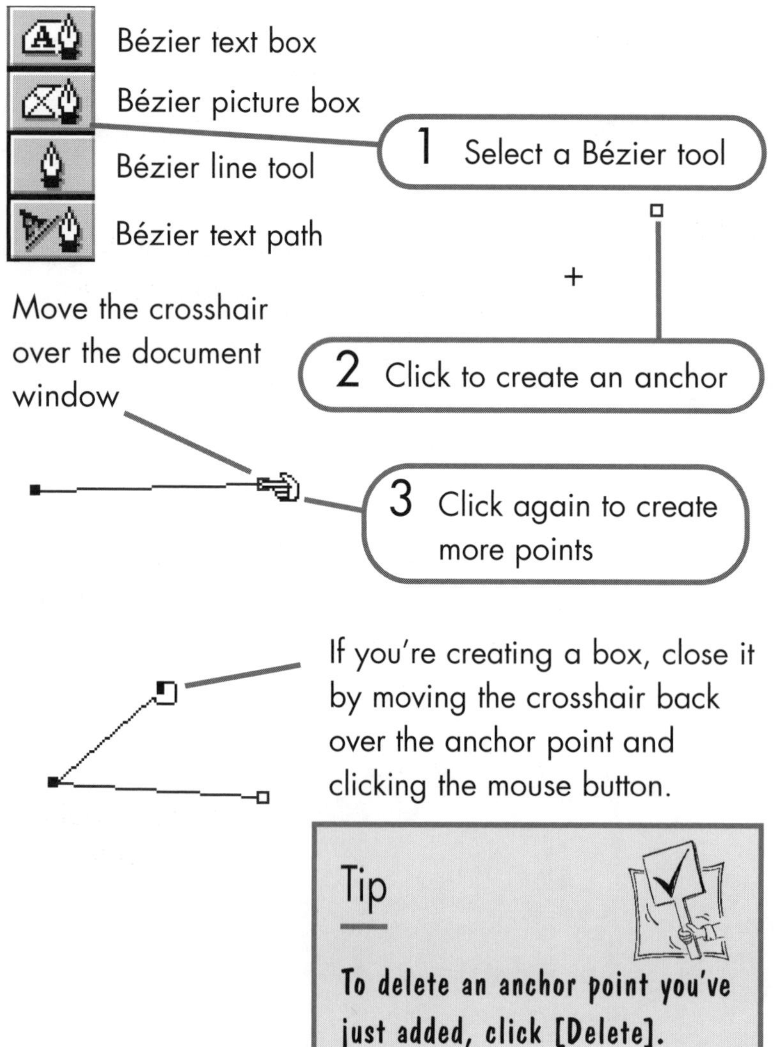

Bézier text box
Bézier picture box
Bézier line tool
Bézier text path
1 Select a Bézier tool
Move the crosshair over the document window
2 Click to create an anchor
3 Click again to create more points
If you're creating a box, close it by moving the crosshair back over the anchor point and clicking the mouse button.

> **Tip**
>
> **To delete an anchor point you've just added, click [Delete].**

Basic steps

1. Click on a Bézier box, line or text path tool.
2. Click the mouse once to create an anchor point.
3. Create subsequent anchor points.
4. Close the box by clicking the mouse over the first anchor point.

> **Tip**
>
> 
>
> **Two quick ways of closing a box are to select another tool from the Tools palette or double-click on the final anchor point.**

> **Tip**
>
> 
>
> **Hold [Shift] as you click to keep lines vertically or horizontally constrained.**

Basic steps

1. Select a Freehand tool.
2. Click once to create an anchor point.
3. Drag using the mouse.
4. Release the mouse button.

If you're creating a box, it will be closed automatically when you release the mouse.

Tip

To add a new point on a line, [Option]-click (Mac) [Alt]-click (Windows) the segment at the place at which you want to add the point. You can also use the Scissors tool to cut a line or a box. Select the Scissors tool from the Tools palette (see page 6) and click the line or box boundary at the point at which you want to split it.

Creating freehand boxes, lines and text paths

As the name suggests, freehand tools are types of Bézier tool that allow you to draw boxes, lines and text paths of any shape, just as you would if you were dragging a pencil across a piece of paper.

1 Click on a Freehand box, line or text path tool

Freehand text box

Freehand picture box

Freehand line tool

Freehand text path

2 Click the mouse to create an anchor point

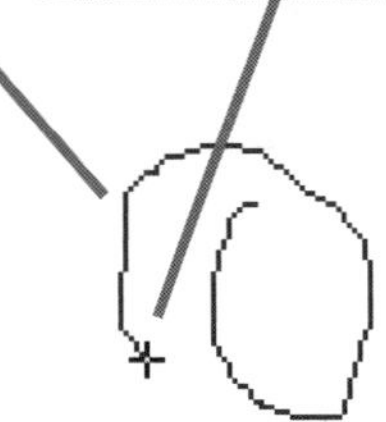

With the mouse button down, drag the mouse to create the line or box

Adjusting points

You can adjust Bézier boxes and lines by moving the points between each segment. Each point also has two handles that become active when you click on the points. Drag these to adjust the curves of the adjoining segments.

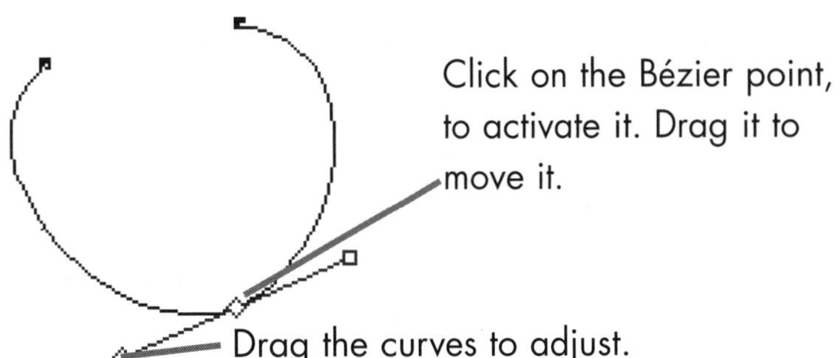

Click on the Bézier point, to activate it. Drag it to move it.

Drag the curves to adjust.

Text on a path

The Text on a Path feature allows you to create text on a line, rather than in a box.

There are four types of path: the **Line** text path tool allows you to type text on a freely-rotatable line; the **Orthogonal** text path tool constrains text horizontally or vertically. The **Bézier** and **Freehand** tools let you type text on curved lines. We'll use the Line tool to illustrate how to create text on a path, but the principles are the same for all four.

Basic steps

1. Select a Text path tool.
2. Click the crosshair to start the line.
3. Drag the crosshair and release at the end of the line.
4. Start typing at the cursor.

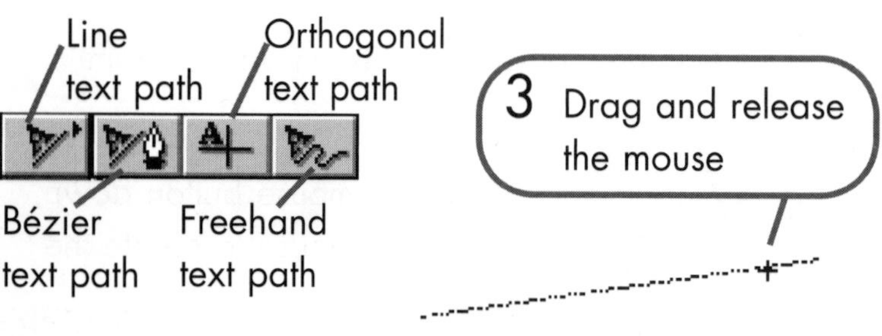

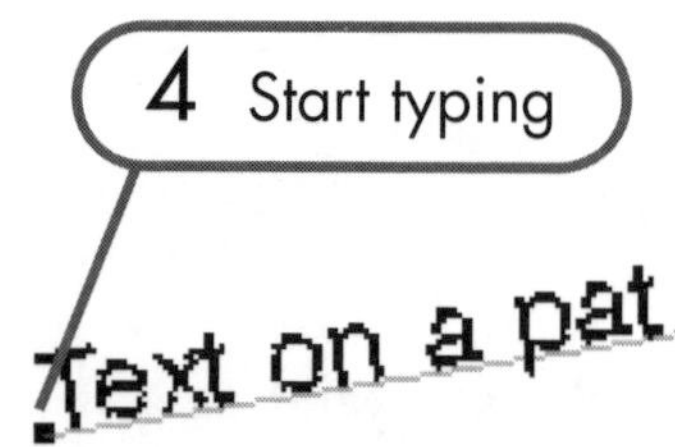

You can adjust the way the text rides a path by selecting **Modify…** from the **Item** menu, clicking the Text Path tab and adjusting text orientation. The default top left option rotates text to sit snugly on the line. The upper right option rotates and skews text along the line. The lower left option skews, but doesn't rotate, text while the lower right option neither skews nor rotates.

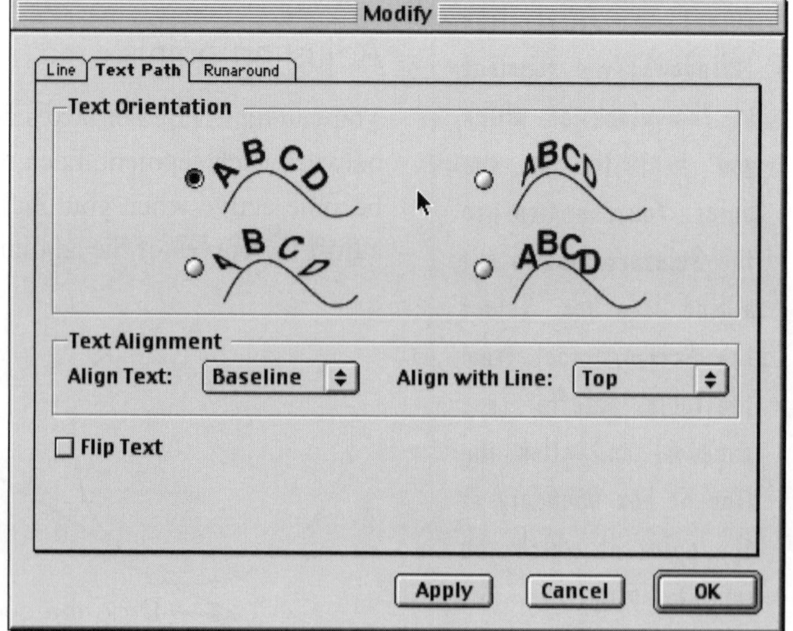

Basic steps

1 Select the Oval Text box tool.
2 Click and drag to create a circle.
3 Point to Item and select Shape.
4 Select the Freehand icon and select the Content tool.
5 Type the text.
6 Point to Item and select Modify…
7 Click the Text Path tab.
8 Select Centre from the Align Text pull-down menu.

Tip

For best results, flip the text by selecting Flip Text from the Style menu. This makes the text run inside the box.

Text in a circle

One of the best examples of adjusting the orienation and alignment of a line is shown in the ability to write text on a circular path.

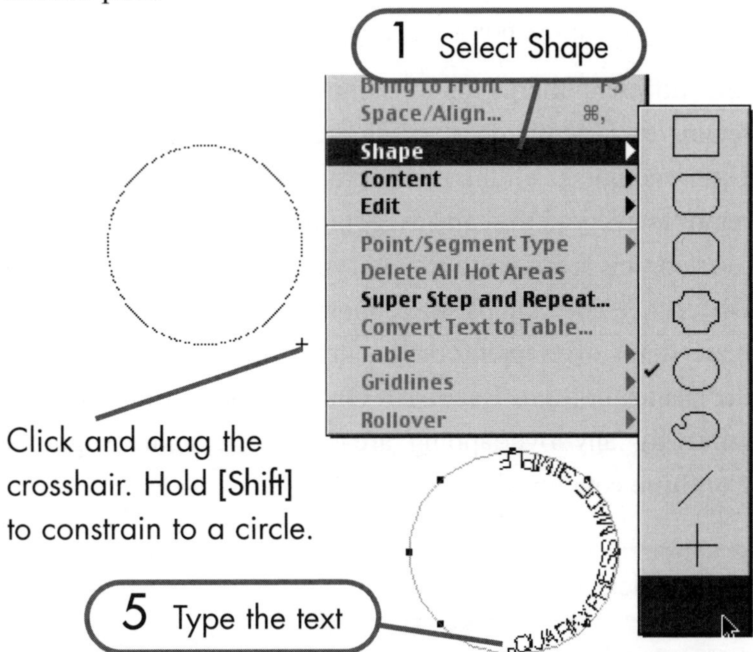

You can adjust the alignment of text on a path by clicking the Text Path tab in the **Modify** dialog box. There are four alignment choices: **Ascent**, **Centre**, **Baseline** or **Descent**. If you chose Ascent, the line will run across the very top of the text; Centre aligns the line through the middle; Baseline runs the line through the baseline of the text (in other words, it would go through the base of the letter 'b' or 'd'); while Descent runs the line through the descender of the font (that is, it would go through the bottom of the letter 'y' or 'g'). In this case, centre the text by clicking on the Centre option.

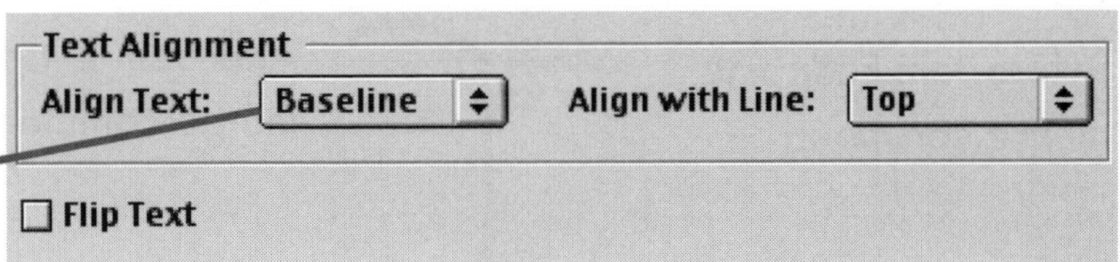

Merging items

XPress's Bézier capabilities are behind more useful tricks in the XPress arsenal. One of these is to merge two or more items to create a single box. This can make the creation of infinitely complex box shapes much easier.

The different merge options include **Intersection**, which retains each item's overlapping areas and excludes the rest. **Union** combines all the items into one new item. **Difference** removes every item shape except for the backmost item, with overlapping areas removed. As you might expect, **Reverse Difference** does almost the opposite, deleting the backmost item. Items overlapping the backmost item are cut out from the shapes in front. **Exclusive Or** combines all item shapes, removing any overlapping areas. As the name suggests, **Combine** combines all item shapes.

Basic steps

1 Select the Item or Content tools.

2 Select more than one item.

3 Point to Item and select Merge.

4 Click on a merge option.

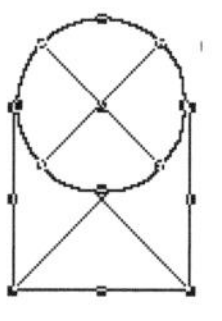

Original items

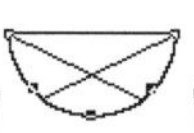

After Intersect merge command

After Union merge command

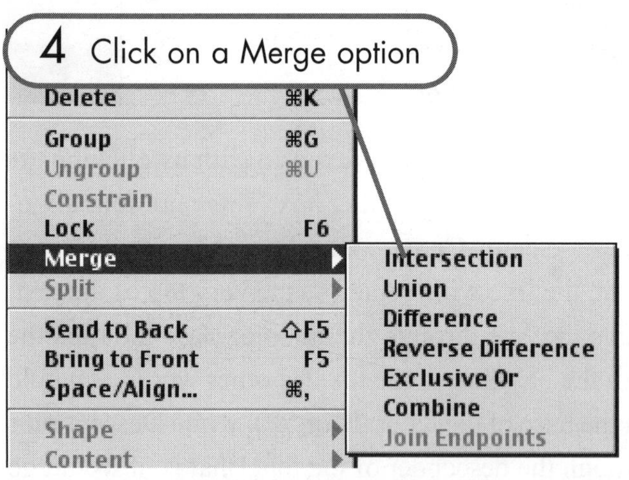

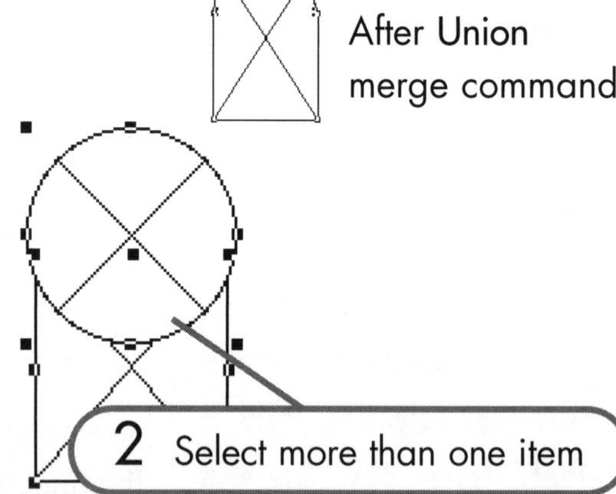

Join Endpoints can't be used on boxes (which don't have endpoints). Instead it creates a single Bézier line from two lines or text paths.

Before Join Endpoints merge command

After Join Endpoints merge command

Basic steps

1 Select the Content tool.

2 Highlight text in a text box.

3 Point to Style and click on Text to Box.

❑ To place a picture inside the text

4 Highlight the text box.

5 Point to Edit and select Get Picture.

❑ To split the text into multiple boxes

6 Highlight the text box.

7 Point to Item, select Split and choose the Outside Paths sub-menu.

Tip

For Text to Box to be most effective, use rounded fonts at large point sizes and remember that it only works for single lines of text.

Text to box

An excellent Bézier effect is Text to Box, which changes text inside a box into an editable Bézier object. You can place pictures inside it, and even make every letter an individual box.

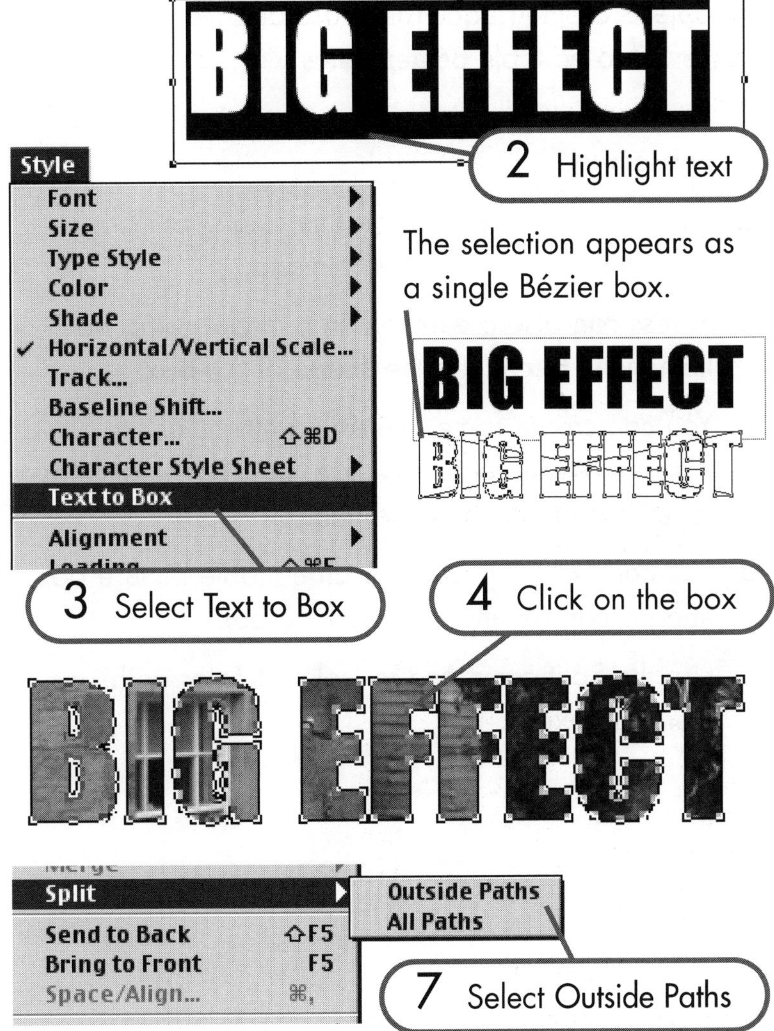

Outside Paths splits only outside paths, while **All Paths** splits every path, so to split a word into individual letters, use Outside Paths. You can now individually manipulate each letter of the word.

Summary

- ❑ Bézier items allow you complete freedom to design your own page elements. You're not restricted to rectangular or oval boxes – you can design your own!
- ❑ Use XPress's Freehand tools to draw your own objects on the page. These are automatically converted to editable Bézier paths.
- ❑ You can split paths or cut box boundaries using the Scissors tool.
- ❑ You can create versatile text items on your page using the Text on a Path command.
- ❑ XPress can also create text in a circle, using the Item menu to change the shape of the box.
- ❑ You can create some interesting effects using XPress's Merge feature, which joins boxes or lines together to make a single item.
- ❑ You can turn your text into an editable picture box. Images can be imported into the box.
- ❑ Use the Split command to isolate Bézier paths in merged boxes.

10 Long documents

Page numbering

Basic steps

1 Open a master page by double-clicking on its icon in the Documents Layout palette.

2 Click inside a text box.

3 Type [Command] or [Ctrl] and [3].

To number pages in your document, you can take the laborious route and manually add numbers to the bottom of each page. But if you move, add or delete pages you will have to painstakingly change each number again. Fortunately, XPress supplies a built-in shortcut that allows you to number pages automatically.

The shortcut uses a special keyboard command: **[Command]-[3]** (Mac) or **[Ctrl]-[3]** (Windows). Pressing these together inserts the current page number into the text. This shortcut becomes more useful used in conjunction with master pages (see page 44). When you type this shortcut on a master page, it will appear as <#>. On every standard page based on that master, this will be replaced by the current page number. This means that as pages are added or removed, their current page number is always correctly shown.

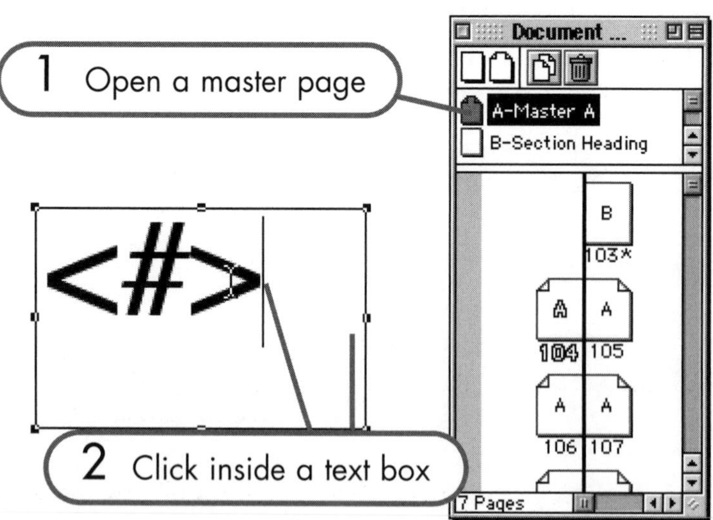

The page number shortcut can be formatted on the master page like any other text element.

Tip

[Command]-[2] (Mac) [Ctrl]-[2] (Windows) automatically enters the page of the previous linked text box, while [Command]-[4](Mac) [Ctrl]-[4] (Windows) enters the page number of the next linked box.

These commands help create Continued On or Continued From text boxes; they are automatically updated if the text boxes move.

Basic steps

Sections

1 Go to the page that you want to start the section from.
2 Point to Page and select Section…
3 Click on Section Start.
4 Enter a prefix.
5 Enter a starting page number.
6 Click OK.

When you number pages, you aren't restricted to Arabic numerals or starting every single document at page 1. By creating sections, you can specify the starting point and style of your page numbers.

Pages following the section start will follow the same numbering format until the document ends or a new section start is created. You can create more than one section in a document; pages that have been specified as the start of a section are indicated in the Document Layout palette by an asterisk.

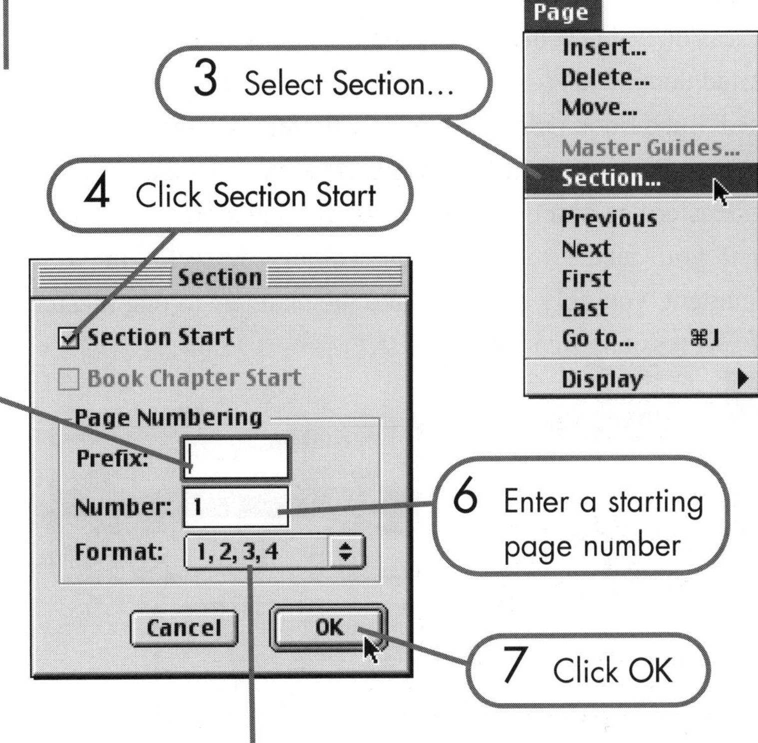

You can add a prefix of up to four letters before the page number.

A range of formats is available from the pull-down menu.

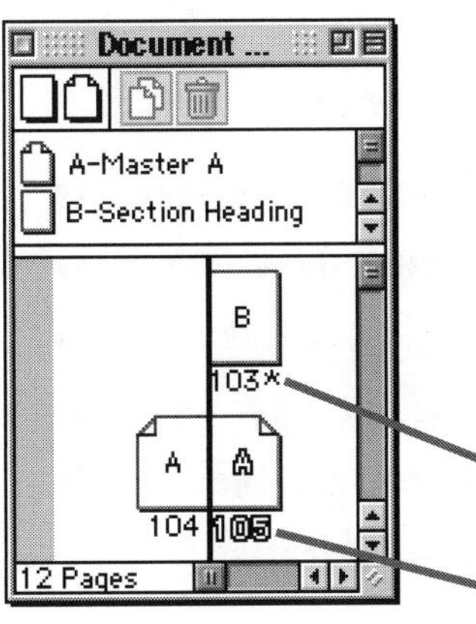

The section start is denoted by an asterisk.

Subsequent pages follow the same numbering procedure.

Books

The longer your XPress document, the more unwieldy it becomes. Changes become more laborious, the file occupies more memory, scrolling is slower and it is more liable to corruption. The obvious answer is to split your document into small files, but then it can be hard keeping colours and style sheets consistent across every document. Fortunately, XPress has a way of allowing you to split large files into smaller parts, while keeping all the text attributes we looked at in Chapter 5, such as page numbering, styles, H&Js, colours and dashes and stripes, looking the same.

XPress does this using the Book palette, which holds a list of related documents (called chapters) and keeps them synchronised. Each Book palette contains a master chapter, by default the first document added to it. Every XPress file added after the master can share its properties through synchronisation. So if you decide to change the colours or styles in your document, you only have to make the changes to one master file: XPress takes care of the rest.

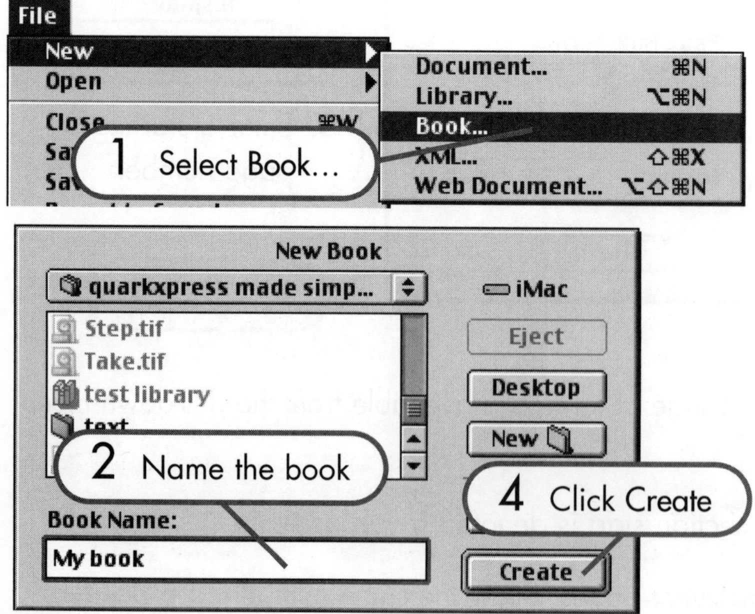

Basic steps

- To create a new book palette

1 Point to File, select New and click on Book... from the submenu.

2 Enter a name for the book.

3 Choose a location.

4 Click Create.

- To add a chapter

5 Click on the New Chapter icon.

6 Select an XPress document to add.

7 Click Add.

Take note

If a chapter is shown as missing, re-attach it by double-clicking on its name in the list and selecting the file's current location.

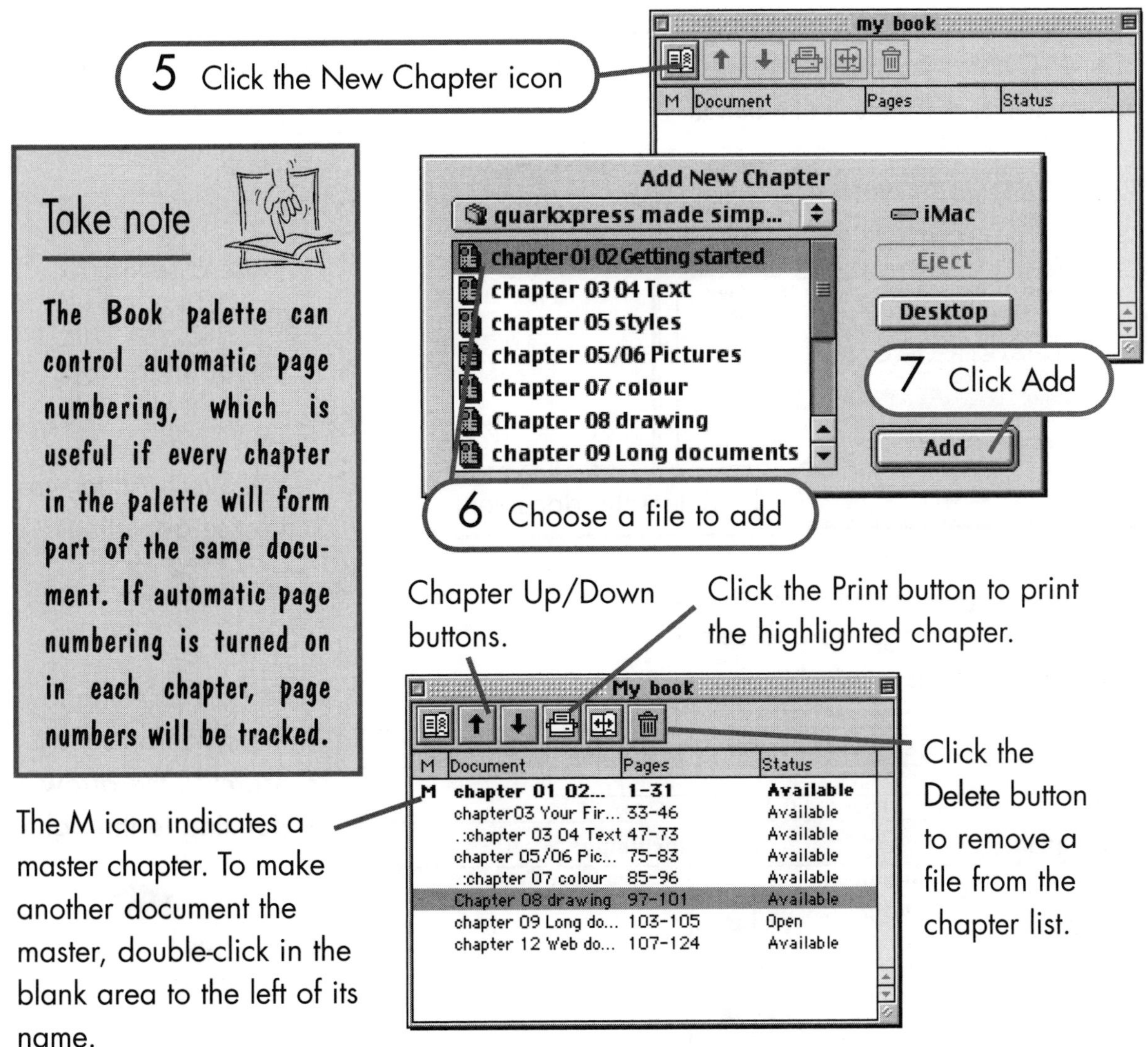

Take note

The Book palette can control automatic page numbering, which is useful if every chapter in the palette will form part of the same document. If automatic page numbering is turned on in each chapter, page numbers will be tracked.

You can move a selected chapter up and down the Chapter list by highlighting it and clicking the Chapter Up or Down buttons. Pagination will be adjusted automatically.

The **Status** column displays a chapter's status. Commonly it shows either Available, which means the document is available for you to edit; or Open, which means the document is open on your computer. The column can also display Modified if you changed the file while the Book palette was closed; Missing, if the file can't be found; or In Use,if you are sharing the chapter file over a network and someone else has the file open.

Synchronising and organising chapters

Synchronising chapters brings style sheets, colours, H&J, Lists and Dashes and Stripes settings in line with those of the master chapter at the touch of a button.

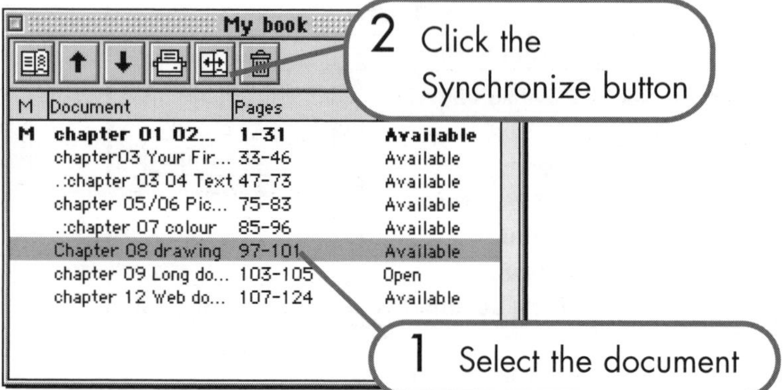

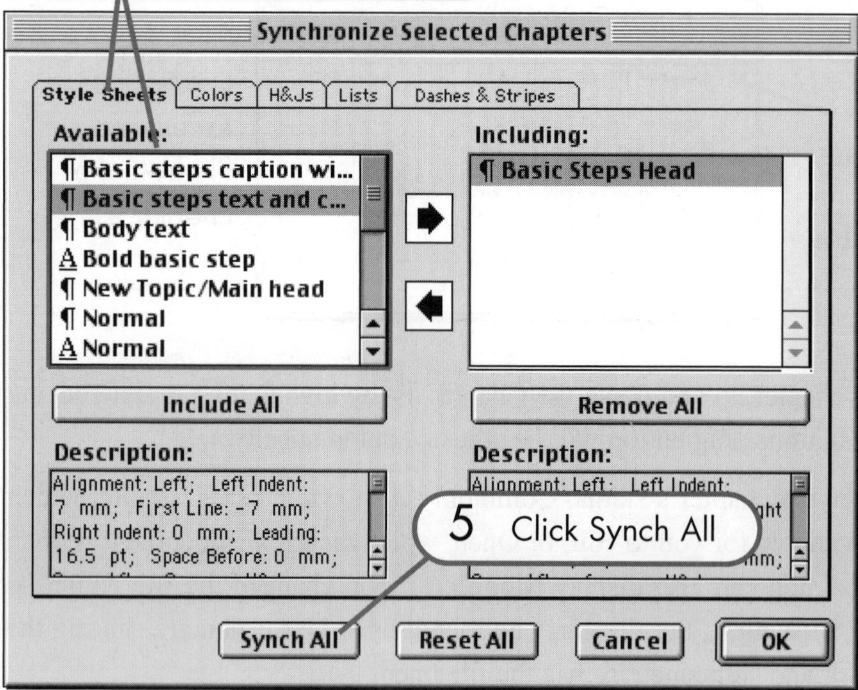

Basic steps

1 Click the document name in the list.

2 Click the Synchronize button.

3 Click on a tab and choose a setting to synchronise.

4 Click on an arrow.

Or

5 Click Synch All to synchronise all settings.

6 Click OK.

To add a setting to the synchronisation list, click the arrow pointing to the right.

To remove a setting, click the lower arrow.

Lists

Basic steps

1. Point to Edit and select Lists...
2. Click New.
3. Name the list.
4. Click on an available style.
5. Click the upper arrow.

continued...

Tip

As with most dialog boxes, you can edit lists by clicking the Edit button, or append from other documents by clicking Append...

Lists are a great way of creating a table of contents or even catalogue listings. They take headings, chapter titles or other text items that are based on a style sheet and assemble them into a list. This list can include page numbers and can be automatically styled.

You can choose from any style sheet created in the current document. Use the scroll arrows to locate the style to use and press [Shift] while clicking to select multiple styles.

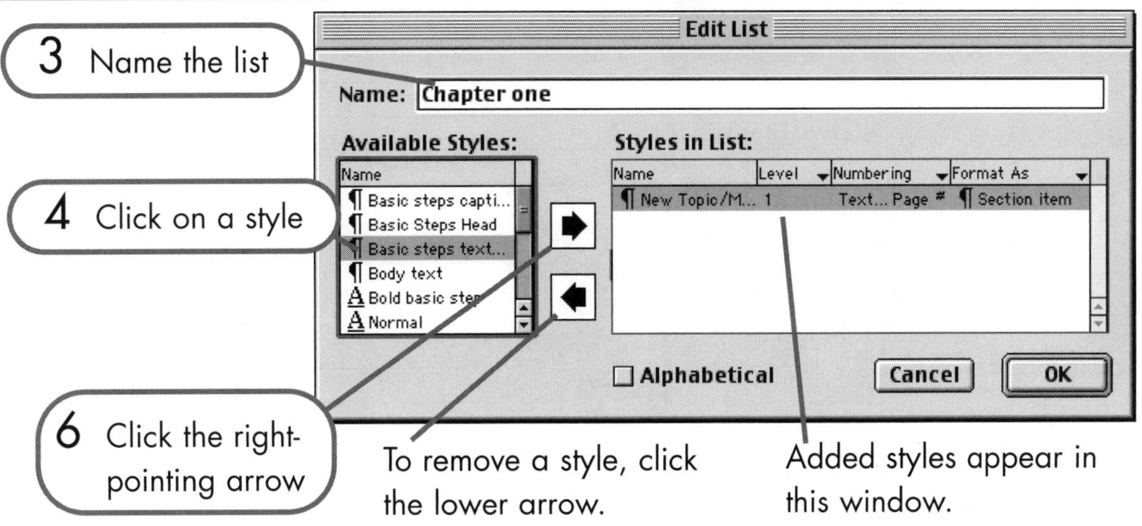

To remove a style, click the lower arrow.

Added styles appear in this window.

Basic steps

(continued)

6 Choose an indent level.

7 Choose a numbering style.

8 Choose the formatting option.

9 Click OK.

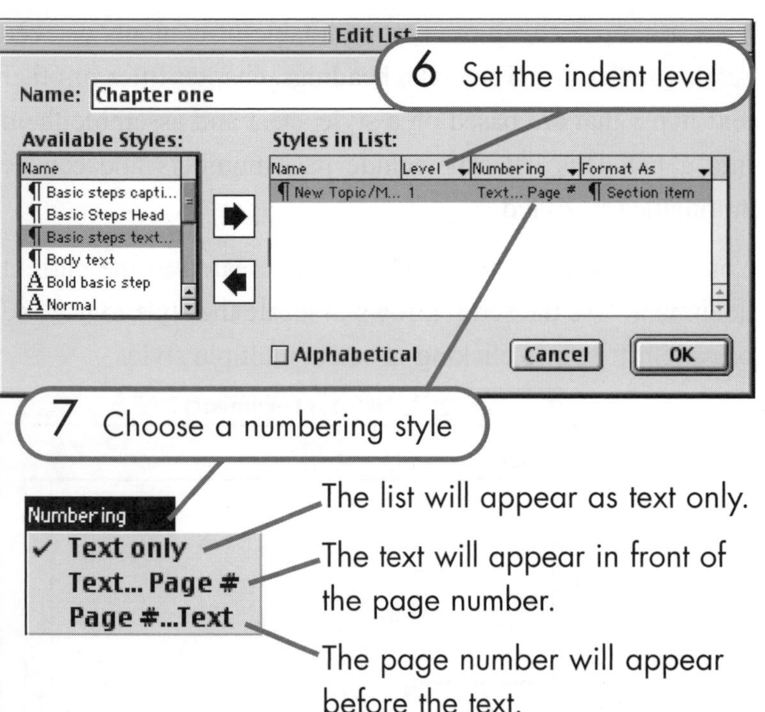

The **Format As** option lets you output the list in any existing style in your document.

Choose an indent level from 1 to 8. The higher the number, the more the text is indented when you build your list.

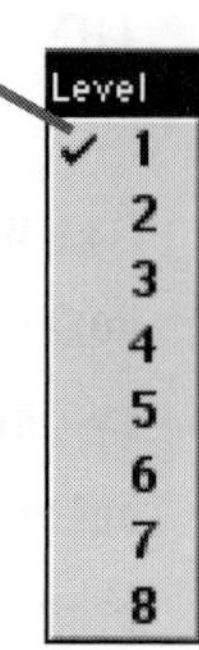

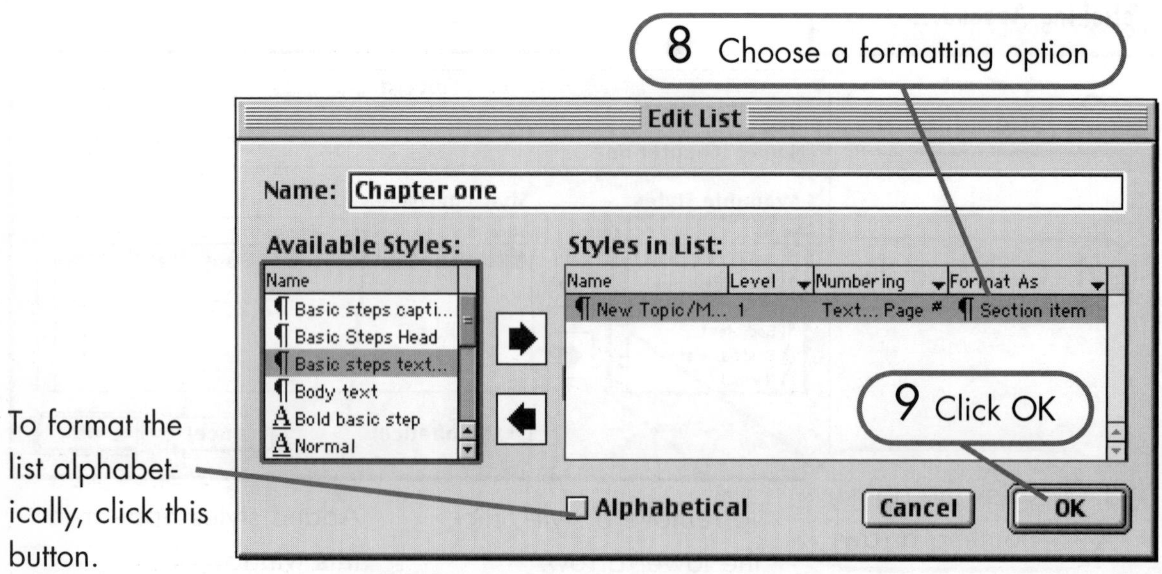

Basic steps

- ❑ To update the list

1 Point to View and select Show Lists.

2 Select the list to view.

3 Click the Update button.

- ❑ To build a list

4 Click on an empty text box.

5 Click the Build button.

Tip

The easiest way to navigate through a document isn't via the pop-up palette at the bottom of the screen. Instead select major document landmarks and create a list based on their style sheets. With the Lists palette open, click on any list item and you will be taken to that heading.

Updating and building lists

The contents of the list are held in a Lists palette. It doesn't automatically update as you add new entries; you'll need to do this manually.

The final step is to build the list, which simply puts the contents of the Lists palette into a selected text box. It will be formatted according to the style you specified earlier in the Lists dialog box.

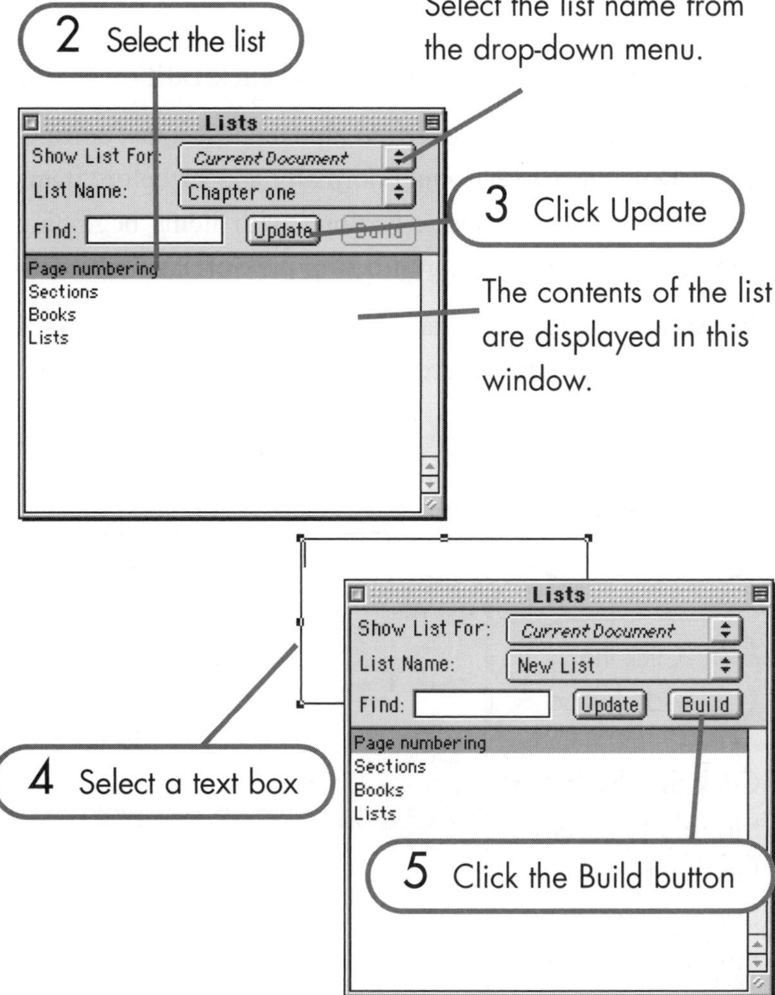

Indexes

Basic steps

Build a document index by adding words in a text box to an Index palette. Once a word has been added to the palette, it is surrounded in the text by non-printing marker brackets, which are visible while the palette is open. You can choose between four indent levels, which define how related entries are inset under one heading. By default, entries are First Level – to create Second, Third or Fourth Level entries underneath, select the level from the drop-down menu. Now click to the left of entry you want to nest the selection under so the arrow appears next to it. Click **Add** and the nested entry will appear under this heading. To edit or delete an entry, highlight it in the Entries list and click **Edit** or **Trash**.

Use the **Sort As** field to override alphabetical index sorting, eg '10 Downing Street' would normally appear before items beginning with A. To index it along with items beginning with T, enter 'Ten Downing Street' in the Sort As field.

The **Style** entry lets you attach a specific character style (see page 84–86) to index references such as page numbers and cross-references.

1 Point to View and select Show Index.

2 Select a word to index in the Text field by highlighting it in a text box.

3 Choose the style and scope of the references.

4 Click the Add button.

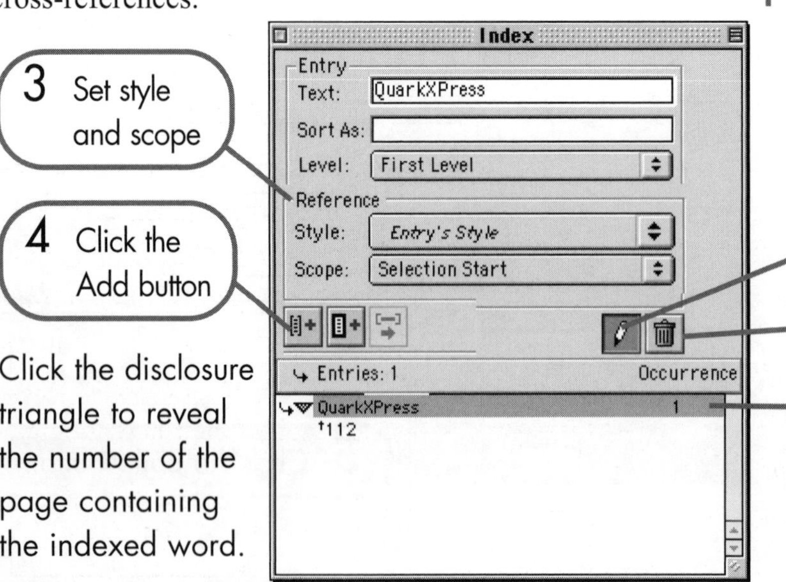

3 Set style and scope

4 Click the Add button

Click the disclosure triangle to reveal the number of the page containing the indexed word.

Edit button

Trash button

The Occurrence column shows the number of times of the word has been indexed.

Basic steps

1 Point to Utilities and select Build Index.
2 Choose index options.
3 Click OK.

The **Scope** pull-down menu allows you to specify the how many pages XPress will look through to find words matching the one you have indexed. There are several options: **Selection Start** records the number of the page that contains the open bracket of the indexed entry. **Selection Text** lists all the page numbers between the index marker's brackets, while **To Style** lists pages from the open bracket to the occurrence of a specified paragraph style sheet. **The Specified #of ¶s** shows numbers through a specified number of paragraphs. **To End Of** up to either the end of the current story or the end of the document.You can also select **Cross-Reference**, which refers to another index entry rather than, or in addition to, a page number.

Building an index

To create an index at the end of your document, first select the master page on which to base your index pages. This master page must have a default linked text box in which to flow the index (to see how to create such a linked box, see page 45).

Choose between nested format, where indented entries appear as indented new paragraphs, or run-in, where indented entries appear in the same paragraph as their parent entry.

Build Index

Format: (•) Nested ( ) Run-in
☐ Entire Book
☑ Replace Existing Index
☐ Add Letter Headings
Style: ¶ Normal
Master Page: A-Master A
Level Styles
First Level: ¶ Normal
Second Level: ¶ Normal
Third Level: ¶ Normal
Fourth Level: ¶ Normal
Cancel OK

To replace an existing index, check this box.

2 Choose Index options

Enter a style sheet on which to base each level of index entry. For more on style sheets, see page 84.

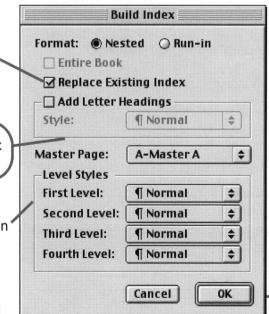

3 Click OK

Summary

- Instead of typing in the current page number, use the [Command-[3] (Mac) [Ctrl]-[3] (Windows) to enter the current page. The number will be updated even if the page moves.
- [Command]-[2] (Mac) [Ctrl]-[2] (Windows) and [Command]-[4] (Mac) [Ctrl]-[4] (Windows) show the page numbers of the previous and following text boxes. It can be useful when creating Continued On and Continued From pages.
- Sections allow you to change the starting point and format of page numbers.
- Books can act as an umbrella for a number of different documents. Use them to keep style sheets and colours consistent and to track page numbers throughout a document.
- Lists are useful for creating tables of contents, but they can also be used to keep a track of catalogue prices, or even to navigate through a document.
- Use the Index palette to create and edit indexes.

11 Printing

The Print dialog box

The Print dialog box, selected by pointing to **File** and choosing **Print...**, contains a raft of options. Some are self-explanatory: you enter the number of copies to print in the **Copies** field, and the number of the page or pages to print in the **Pages** field. A range of pages is selected by typing the first and last page numbers, separated by a hyphen. To print non-continuous pages, separate each with a comma. The **Separations** checkbox lets you choose between printing separations for each colour in your document, while checking the **Print Blank Pages** box, prints pages even if they have no content on them. **Back to Front** reverses the print output so the last page prints first – handy for multi-page documents.

There are other important tabs in the dialog box. **Output** lets you set print colour options and resolution for your document. Under **Preview**, you'll see a thumbnail of your document as it would print with the selected printing options.

Take note

You may often be asked to supply printouts with registration marks if you are sending files to the printer. If so, make sure either Centred or Off Centre is selected in the Registration pull-down menu.

For more about Print Styles, see page 136.

Choose to print only odd or even pages by selecting the Odd or Even options from the drop-down Page Sequence menu.

Go to the Page Setup dialog box.

Displays or edits printer settings.

Closes the Print dialog box, but stores the settings you have created.

Tiling

If your printer can only print A4 pages, how do you create a poster-sized document? XPress supplies the answer in the form of tiling, which allows you to print large documents in sections so you can reassemble them later.

If **Automatic** tiling is selected XPress chooses the number of tiles that will make up your page based on the document size.

Manual tiling lets you specify where tiles will be created. The tiles are created using the Document Origin icon at the top left of the document window.

To manually tile, drag the Ruler Origin icon across the page to set the borders of the tile.

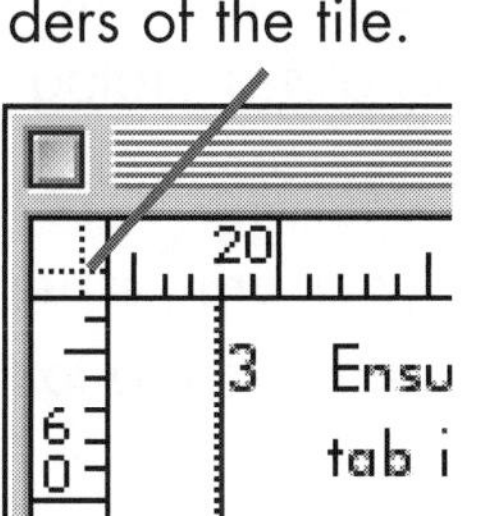

If you choose Automatic Tiling, enter the amount by which each tile will overlap.

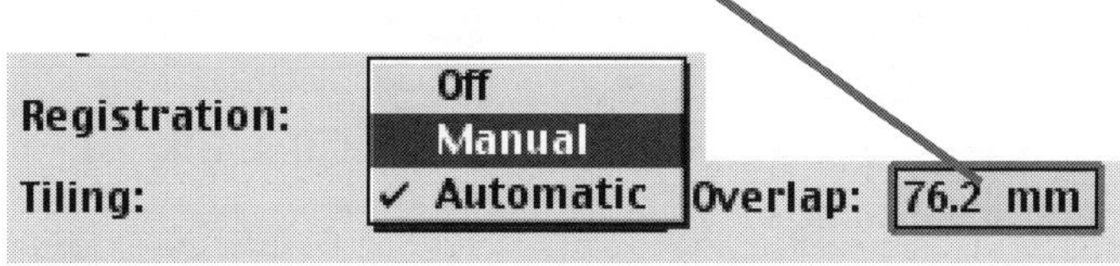

Print Setup

Vital print options are available under the Setup tab, including page size, orientation – either landscape or portrait – and an option to reduce or enlarge the printed document.

Select a paper size. If supported by the printer, you can also enter a specific width and height for your page.

Select your printer from the list. If it doesn't appear, choose the generic printer option.

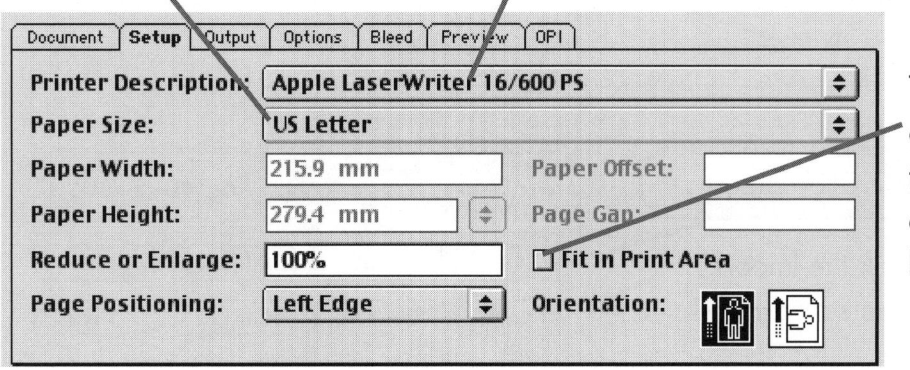

To force the printout to stay within the available print area, check this box.

Print styles

Basic steps

A print style is a collection of print settings that are created, saved and applied via the drop-down menu in the Print dialog box. Print styles are a time-saver, as they allow you to store different settings for each printer that you print to. As styles can be imported and exported, you can make sure your printing setup is consistent wherever you are.

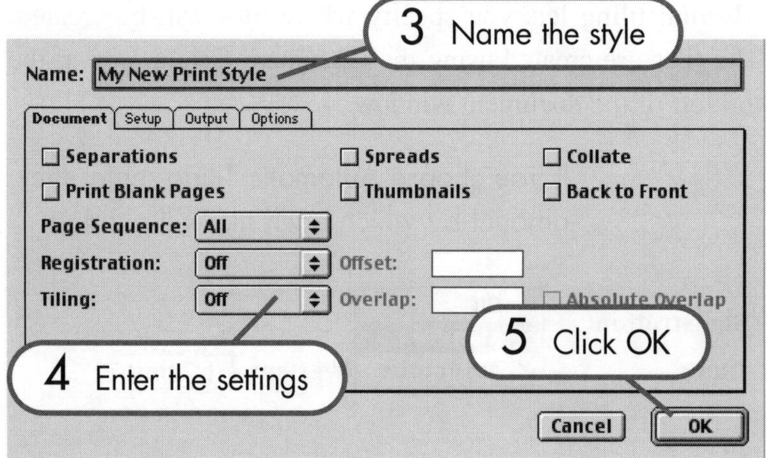

These are the same settings options available in the main Print dialog box.

1 Point to Edit and select Print Styles...
2 Click New.
3 Name the style.
4 Select the style settings...
5 Click OK.
6 Click Save.

- To export a print style

7 Select Export... from the Print Styles dialog box.
8 Name your print style and choose where to save it.
9 Click Save.

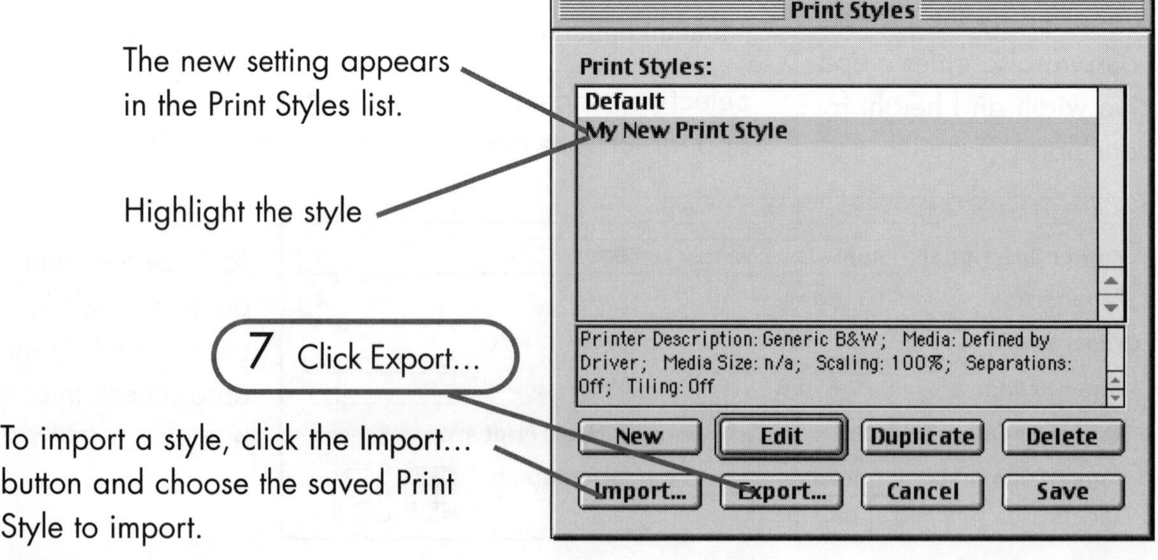

To import a style, click the Import... button and choose the saved Print Style to import.

Basic steps

1 Point to File and select Collect for Output…
2 If prompted to save the file, click Save.
3 Choose the items to collect. If in doubt, check all the boxes.
4 Click Save.

Collect for Output

Whether you're sending your XPress document to a repro house or transferring it to a computer in the next room, you need to make sure that all the images and fonts used in the document are included alongside it, otherwise the recipient might encounter missing file or picture messages. The **Collect for Output** command does this housework for you.

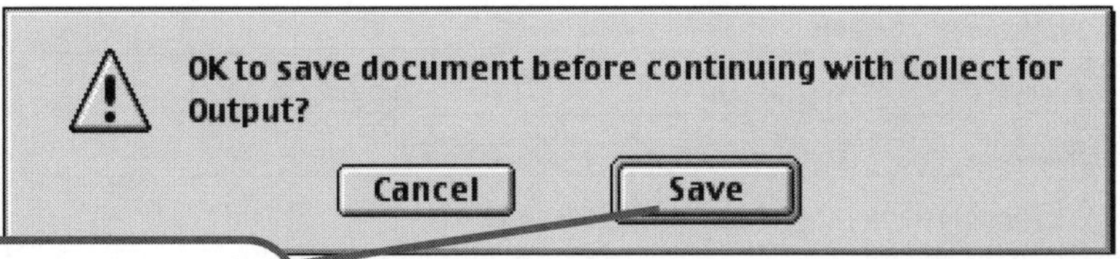

OK to save document before continuing with Collect for Output?

Cancel Save

2 If prompted, click Save

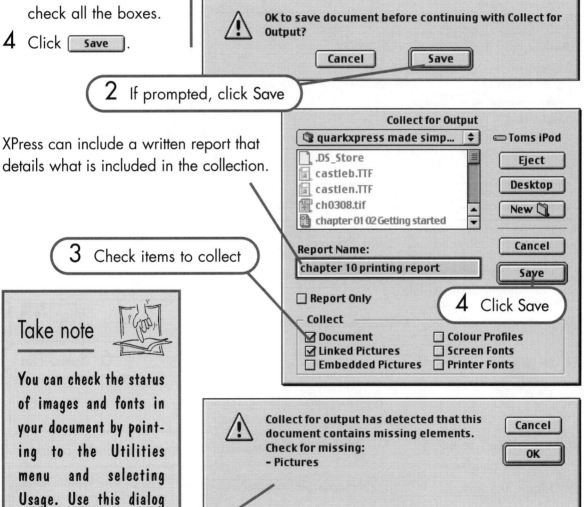

XPress can include a written report that details what is included in the collection.

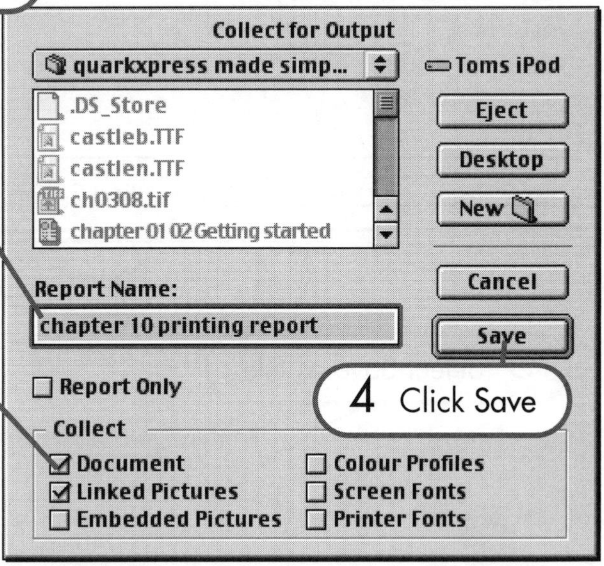

Collect for Output

quarkxpress made simp… Toms iPod

.DS_Store
castleb.TTF
castlen.TTF
ch0308.tif
chapter 01 02 Getting started

Eject
Desktop
New
Cancel
Save

Report Name:
chapter 10 printing report

Report Only

Collect
Document
Linked Pictures
Embedded Pictures
Colour Profiles
Screen Fonts
Printer Fonts

3 Check items to collect

4 Click Save

Take note

You can check the status of images and fonts in your document by pointing to the Utilities menu and selecting Usage. Use this dialog box to inspect missing images or fonts.

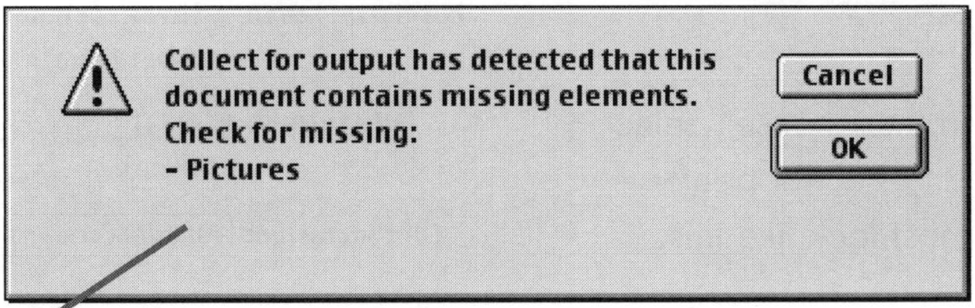

Collect for output has detected that this document contains missing elements. Check for missing:
- Pictures

Cancel
OK

If Collect for Output can't find an item to include with XPress, it will display a warning box.

Creating PostScript files

Basic steps

Printing your document as a PostScript file doesn't actually print it out. Instead it is written to a single file which contains the document, images, fonts and printer settings. The procedure for creating such a file varies according to the platform you're using.

- ❑ Using a Mac

1 Point to Apple menu and select Chooser.

2 Select a PostScript printer, such as a LaserWriter.

- ❑ In XPress

3 Point to File and select Print…

4 Click Printer…

5 Select Save as File.

6 Select File as the destination.

7 Enter the PostScript options.

8 Click [Save].

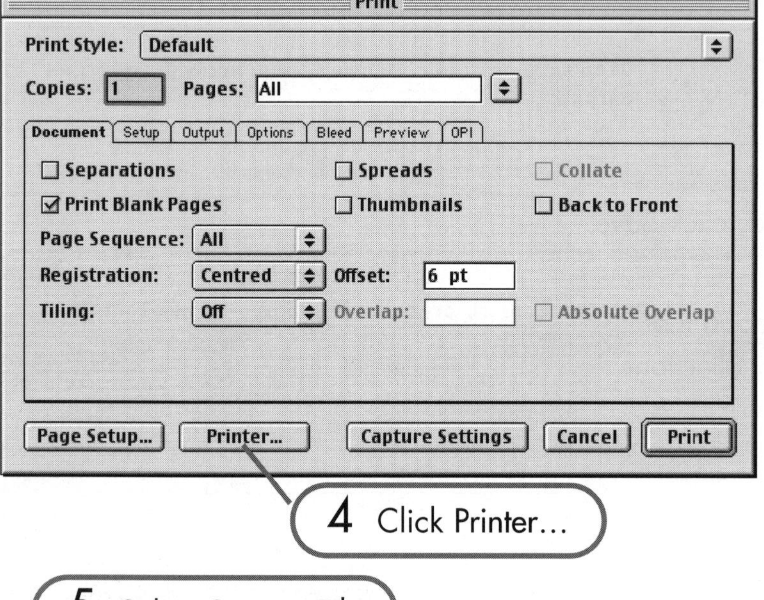

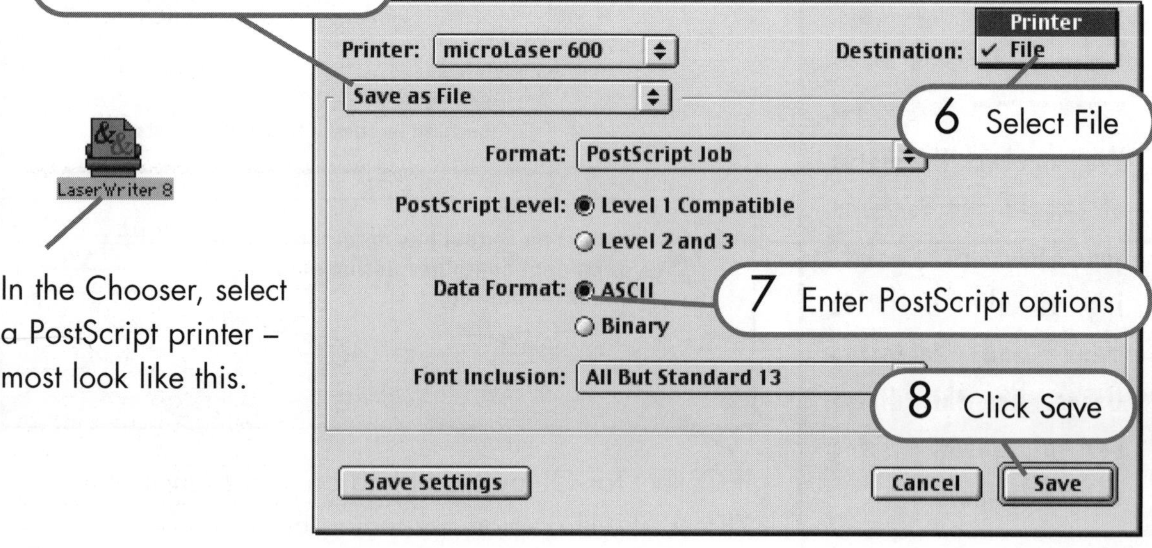

In the Chooser, select a PostScript printer – most look like this.

Basic steps

- Using Windows

1 Open the Printer folder on your hard disk.

2 Click Add Printer and step through the Add Printer Wizard.

3 Select Local printer.

4 Choose File as an output port.

Take note

What PostScript settings should you apply? PostScript Level 1 ensures compatibility with most PostScript printers; Levels 2 and 3 are faster. Check what your printer supports. Unless told otherwise, leave the Data Format field as it is. The font field should be set to Include All, unless you know the destination printer already has those fonts.

QuarkXPress under Windows uses a different method. Here you create a specific printer to 'print' your documents as a PostScript file. Windows' Add Printer Wizard steps you through the creation of the printer. The important selections are to choose a local printer and when it comes to choosing a port for the printer, select **File**.

As with any other printer you create, this PostScript file printer now appears inside the Printers folder. When you print a document and select this printer, the document will print as a PostScript file.

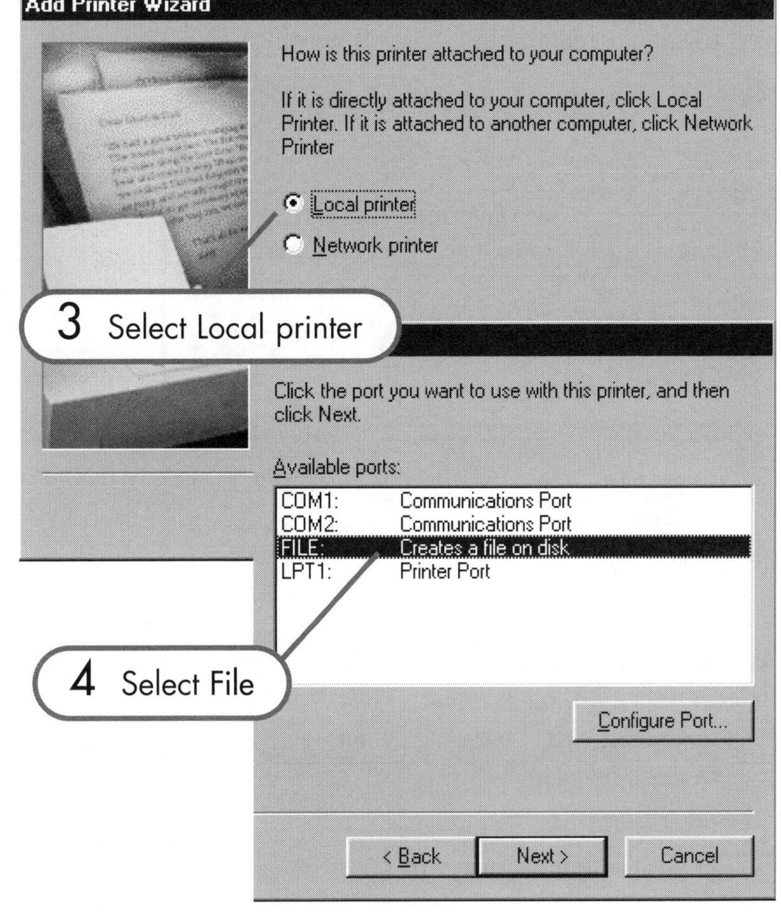

Save as EPS

Saving a page as EPS (Encapsulated PostScript) shouldn't be confused with saving a document as a PostScript file. Unlike PostScript files, pages saved as EPS files can be imported into other DTP and illustration files as images and can even be edited in some illustration programs. There are some restrictions: you can only save one page at a time as an EPS, although if you click the Spreads box, XPress will save two pages next to each other.

The Save Page As EPS dialog box contains three tabs. Aside from the main tab, The Bleed tab allows you to set the bleed amount of your pages – if your document has images or text overlapping the edge of the page and your printer requires you to set a bleed amount, enter it here.

Basic steps

1 Point to File and select Save Page As EPS....
2 Name the page
3 Choose where to save it.
4 Enter the page number.
5 Click 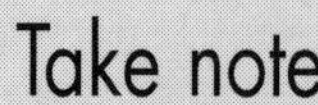.

Take note

The OPI settings are used by high-end printers so in most cases, you should leave these are they are.

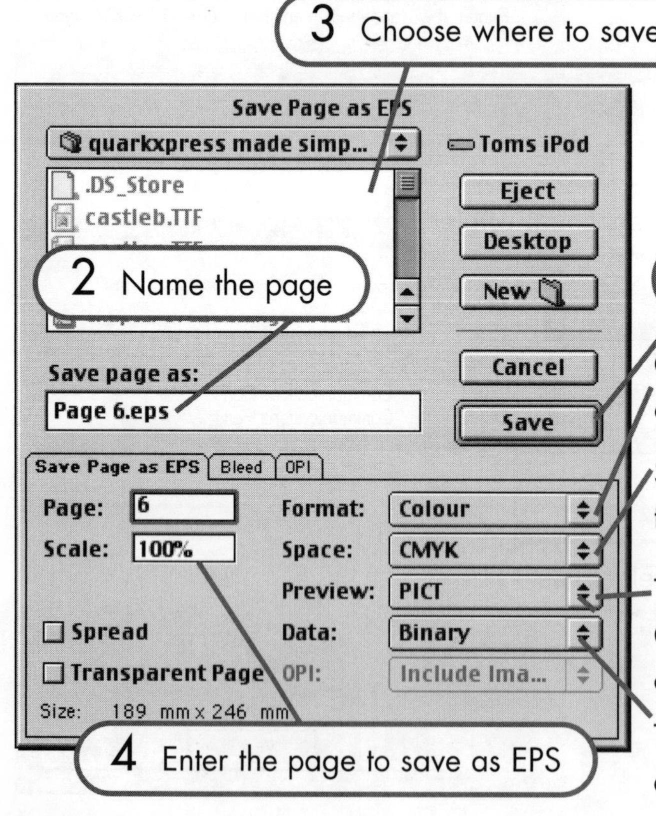

5 Click Save

Choose colour to create a colour EPS, or B&W to save in black and white.

Select CMYK if the document is going to be professionally printed in colour.

The format of the thumbnail preview. Choose TIFF for best cross-platform compatibility.

This determines how TIFF images are encapsulated. Binary is usually best.

Basic steps

Exporting to PDF

1 Point to File and select Export Document as PDF.

2 Type a file name and choose the pages to export.

❑ To adjust options

3 Click Options.

4 Enter settings for the PDF export.

5 Click OK to return to the main dialog box.

6 Click Save.

PDF (Portable Document Format) is a popular cross-platform format, suitable for Web or print. Although XPress can export to PDF, it does so indirectly – you'll need an extra tool, such as Adobe's Acrobat Distiller, to help create the PDFs.

Export as PDF
quarkxpress made simp...
Toms iPod
Eject
.DS_Store
castleb.TTF
castlen.TTF
ch0308.tif
chapter 01 02 Getting started
Save current document as:
chapter 10 printing.pdf
Cancel
Save
Pages: All
Spreads
Options...

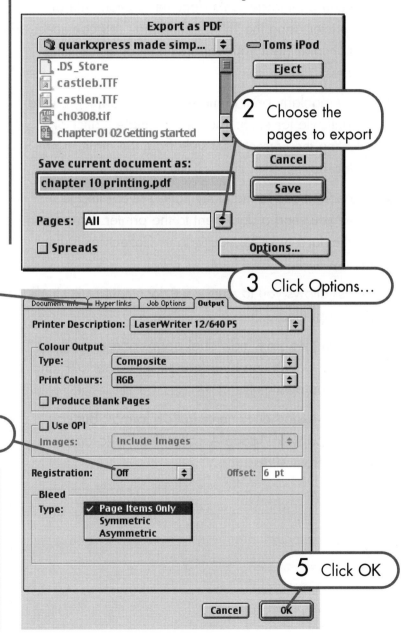

2 Choose the pages to export

3 Click Options...

Use the options in the Hyperlinks tab to include hyperlinks in your PDF.

Document Info | Hyperlinks | Job Options | Output
Printer Description: LaserWriter 12/640 PS
Colour Output
Type: Composite
Print Colours: RGB
Produce Blank Pages
Use OPI
Images: Include Images
Registration: Off
Offset: 6 pt
Bleed
Type: ✓ Page Items Only
Symmetric
Asymmetric
Cancel
OK

4 Enter export settings

5 Click OK

Take note

You can adjust default PDF settings in the Preferences dialog box.

Summary

- To print a document, select Print from the File menu.
- Store a printer's settings by clicking the Capture Settings button.
- You can print large scale documents even with an A4 printer using the Tiling command. You can specify manual tiling if you want full control of the tiling process.
- If you regularly print to more than one printer, create a print style for each. Then it's a simple matter of selecting the correct print style from the main print dialog box.
- You don't need to manually collect every image when you send a document to the printer. XPress can do the hard work for you with its Collect for Output feature.
- XPress allows you to save your document as a single PostScript file.
- You can also save individual pages and spreads as EPS files, which can be imported into other DTP and illustration documents.
- You can export documents in PDF format, but you need a copy of Adobe Acrobat Distiller to do so directly from XPress.

12 XPress on the Web

Web documents

Creating a Web document is similar to creating a print document. You can use virtually all the same tools. The only significant difference is the appearace of a Web tools palette, which allows you to create image maps and interactive forms for your Web site.

The Web palette

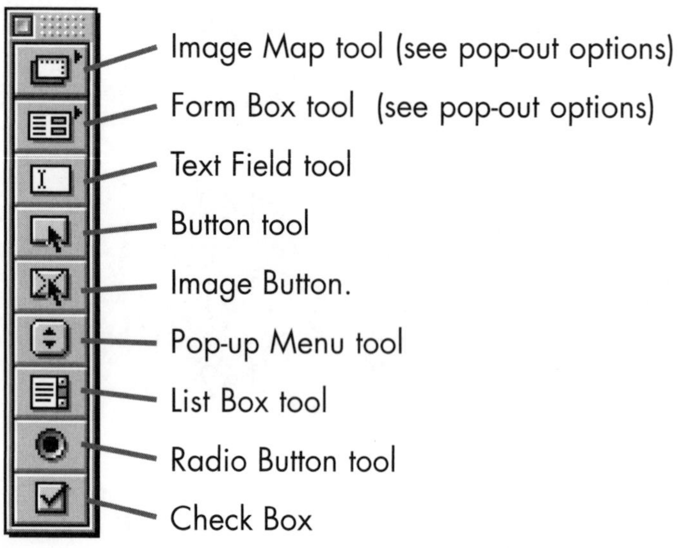

The Image Map and Form box tools feature pop-out options.

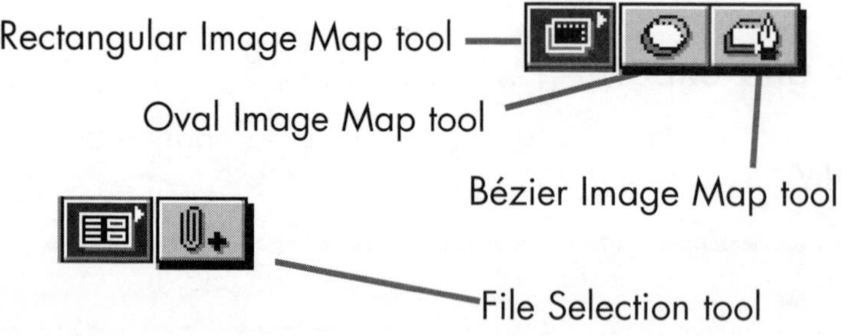

Take note

While Web and print documents share many features and are created in similar ways, there is no easy way to generate a Web page from a print document. You can move items between Web and print documents,though. Using the Item tool, you can drag items between open Web and print documents. Text boxes transferred to Web documents are automatically converted to images, and linked text boxes on facing pages appear as separate text boxes on the same Web page. Note that form boxes, rollover images and image maps won't transfer to from Web to print documents.

Basic steps

1 Point to File and select New and Web Document…

2 Choose the colour of the text, background and links.

3 Set the width of your page.

4 Click [OK].

Creating a document

XPress Web and print documents don't mix easily. To create a Web page, you must open a Web document, rather than use a standard XPress document – you can't convert one type into another. The setup dialog box for creating Web pages is similar to that used for print documents.

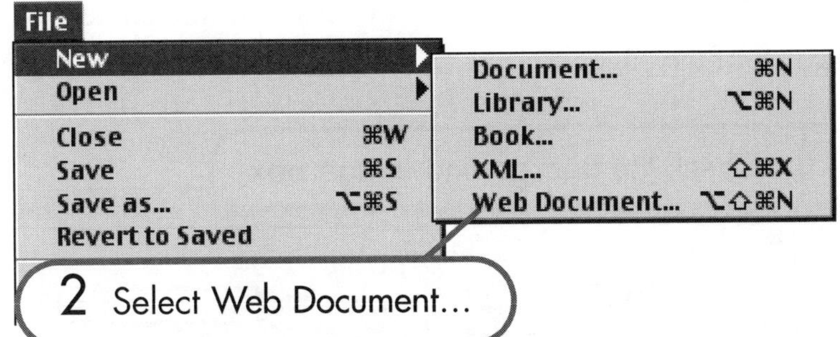

Check the **Variable Width Page** box to make the document width resizable in a browser. This means elements in your page will automatically adjust their positions when the page is narrowed in a browser, but you can limit its effect on page layout by entering a minimum pixel width for the page.

3 Choose basic settings

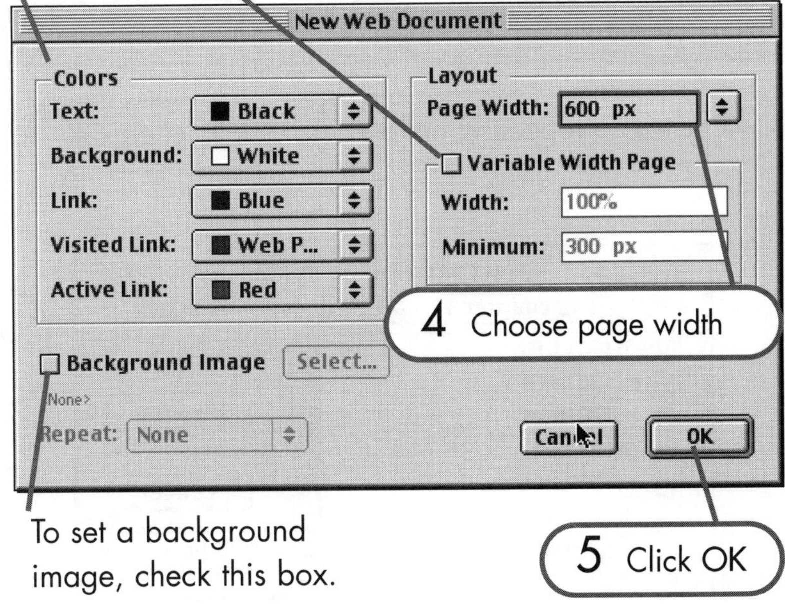

To set a background image, check this box.

Tip

600 pixels is a safe choice for page width, as it fits the most common monitor resolution (800 x 600) used by Web surfers. By keeping it this size, you ensure that anyone viewing your page can see all its content without having to scroll.

Setting a background image

A background image, if carefully used, can add impact to your page.

Background images can be repeated behind foreground text and pictures, either in horizontal or vertical rows, or tiled to repeat in both directions. Use a subtle background image when repeating, so that it doesn't overwhelm the content of the rest of the page.

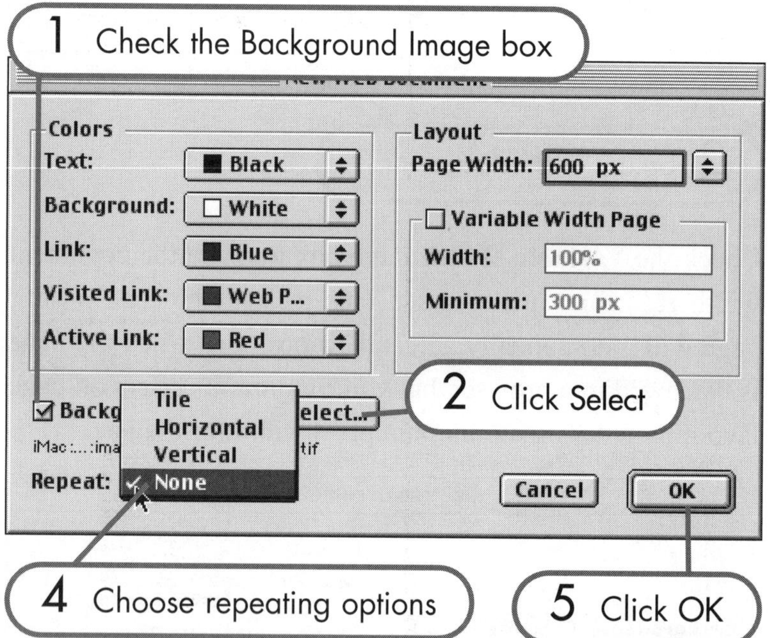

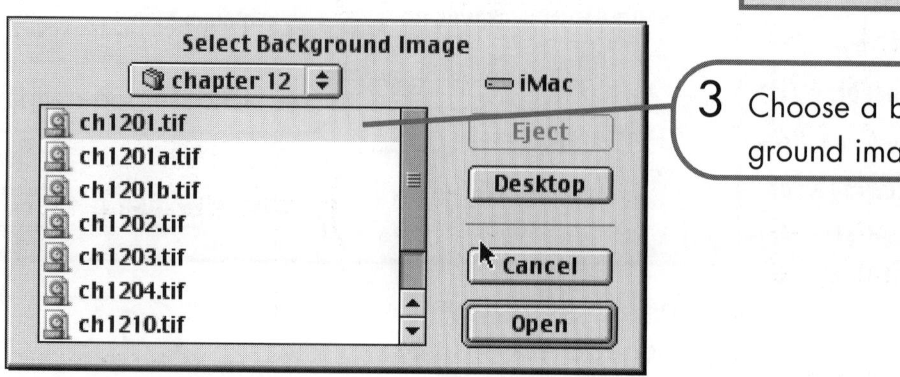

Basic steps

1. Click on the Background Image box.
2. Click Select (Mac), or Browse (Windows).
3. Choose a background image.
4. Choose if you want the background image to repeat.
5. Click OK.

Take note

Repeating options let you choose how you want a background image to display. Set it to none, and only a single image will show.

Hyperlinks

Basic steps

1 Point to View and select Show Hyperlinks

2 Select the Content tool.

3 Select the text you want to link from.

Or

4 Click on the picture box to link from.

5 Click the New Hyperlink button.

6 In the New Hyperlink dialog box, enter the destination address.

7 Click OK.

Take note

You can type other destination types, such as FTP, in the URL window. Use the drop-down arrow menu to the right of the URL field to quickly select a URL type.

Text and picture boxes are created in the same way in Web documents as they are in print documents. But the Web is interactive, making use of features such as hyperlinks, which provide a link between the Web document and other files, sites on the Internet or email addresses. Hyperlinks aren't exclusively used in Web documents: PDFs (see page 141) also support hyperlinks.

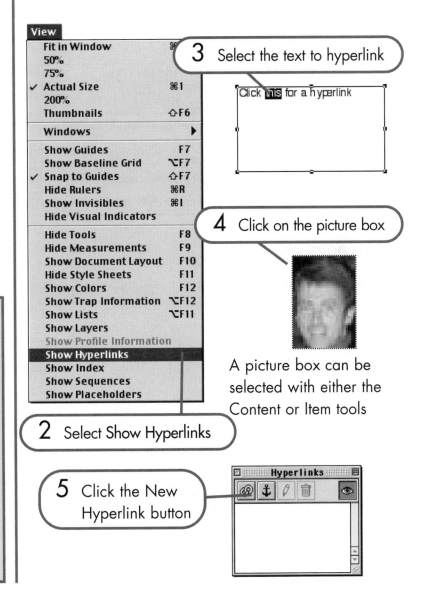

3 Select the text to hyperlink

4 Click on the picture box

A picture box can be selected with either the Content or Item tools

2 Select Show Hyperlinks

5 Click the New Hyperlink button

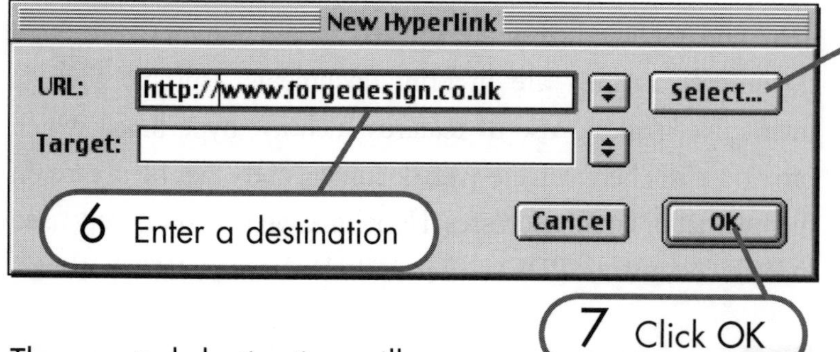

The Select... button, opens up a dialog box to let you link to selected local files – such as those on your hard disk.

The created destination will now be listed in the Hyperlinks palette.

Click the disclosure icons ▶ (Mac) or ⊞ (Windows) to reveal the hyperlinks in the current document.

Take note

Hyperlinks are only clickable when you export the Web document.

Choosing a target

The Target field lets you specify how a link should be opened. If you leave the Target field blank, the link will open in the same browser window. There are three other options:

- _blank: This will open the target page in a new window without closing the original window. This is a good idea if you are linking to anothersite, but want visitors to keep | your site's window open.
- _self: The target page will be opened in the same window.
- _parent: In Web pages with frames, this type of target ensures that the link opens in the parent window of the page containing the link.
- _top: The link will remove all frames in the target document.

Take note

An XPress-created Web document is not an HTML file from the outset, which means you can't open a Web document in a text editor and add extra code to it. XPress only generates the necessary HTML when you press the Publish button.

Anchor links

Basic steps

1 Select the Content tool and click inside a text box at the point at which you wish to create the anchor.

Or

2 Click on a picture box.

3 Click the Anchor button.

4 Name the anchor.

5 Click [OK].

Standard hyperlinks link to entire pages; anchors link to particular points on a page. To create a link to an anchor, you must first create the anchor itself.

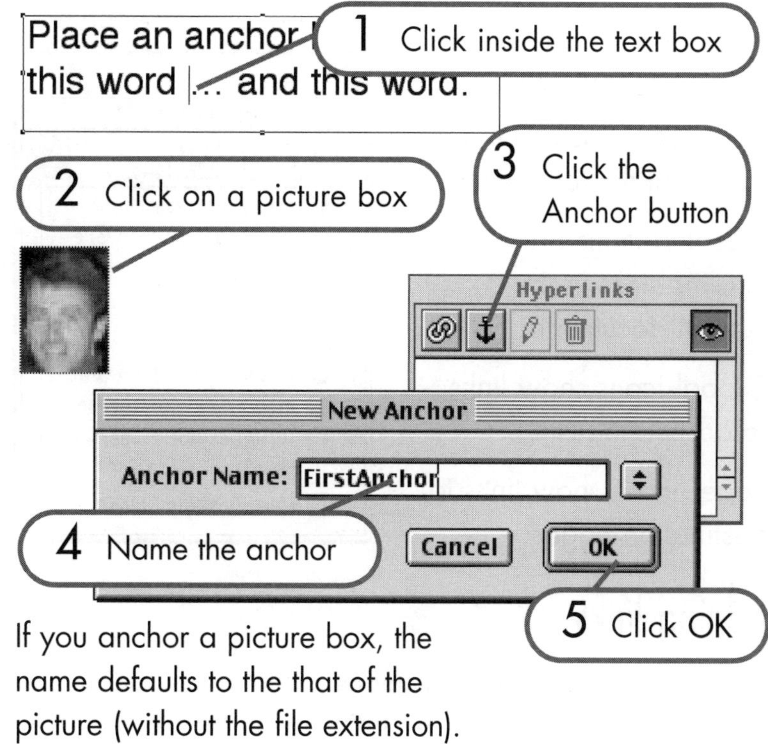

If you anchor a picture box, the name defaults to the that of the picture (without the file extension).

Take note

Anchor names can only comprise a single word.

Tip

More anchor names can be added without closing the New Anchor dialog box by holding [Shift] when you click [OK].

An anchor icon appears in the picture or at the point in the text where you created the anchor.

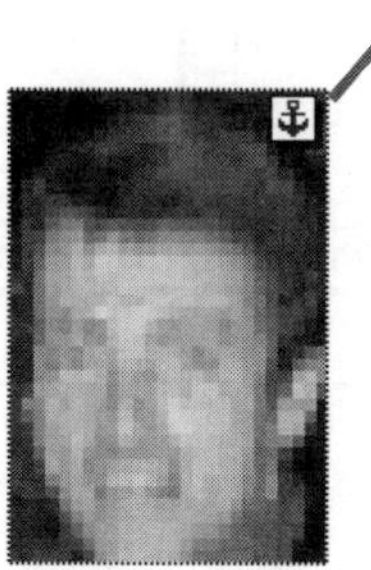

Once the anchor has been created, its name will appear in the Hyperlinks palette.

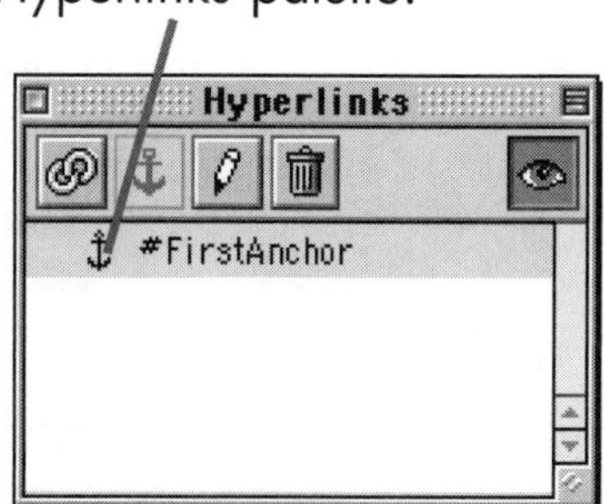

Linking to existing hyperlinks and anchors

Once you have created a hyperlink or anchor, you can add further links to it by selecting it in the Hyperlinks palette.

3 Click on the hyperlink

Destinations linked from the current document are shown at the top level.

Indented items are existing links in the current document.

Global icons show links to destination URLs.

Page icons show links to destination pages.

Hyperlinks

http://accessaccounts.c...
accounting software
years
companies
Finance
http://www.apple.com
http://www.pictureson...
iMac:Desktop Folder:Ac...
when
iMac:Desktop Folder:tes...

Editing links

The Web is a constantly changing environment and hyperlinks and anchors would be little use if they couldn't be changed. They can be edited from the Hyperlinks palette.

Basic steps

- ❑ Linking to existing hyperlinks and anchors

1 Select the Content tool and select text from inside a text box.

Or

2 Click on a picture box.

3 Click on the hyperlink that you want to apply to it.

- ❑ Editing links

4 Click the link to edit.

5 Click the Edit button.

6 Edit the URL or anchor.

7 Click OK.

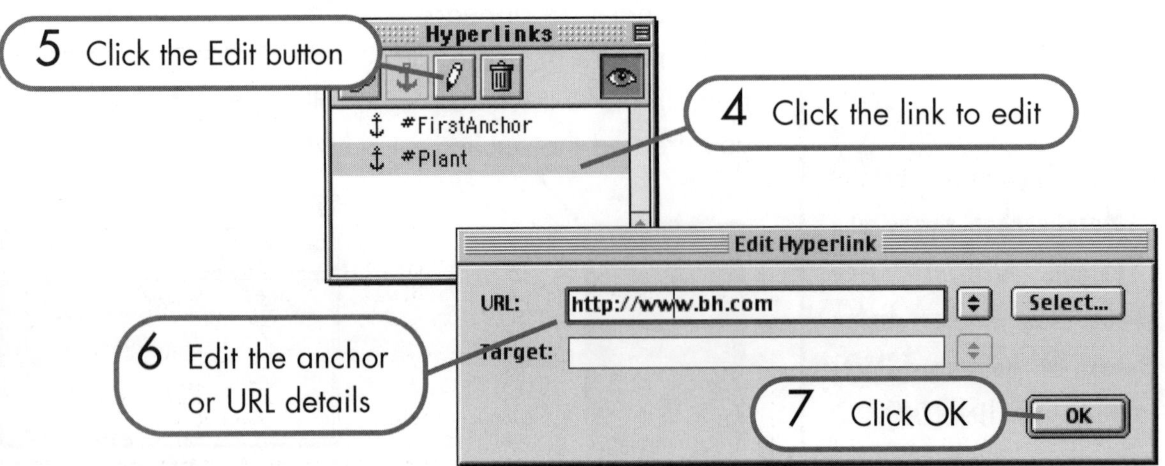

Deleting links

Basic steps

1 Highlight the link to delete.

2 Click the Delete button.

3 Click OK if you are presented with a warning message.

Tip

You can use the Hyperlinks palette as a navigation tool. Double-click on a link in the palette to navigate to that point in the current document.

Tip

The Show/Hide button in the Hyperlinks palette lets you view and hide hyperlinks and anchors in the active document.

It's equally easy to delete a hyperlink or anchor from your Web document: just select the link to delete in the Hyperlinks palette and click the Delete button

Relative and absolute links

When using the Hyperlinks palette it helps to understand the difference between absolute and relative links. An absolute link – an example is http://www.quark.com – links to a specific address on the Internet. A relative link, however, points to a document in the same Web site, and is most commonly used to link Web documents in the same directory.

When entering relative links, you don't need to add the full URL, just the path to the link relative to the current document. Be careful, though: while absolute links always point to the same address, relative links may need to be adjusted if you move pages into different directories on your Web site.

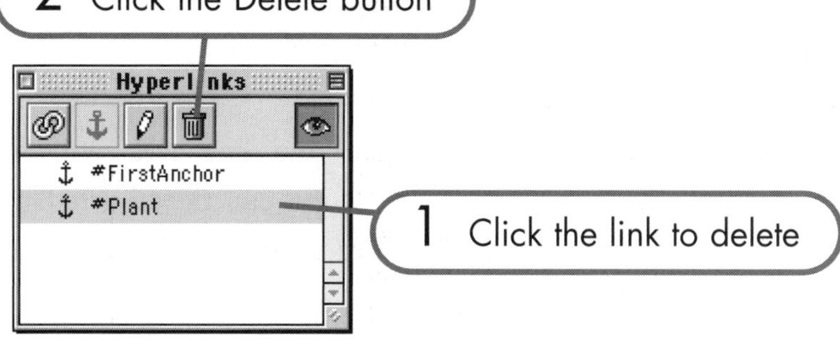

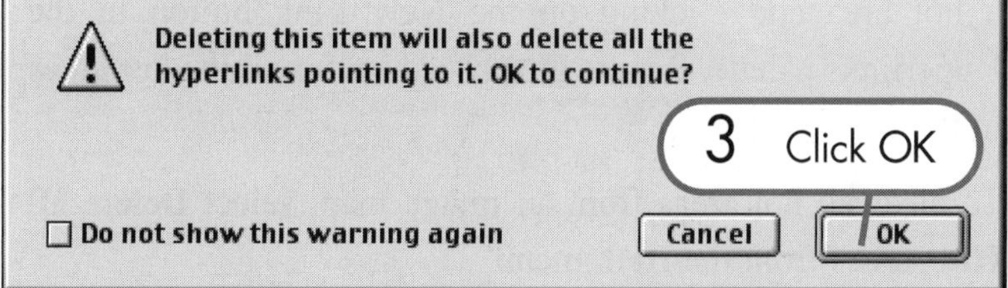

Deleting this item will also delete all the hyperlinks pointing to it. OK to continue?
3 Click OK
Do not show this warning again
Cancel
OK

Image maps

Image maps allow you to create 'hot' areas inside an image that each provide links to different destinations. Creating an image map in XPress is simple.

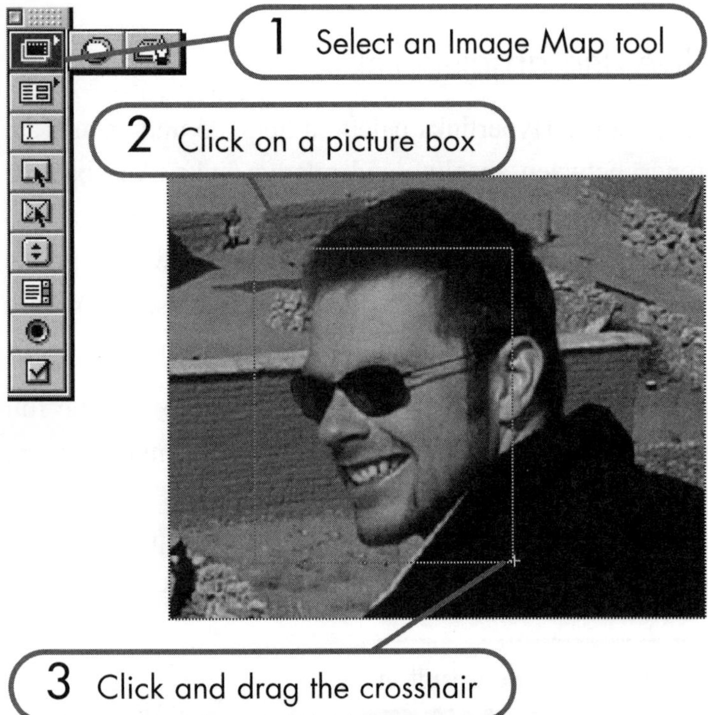

When you let go of the mouse, the hot area will be highlighted by a red border. Its scope can be adjusted by clicking on its handles and dragging to resize.

Once you have created individual hot areas to make up an image map, you can create hyperlinks from each by selecting a hot area and clicking on the New Link button in the Hyperlinks palette. Repeat the procedure for all the hot areas in the image map.

To clear all hot areas from an image map, select **Delete all Hot Areas** from the **Item** menu

Basic steps

1. Select an Image Map tool.
2. Select a picture box or import a picture into a new picture box.
3. Drag the crosshair over the part of the image that you want to define as a hot area.
4. Repeat for other hot areas.

Tip

Hot areas can be viewed by clicking on the View menu and selecting Show Guides. To hide hot areas, choose Hide Guides from the same menu.

Basic steps

1. Select a picture box.
2. Point to the Item menu and choose Create Rollover…
3. Enter a file path to the default image or click the Select or Browse buttons.
4. Enter a file path to the rollover image or click the Select or Browse buttons.
5. Enter the details of the location that the browser will go to when the button is clicked.
6. Click OK.

Rollovers

Rollovers, where picture boxes change their contents as the mouse moves – or rolls – over them, are common Web navigation elements. QuarkXPress lets you create basic rollovers in a simple dialog box, comprising three basic options.

The default image displays in the selected picture box when the page is first loaded. The Rollover Image displays in the box when the pointer is over the box. The third element of the rollover is the hyperlink field. This lets you choose a URL to link to when the rollover is clicked.

Delete All Hot A…
Super Step an…
Convert Text to Table…
Table
Gridlines
Rollover
Create Rollover…
Delete Rollover

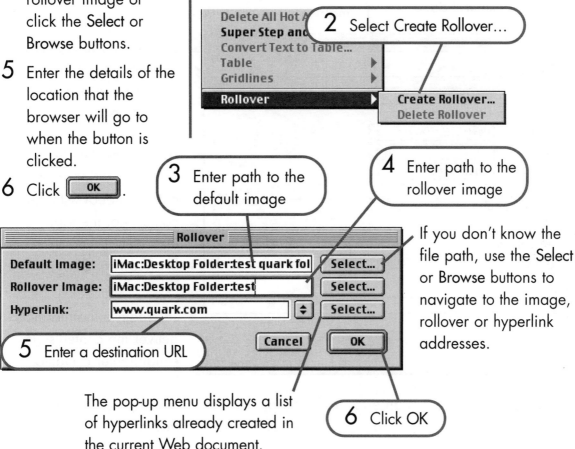

2 Select Create Rollover…

3 Enter path to the default image

4 Enter path to the rollover image

Rollover
Default Image: iMac:Desktop Folder:test quark fol Select…
Rollover Image: iMac:Desktop Folder:test Select…
Hyperlink: www.quark.com Select…
Cancel OK

5 Enter a destination URL

If you don't know the file path, use the Select or Browse buttons to navigate to the image, rollover or hyperlink addresses.

The pop-up menu displays a list of hyperlinks already created in the current Web document.

6 Click OK

Forms

Interactive forms are used in Web sites to allow visitors to provide feedback, shop or even browse online databases. XPress 5 includes some decent form creation tools. The process of creating a form begins with the Form Box itself, which is made up of a number of elements that can be viewed in Quark's **Modify** dialog box in the **Item** menu.

Name: this field contains the name for the form. Any descriptive title will do.

Method: Get asks the user's Web browser to add form data to the end of a URL, while Post asks the browser to send form data to a script or application separately. The difference between them is minimal; you can use either.

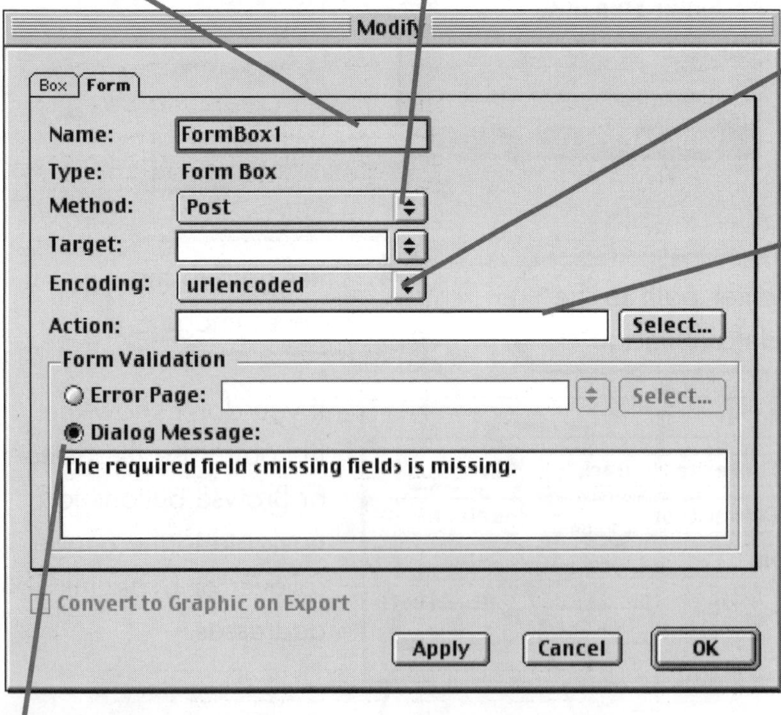

Encoding: You can specify whether the form data should be encoded for greater security.

Action: This line lets you specify a script or application to deal with the contents of the form – use the Select (Mac) or Browse (Windows) to select a local application.

To create a mail form to deliver the contents via e-mail, enter a mailto: HTML tag, followed by the required e-mail address.

Form validation: if there is an error in the script you can choose to automatically load an error message or generate a user-defined error message that you set here.

Basic steps

1. Click the Form Box icon.
2. Click and drag across the Web document to create the Form Box.
3. Point to Item and select Modify...
4. Give the form a name and enter its basic details.
5. Click OK.

Tip

A quick way to create a form box is to drag a form element, such as a text field, onto the page. The form box will be created automatically.

Creating a Form Box

The first step in creating an online form is to create a Form Box to hold the form elements.

Remember that complex forms often require powerful scripting languages, such as CGI or PHP to work successfully.

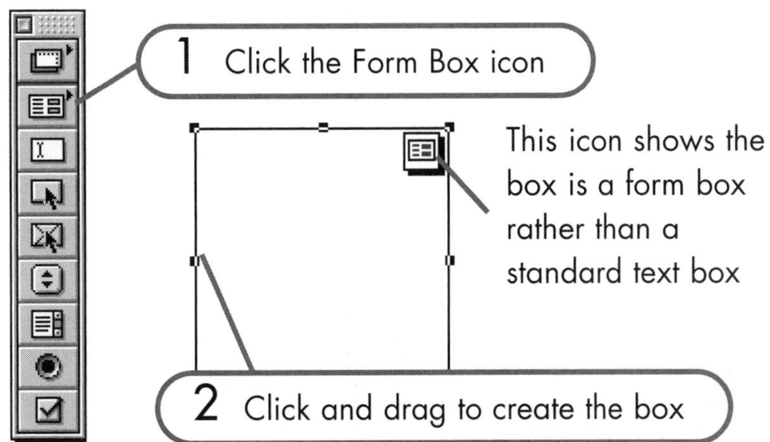
1 Click the Form Box icon
This icon shows the box is a form box rather than a standard text box
2 Click and drag to create the box

4 Enter form properties

Modify

Box | Form

Name: FormBox1
Type: Form Box
Method: Post
Target:
Encoding: urlencoded
Action: Select...
Form Validation
Error Page: Select...
Dialog Message:
The required field ‹missing field› is missing.

Convert to Graphic on Export

Apply | Cancel | OK

5 Click OK

Adding form elements

Basic steps

Text fields

Text fields can comprise text, password or hidden field types. Text appears to the reader as plain text; while password are displayed on a web page as a series of asterisks. Hidden fields submit a value when a form is submitted without showing it to the reader.

1. Click the Text field tool.
2. Click and drag inside the Form box.
3. With the box selected, point to Item and select Modify...
4. Click the Forms tab.
5. Give the text field and choose a type of text element.
6. Click OK.

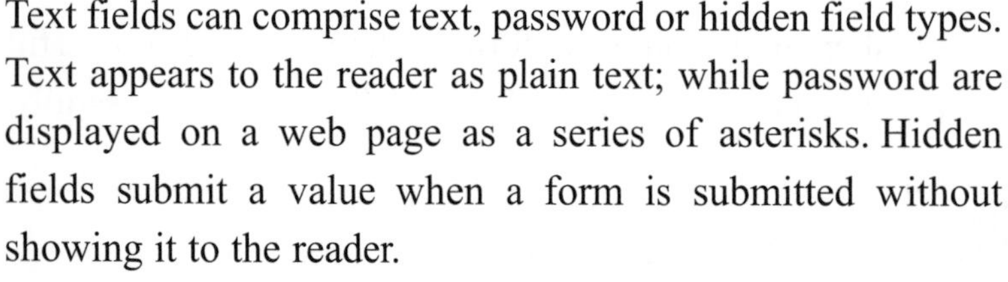

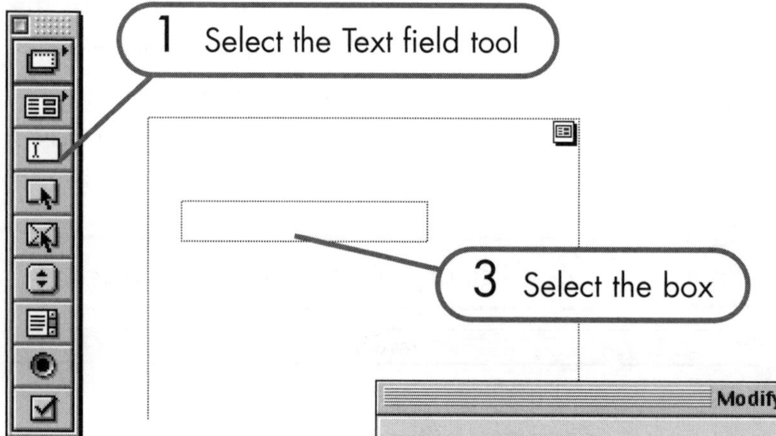

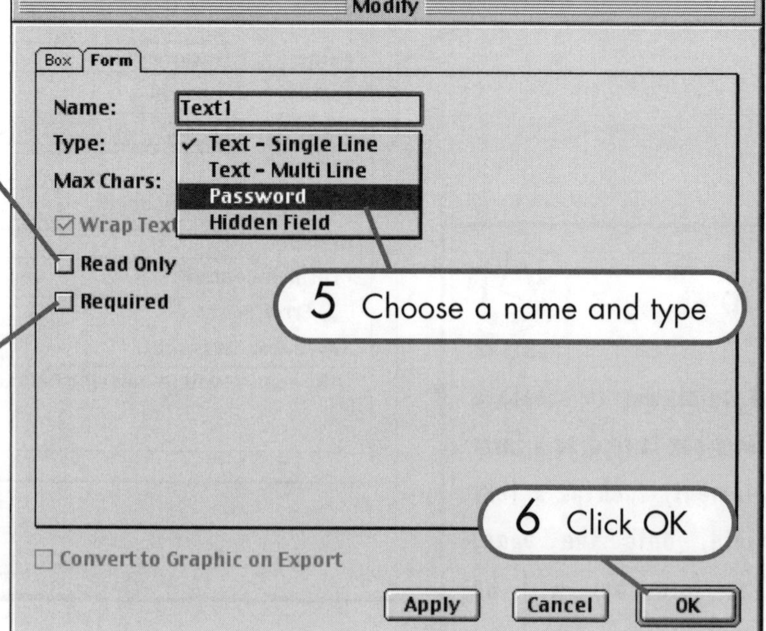

Make a field read only if you don't want its contents to be editable.

If a text field must be completed before it is sent, check the Required field box. If you don't check this, fields in your form may be left blank.

Basic steps

1 Click the Button tool.
2 Click and drag across the inside the Form Box.
3 Click on the button and add a descriptive title for the reader
4 Point to the Item menu and select Modify…
5 Click the Form tab.
6 Name the button.
7 Choose between Reset and Submit.
8 Click OK.

Take note

Pop-up lists and menus allow the reader to make multiple selections, while checkboxes and radio boxes let you make single choices.

Submit and Reset buttons

There are two types of buttons used in forms, and their function is clear. A **Submit** button sends the contents of the form to a script or application; the **Reset** button allows the reader to reset fields to their original state.

Naturally, every form should contain both.

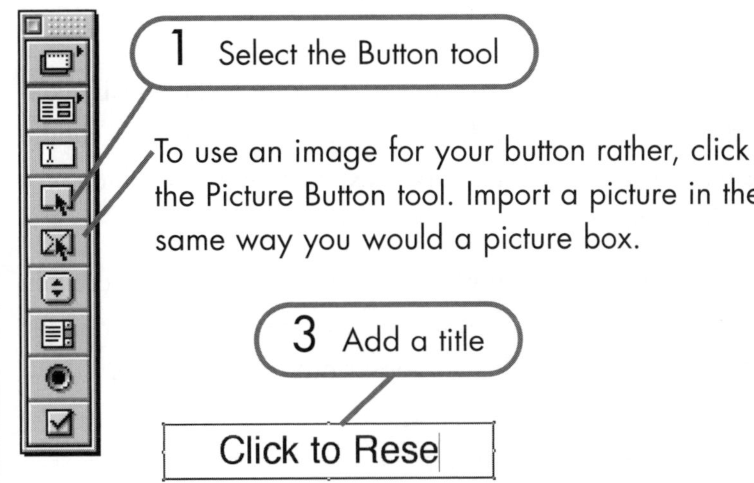

1 Select the Button tool
To use an image for your button rather, click the Picture Button tool. Import a picture in the same way you would a picture box.
3 Add a title
Click to Rese

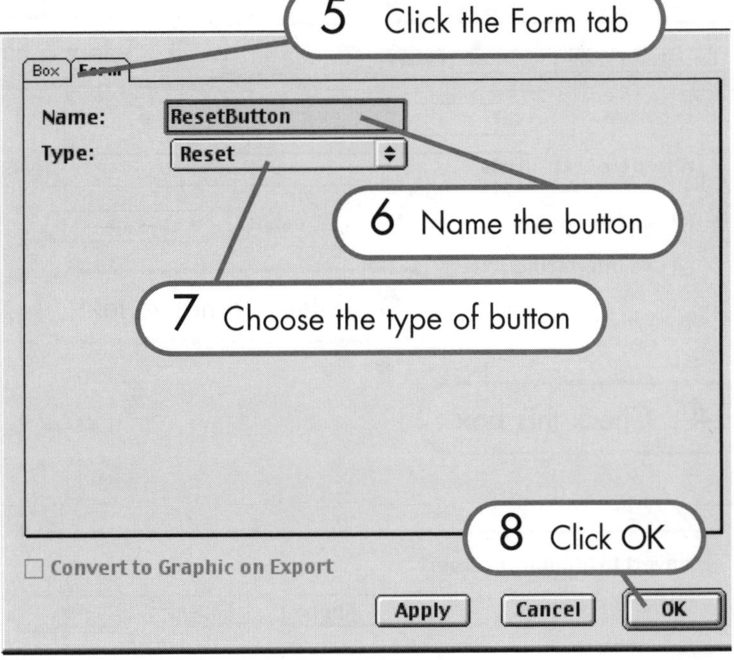

Preview and export

Basic steps

1 Select a text or image box with the Content or Item tools.

2 Point to the Item menu and select Modify...

3 Click the Export tab.

4 If the item is a text box, click on the Convert to Graphic on Export button

5 Choose a file format.

6 Enter alternative text.

7 Click OK.

Exporting text and image boxes

You have some control over the conversion of text and image boxes when you publish your document. Normally, when you create a text box, it will export as HTML text. But if the box contains styles that may be lost in the conversion, you can choose to export it as a graphic.

Exporting image boxes is simpler: these are automatically converted to a Web-ready format if necessary. You can choose between JPEG, PNG and GIF – experiment to see which produces the best results for your needs.

Images and text exported as an image should contain alternative text that appears in the viewer's browser if the images don't. Make this text descriptive, but concise.

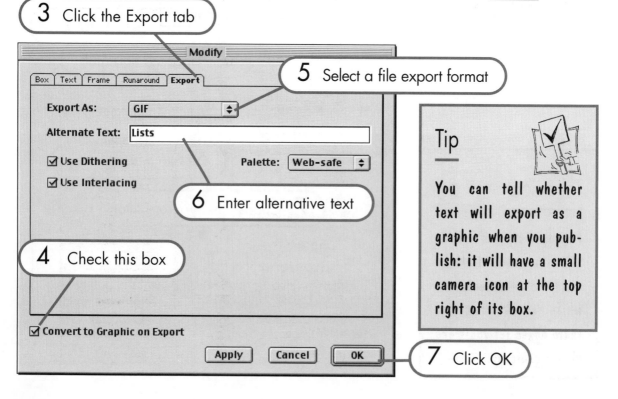

3 Click the Export tab

Modify

Box | Text | Frame | Runaround | Export

Export As: GIF

Alternate Text: Lists

☑ Use Dithering   Palette: Web-safe

☑ Use Interlacing

☑ Convert to Graphic on Export

Apply Cancel OK

5 Select a file export format

6 Enter alternative text

4 Check this box

7 Click OK

Tip

You can tell whether text will export as a graphic when you publish: it will have a small camera icon at the top right of its box.

Basic steps

- ❑ To preview a page

1 Click and hold the Preview icon.

2 Select a Web browser from the list.

- ❑ To export a page

3 Point to File, select Export and choose HTML... from the sub-menu.

4 Enter the page range to export.

5 Select a folder in which to store your exported pages.

6 Click Save.

Take note

You can add more Web browsers to XPresss default choice — or set one if XPress doesnt display a browser next to the Preview button — from the Preferences pane in the Edit menu.

Previewing a page

One final step before publishing your site is to check that it will look the same on the Web as it does in XPress. When you press the **Preview** button, XPress provides a preview of the current document in your selected Web browser.

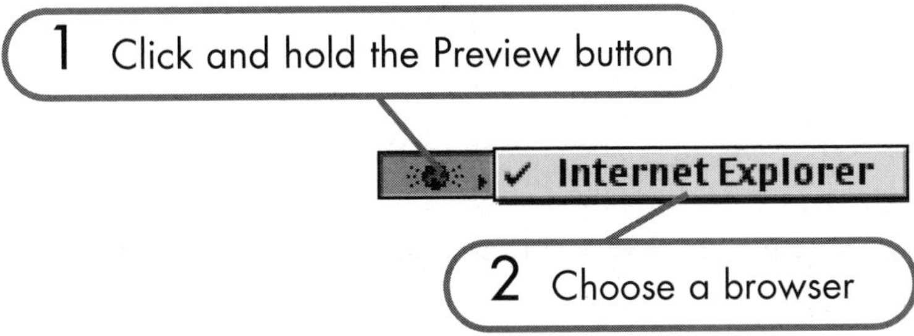

Exporting a page

The final stage in producing Web documents is to export them. The export process turns the pages into HTML pages suitable for uploading to your Web site.

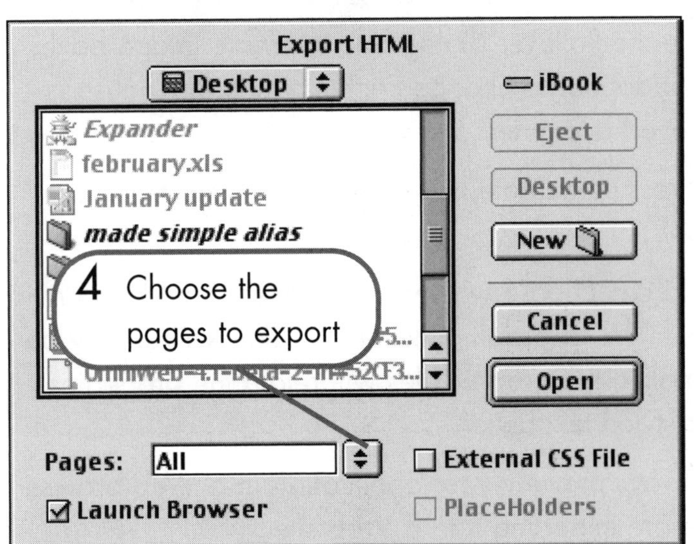

Summary

- ❑ Web documents aren't the same as print documents – you can't take the same document and produce print and Web versions easily.
- ❑ You create a Web document in almost exactly the same way as you produce a print document. The same techniques apply.
- ❑ When creating a Web page, don't make it wider than 600 pixels without good reason.
- ❑ Images can be used as a background to your text. But use this effect sparingly and be careful not to overwhelm the text.
- ❑ Use the Hyperlinks palette to create or amend links in Web documents – you can also use them in print documents destined for PDF output.
- ❑ Delete a link by selecting it in the Hyperlinks palette and clicking the Delete button.
- ❑ The image map tool creates image maps in picture boxes inside Web documents.
- ❑ Use the Rollover dialog box to create image boxes that appear to change content when the mouse is moved over them.
- ❑ XPress can create powerful forms using its form tools.
- ❑ You can choose whether text boxes should export as HTML or graphic files. HTML files will usually be smaller, but graphic files will retain the properties of styled text better.
- ❑ Always preview your application in a Web browser before exporting it to a Web site.

Index

R

S

T

U

V

W

X

Z